Barry Sheene

Haynes Publishing

Dedication
To Jennifer

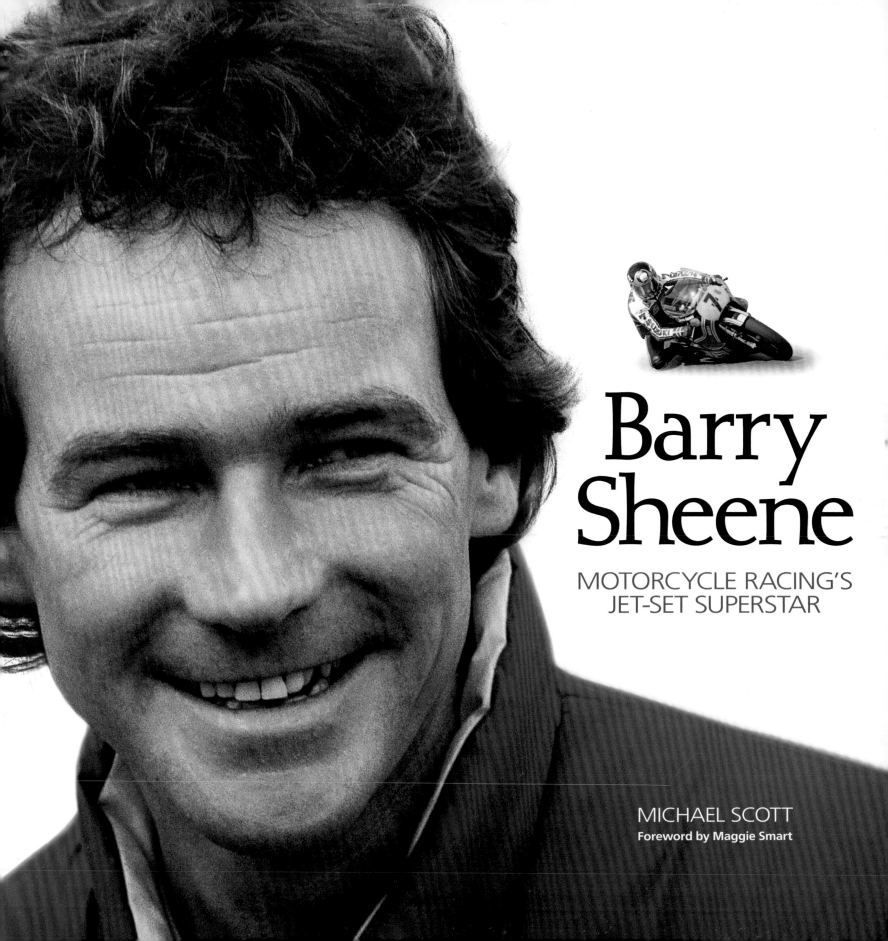

Barry Sheene

MOTORCYCLE RACING'S JET-SET SUPERSTAR

MICHAEL SCOTT

Foreword by Maggie Smart

First published in June 2006

A catalogue record for this book is available from the British Library

ISBN 1 84425 013 X

Library of Congress control no 2006921751

Published by Haynes Publishing,
Sparkford, Yeovil, Somerset BA22 7JJ, UK
Tel: 01963 442030 Fax: 01963 440001
Int.tel: +44 1963 442030
Int.fax: +44 1963 440001
E-mail: sales@haynes.co.uk
Website: www.haynes.co.uk

Haynes North America Inc.,
861 Lawrence Drive, Newbury Park, California 91320, USA

Design and layout by Richard Parsons
Edited by Flora Myer
Consultant editor Julian Ryder

Printed and bound in Britain by J. H. Haynes & Co. Ltd.,
Sparkford, Yeovil, Somerset BA22 7JJ, UK

Author's acknowledgements

Material for this book was collected over many years, from the 1970s to the present day. The names of those who assisted are in the book. To them my warmest thanks, and especially to Paul and Maggie Smart, Don Morley, Chas Mortimer, Garry Taylor, the late John Cutts, Steve Parrish over the years, Will Hagon, and to the many other people who have shared their memories. Thanks also to Julian Ryder for picture research and advice, and Jennifer Scott for motorcycle press cuttings, proof-reading and support.

Photo credits

Peter Barnes, Helivision: 210
BBC: 108 top
Ian Beacham: 110-111
Jacques Bussillet: 44-45
John Colley: 190, 191
Emap: 71, 180, 201 top
Richard Francis: 169
Fremantle Media: 108 bottom, 109
Getty Images: 12 top, 16-17, 32, 62, 84, 96 bottom, 97, 103 bottom, 112, 113, 115, 126, 127 top and bottom, 130 top, 152, 153, 167, 215 top
Gold & Goose: 200, 201 bottom, 215 bottom, 216 top
Stewart Kendall: 159
Henk Keulemans: 10, 28-29, 72-73, 76, 77, 85, 92-93, 95, 128-129, 132, 135, 136, 137, 140-141, 142, 148-149, 154-155, 160, 161, 162-163, 164 top and bottom, 172-173, 174 top and bottom, 192-193, 194,195, 196, 197, front cover inset
LAT Photographic: 114
Phil Masters: 9, 13, 67, 176-177, 202, 203 top and bottom, 206, 207, back cover right
Mirrorpix: 106-107, 116, 119, 121 top
John Mockett: 216 bottom
Don Morley: 8, 11, 86-87, 88, 98-99, 100-101, 102, 134, 146, 151, 158, 165, 166, 167 top, 168, 170, 171, 179, 182, 182-183, 184, 187, 188, 189, front cover portrait, back cover middle
Nick Nicholls Collection at Mortons Media Archive: 24, 25, 27, 30, 34, 35, 40, 48 top, 49, 63 bottom, 94, 103 top, 123, 130 bottom, 131, 143, 144-146, back cover left
Stan Perec: 104 top, 185 top and bottom, 186, 198, 204, 205, 211
Rex Features: 80, 80-81, 120-121, 178, 217
Maggie Smart: 6, 7, 12 middle and bottom, 18, 19, 20, 21 top and bottom, 22, 23, 58-59
Paul Smart: 74-75
Rob Stanley: Advertisements and memorabilia
Mick Woollett: 33, 36-37, 38, 39 top and bottom, 41, 42, 46, 47, 48 bottom, 50-51, 52, 54, 55, 56-57, 59, 60-61, 63 top, 66, 68-69, 78, 79, 82, 83, 90, 90-91, 96 top, 138, 156, 157, 175

CONTENTS

———— BARRY SHEENE ————

	Foreword by Maggie Smart	6
	Introduction	8
1.	Very Nearly Cockney	16
2.	A Star is Born	28
3.	Fame through Pain	50
4.	Square Four	72
5.	The Glory Years	86
6.	The Playboy	106
7.	Into the Doldrums	128
8.	The Yamaha Years	148
9.	Time to Retire	176
10.	Family Guy	192
11.	The Big C	208
	Appendix: Race Results 1968–2002	218
	Index	222

FOREWORD

BY MAGGIE SMART

Whenever I was asked what it was like to have Barry Sheene as my brother, I would say, 'Well, do you have a younger brother or sister?' They would normally make a face and say that they did. 'Well, that's what it's like for me!'

I wasn't really enamoured with Barry's arrival in my life, as I had been the focus of all the attention for the previous five and a half years. Then one day Mum arrived home after a few days in hospital with a brand new baby boy who was to take up all the time and attention. So I guess I didn't like him too much! To make matters worse he was a bit of a sickly child, with infantile eczema, and as if that wasn't bad enough the eczema went and the asthma arrived – something he would use in later life to his advantage.

In his early years he wasn't naturally blessed with balance and co-ordination, and this was highlighted on the fateful day when he tripped over his pyjama trousers, falling on my pet budgie, killing him instantly – poor old Peter.

He also didn't always do as he was told. There was the time Mum told him to spit out his chewing gum before going to bed. Barry awoke the following day with his eyes glued firmly shut by the said gum, having stuck this on his eyelids (presumably because it seemed a safe place) before going to sleep. He managed to lose all of his eyelashes with the effort of getting it off, not to mention large chunks of his locks.

Barry will always be remembered for many reasons, some good, some not so good – the colourful language, the girls and, of course, the fags. The first time he was caught smoking, at the age of 11, he told Mum that I'd given him the cigarettes – the little shit was known to tell a few fibs too!

With all that said, we did have an extremely happy childhood together, apart from the occasional fights – which I usually won as I was older and bigger.

His racing years are now legend and very well documented in the following pages, so I've no need to talk about them. However, another side of Barry's character was his compassion. He would be watching the news and see a tragic story and feel he had to do something to help – and did so on several occasions. One time in particular concerned a young girl (of roughly the same age as his daughter, Sidonie), who had been very badly burned in a house fire, having returned to the flames in order to save her young niece. Barry managed to get in touch with this remarkable young lady, even flying to visit her once she had been released from hospital. Having had first-hand experience of rehabilitation, he offered her all he could – advice, comfort and support.

He also had an amazing ability to remember names and faces, and would quite often remember a person he had signed an autograph for years before – I'm sure some of you may be able to vouch for this.

Barry was an excellent helicopter pilot and I (along with all the family) loved to fly with him. When I think of him now, I like to picture us flying back from Switzerland together in his newly purchased Agusta A109C. Sadly this was the last time my brother and I got to spend any happy, carefree time with one another prior to the shadow of his cancer diagnosis.

I hope you all enjoy reading this book. I have certainly enjoyed re-living many of the wonderful memories we have shared over the years. He may well be gone, but he will never be forgotten.

Maggie

INTRODUCTION

The wind plays games with sound at Phillip Island. And there's almost always a wind, close to the island continent's most southerly point – not for nothing did adopted Australian Barry Sheene call the atmospheric ribbon of fast tarmac 'Gateway to Hypothermia'.

What you hear, from the pits-and-paddock nerve centre of the Grand Prix circuit, depends which way that breeze is blowing. From the sea, it swallows it all up. But from landward, it takes the sound, rolls it around, and funnels it back to you. And the noise this Sunday morning was not the howl of the new MotoGP four-strokes accelerating through the final corners … that would come later. Now it was a human sound, almost eerie, the sound of many voices, of appreciative yelling, whooping and cheering. The sound of admiration, of respect. And even of love.

The cheers were for one man, heading the motorcade of drivers on a pre-race lap of honour for the 2002 Australian MotoGP, and he wasn't even riding in it. They were cheering Barry Sheene.

A few people who had raced against Barry were there. Kenny Roberts for one. The main one. And Angel Nieto, Franco Uncini, Randy Mamola …

Many more had known Barry as a racer, had worked with him, for him or against him in rival teams. Fellow TV commentators were there, mechanics, journalists and photographers, the riff-raff of paddock life. As always, Barry had a personal word for all of them – a gibe, often as not, but affectionate enough, and most especially personal. In this way, Barry touched almost everybody who had flown down to Australia for the race.

Britain's last motorcycle Grand Prix World Champion had also flown down – not so far, now that he lived in Australia, though it was still more than a five-hour journey, even in the beautiful Agusta A109C helicopter he'd had delivered to Australia barely two months before.

Barry loved helicopters. They were flash and jet-set and millionaire, at the same time as being knavish, renegade and cheeky. Just like himself, really. He liked the way you could go anywhere, set down anywhere. Take off again when you liked … a habit that now and then put him in conflict with the aviation authorities. Then again, he'd been in conflict with the authorities since he'd started at school.

Barry had flown down with his son Freddie by his side. Freddie was 13; it was quite a schoolboy outing. Everywhere Barry went, so too did Freddie. And everywhere Barry went, he was surrounded by eager conversation, by crowds of people. As always, Barry was frank, and spoke openly about his illness – cancer of the

Sheene in his element (left), champion of the world, and having the last laugh (opposite) on the day he announced his retirement – Barry had sold 'Motor Cycling Weekly' a dummy.

LEFT *Sheene on the Number 7 Suzuki, an instantly recognisable image.*

oesophagus – and the unconventional treatment he had espoused. And of his confidence that he would beat it, like he'd beaten everything else in his life. But there was something unsayable in the air. By Barry, or by his companions. Everybody, deep inside, knew they were saying goodbye.

The same applied to those tens of thousands of fans who cheered him to the echo. And you couldn't help feeling it was them, as much as his old rivals and friends, to whom Barry had come to bid farewell.

That was in October 2002. Barry continued to fight his cancer, but it was a losing battle. Within six months he would be gone. His last three days were spent in hospital close to his home in Queensland. Even there, Barry was still signing photographs for his fans. It was a love affair that lasted to the death. For those left behind, it is Barry Sheene's memorial.

This is a story of a motorbike racer. It's a game of grafters and twisters, if you like. Plenty of that, at every level. Plenty of pretence and subterfuge and trickery, and Barry Sheene was a past master of it. But it's an honest sport in the end. What you see is what you get. The stopwatch may sometimes flatter to deceive, but it never lies.

What you saw with Barry Sheene was a rider of skill and courage, never reckless, often dominant. And a career somewhat betrayed by circumstances, as often as not of his own making.

When Barry won the 500cc World Championship two years straight, in 1976 and 1977, it was all too easy. When he lost it, especially over the next three years to Kenny Roberts, it was all too difficult. He was riding harder and better than ever, but one thing after another conspired against him to make each subsequent year more challenging than the last.

In retrospect, Barry's most costly decision was to leave Suzuki at the end of 1979. That finally closed off any chance he might have had of regaining the crown. It happened, at least partly, by accident – driven by Sheene's overwhelming self-belief, and his desire to run his own independent team.

But not winning, curiously, didn't really make any difference. Sheene was in that sense bigger than his sport. His career as a celebrity, as a TV commentator and presenter, and as a playboy, flourished even as his championship chances waned. He rode some fine races – his skill never lessened, especially when wet weather reduced the advantage of rivals on more powerful

OPPOSITE *Sheene takes off for the fastest ever motorcycle road race, the Belgian GP of 1977. He averaged more than 135mph. Behind him are Wil Hartog (19), Alan North (33), Steve Parrish (11) and, in the distance, ultimate challenger Michel Rougerie (31).*

machines. But his popularity was not linked to his finishing positions.

Sheene's character carried his fame. He had an overwhelming charisma. Call it star quality. Sheene's presence was so powerful and so magnetic that he had only to walk into a crowded room and you would know at once that he had arrived. His sharp-featured grin was easily the most noticeable thing in any company; his razor-sharp wit could reduce friends to helpless laughter and cut enemies to the quick. Barry had a knack of making everyone feel that there was something personal between him and them. No matter how small, it was enough to make everybody feel a little special, and for Barry to be forever special to them.

Sheene's fame had been kick-started by his racing, but it was misfortune that gave him a better chance to win the hearts of the public … in the shape of a horrendous high-speed crash, the fastest ever recorded, on the banking at Daytona in America in 1975, the year before his first World Championship. Barry not only survived, his broken femur and other bones pinned and screwed, but fought back with a courage that was genuinely awe-inspiring. He was

*Star quality – the
Sheene publicity
machine spawned a
minor industry of
spin-off publications.*

back on a racing bike within seven weeks, and winning races not long after that. As if that was not enough, he was called upon to do the same again, from even worse leg injuries, after he was an innocent victim of another high-speed crash, at Silverstone in England in 1982.

He was a genuine hero, and the times were ready for him – for his Cockney manners and cheeky, crooked grin, for his clever chat and skilful self-promotion, for his fashionable disco-era flares and flashiness, and for his devil-may-care looks. And Barry was clever enough to make the most of every opportunity. Combine these ingredients with a will to win so fierce that it could drive him to almost superhuman feats of determination and you have a superstar in the making.

Sheene's will to win was staggeringly strong. And not just to win. To those up against him, it went even further. For Barry, victory alone wasn't enough. He liked the other man also to lose. But he was a complex character, and not to be drawn only in black and white. Barry also had a real heart, and real generosity. If he felt you were on his side, he would never cease in his support.

Barry's generosity reached out also to the hundreds and thousands of fans around the world. This was shown from the start, when he was still becoming famous. No rider, possibly no other sportsman of such status, would spend as long with his fans, giving them all the time he had, until every last scrap of paper had been signed. Barry, of course, took it further. He had a phenomenal memory for names and faces. He would remember snippets of information. A fan might present a grubby autograph book one year at Mallory Park to be greeted: 'Ullo Bill. 'Ow's your little sister getting on then?' Barry would remember them from the previous year.

This fine mental gift served him in every way, especially in business, in self-interest. But let's not forget the generosity. Sheene hated hospitals, feared infirmity, and had a horror of amputation. But he would swallow all that to visit children's wards, charming the nurses and utterly captivating the young patients. He knew his own recovery from injury was inspiring, and he willingly shouldered the responsibility that brought. Many sick or injured people looked to Barry for words of comfort and encouragement. None, and most especially not the children, would ever be turned away. In special cases, Barry would take an even closer personal interest – writing, calling and sometimes visiting. Even in his final illness, Sheene thought also of others. If I am successful in beating cancer, he would say, I will spend all the money I have telling people that they can do it too.

Sheene had made plenty of money. He was clever that way, and highly motivated. By the time he died, at a ridiculously premature 52, he had built up successful property empires in Britain and Australia, where he had emigrated for health reasons in 1987. He had also become an iconic TV commentator in his new homeland.

Barry made a fine life for himself and his family, on Queensland's Gold Coast, where the warm winters eased the pain in his legs and wrist, still held together by titanium plates and almost 30 screws. He and Stephanie had been together since their scandalous love affair had hit the headlines in 1976 – she was a glamour model, and happened to be a married mother at the time.

Barry kept putting off the wedding ... until 1984, as it turned out. The formality didn't matter to him. It was,

for both, the love of a lifetime. Just over nine months later their first child, a daughter called Sidonie, was born.

Freddie came four-and-a-half years later, after they had moved to Australia. There the children were raised in an idyllic lifestyle, in a Spanish-style villa built on a riverside stretch inland from the Gold Coast. Both sets of grandparents lived on the property; the workshop, and even the hallway, were full of Barry's old racing motorcycles; and the jet-skis were parked at the bottom of the garden.

Sidonie and Freddie were at boarding school near Melbourne when Barry was diagnosed with the cancer that would kill him. Telling his children was the hardest thing he had to do, he said. And the most touching.

Barry is survived in Australia by his father, his wife and their two children. At the time of writing, Stephanie was still living in the Carrara villa. Franko, Barry's father, was in an old-age home nearby. Sidonie was working for the Australian Grand Prix Corporation, where Barry had been a director; Freddie was finishing his schooling in Queensland.

And Barry's legacy lives on, his legend as powerful today, three years after his death, as it was in life.

This is his story.

At home in Charlwood in 1982. Sheene, walking sticks at the ready after his Silverstone crash, illustrates a point to the author.

CHAPTER ONE

VERY NEARLY COCKNEY

Barry would always claim to be a Cockney.

Looking back, this was part truth, part smart branding – the sort of thing Barry understood perfectly, long before the marketing term had been invented. Well, he would, as a Cockney. As importantly, being a Cockney was something understood all over the world; it gave Barry a card to play. Cheeky, cheery, chirpy – and sharp as a needle.

Spiritually, bang on; geographically he was more Bloomsbury than Barking, home was within walking distance of the West End rather than earshot of Bow Bells. The four-bedroom flat in Queen Square, Holborn, London WC1, came with Frank Sheene's job.

Frank Sheene had found himself a plum spot in the heart of the capital. Originally from Hertfordshire, he worked at the examination halls of the Royal College of Surgeons, in a quiet little enclave surrounded by teaching hospitals. He was the maintenance engineer … everything from central heating to broken surgical equipment. His wife Iris, from Bromley, was housekeeper, catering all week for visiting doctors writing surgical exams or attending conferences. World War Two brought a break, Frank working as a station

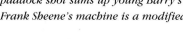

Aged eight, and hands on – this Crystal Palace paddock shot sums up young Barry's world. Frank Sheene's machine is a modified 50cc Itom.

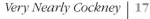

officer in the fire service and then in a top-secret radar factory; Iris moving to Brighton at the height of the bombing. It was there, early in 1945, that their first child was born – Margaret, who would grow up to become the attractive and vivacious Maggie, and to marry renowned motorcycle racer Paul Smart.

As well as the Holborn flat and use of an extensive and virtually private yard, Frank also had a workshop out the back. A glorified lean-to, really, but generously sized, equipped with a lathe and a tower drill and all you might need for general light metalwork and maintenance. There was not only the space and facilities to keep and work on racing motorcycles, but also sufficiently indulgent employers who allowed him to do so. Frank's

little one-man workshop was already a hive of racing activity before Barry was born. Its influence on the new kid would ultimately be of huge significance to the future of motorcycle racing.

Frank had been given to motorcycles ever since learning to ride on the fields of the farm. While his brother Arthur took to the Speedway tracks, Frank concentrated on road racing. Not to any particularly high level, but as an active clubman he rode at Brooklands at the last meeting before World War Two (gaining a trophy on a 250 Excelsior), and five times at the Isle of Man both before and after it. Frank's last race was the Manx TT in 1956, when Barry was five. But by then Frank was already making a name preparing and entering machines for other riders, becoming something of a specialist with the 50cc Itoms from Italy … early harbingers of racing's forthcoming two-stroke revolution.

Throughout Barry's childhood, the family's spare time was focused on racing, on weekend trips in the Ford Thames van out to Brands Hatch, Mallory Park, and further afield to holidays on the Isle of Man during TT time. Racing, and that workshop. There, during the week, Frank would tune and modify his own racing machines, and work on bikes and engines for others in racing. It wasn't really a business, even after he became a special agent for racing Bultacos from Spain, and added go-kart engines to his range … more of a hobby that could pay its own way.

The Queen Square flat was a well-trodden path for a large cross-section of the racers of the day. As Iris told me years later, there would be a steady stream turning up at the door in the evenings. Iris might be cooking the family tea, or bathing one of their two children in the big kitchen sink ('we had no central heating, so it was nice and warm there'). She would wave the visitors through to the workshop. As soon as he could, Barry would be in there too, steeped from earliest boyhood not only in the technical side of motorcycles, but also the racing milieu. And racing people, Frank told me once, are 'good people'. As everyone in racing would find out, Barry would run rings round them all.

Barry was born in the evening of 11 September 1950. He made his presence felt directly. While fashionable London flocked to see *The Third Man*, and to dance to its Harry Lime Theme, Barry kept the household awake – for more than three years, Iris recalled. First, it was infantile eczema, but soon afterwards chronic asthma had him wheezing as well as scratching and crying. Iris told me another story, of how she had been bathing him, aged four, in the sink after a day out racing at Brands Hatch. She'd turned away for a hot towel. Toddler Barry, playing with a clockwork train, had somehow trapped his foreskin in the toy. The serrated gear wheels steadily pulled the infant manhood into the tin toy before the spring finally jammed. They rushed him, wrapped in a towel and howling with pain, to the nearest hospital where Frank took over, using bone-cutters and his technical experience to dismantle the mechanism without releasing the still-taut spring. This was the Homeopathic Hospital, the closest to Queen Square (the Paediatric Hospital, the National Hospital for Nervous Diseases, the Italian Hospital and the Great Ormond Street Hospital for Children were also nearby), and

possibly not the best for such an emergency. 'The doctors were worse off than I was,' Frank said.

Asthma returned spasmodically for some years. It became acute when Barry was five, with the family on the Isle of Man where Frank was running a couple of bikes. In the cold guest house, Barry had such a severe attack that he turned blue, and was rushed to an oxygen tent at Nobles Hospital in Douglas, where he was kept for the next two nights. It was the start of an unhappy association between the one-time pinnacle of the motorcycle World Championships and one of its future icons.

Surgery eased but did not cure the asthma, but Barry was hyperactive all the same – in and out of the workshop and buzzing up and down the yard of the examination hall, stuck in first gear on a little bike Frank had built up for him, fitting a two-speed four-stroke 50cc Ducati engine in a miniature frame (a mini-moto prototype decades before they became popular). His

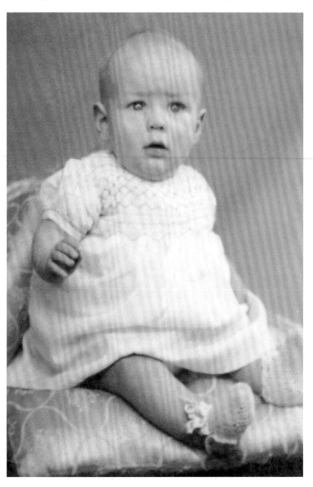

He might have been a beautiful baby …

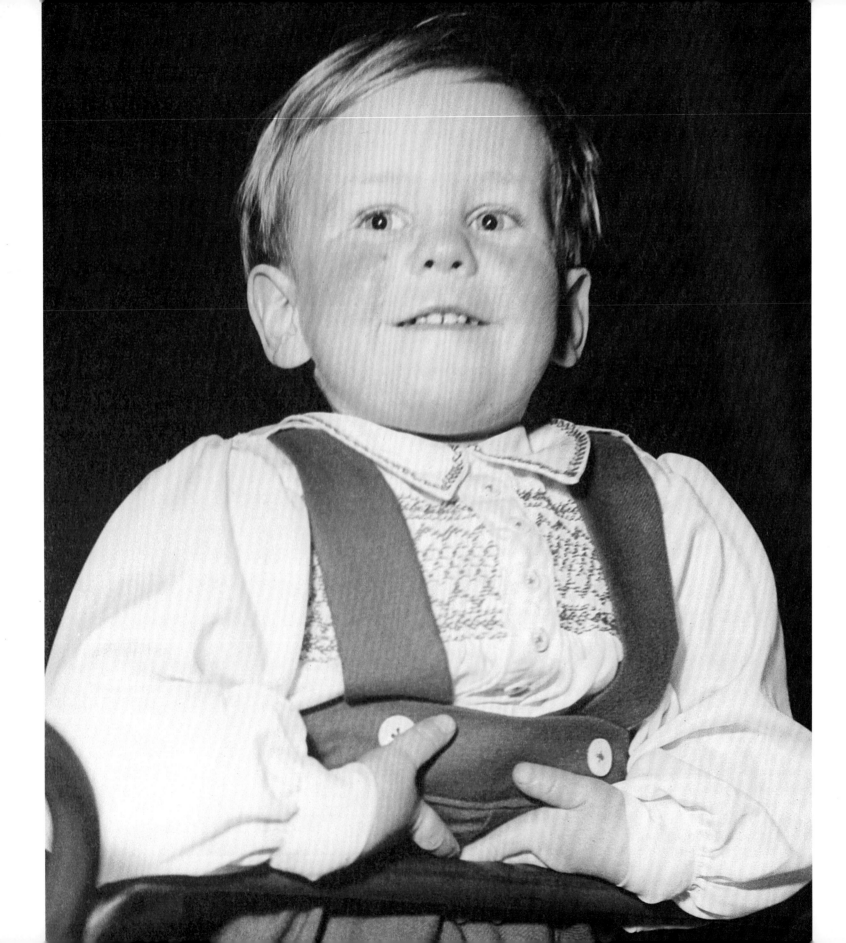

first fracture was soon to follow – though in fact it was a fall from a bicycle that put his arm in a cast. Iris recalled the trip home from the hospital. He told her: 'I've always wanted to break my arm, mum.'

The break was not serious, and Barry was quick to heal – a trait that would always stand him in good stead. And within days the family was off for their first foreign holiday – to Barcelona.

Frank Sheene being Frank Sheene, the holiday coincided with a motorcycle race, the Barcelona 24-hour event at Montjuich Park – an increasingly important event that had started in 1954, and attracted a hard core of British interest. Nosing around the pits, Frank struck up a friendship with the head of the new Bultaco team, Francesco Bulto, who had led a breakaway from the established Spanish Montesa concern when that had withdrawn from racing. The wiry, sharp-featured Londoner obviously got on with the well-born Don Paco, and the consequence was a specially favoured position. For the next several years, Frank Sheene would be supplied each season with new 125 and 250 Bultaco racers, which he entered under the name Sheene Bultaco, and he would act as Bultaco's racing importer and agent, in an informal way.

OPPOSITE *Scrubbed and shiny – it wouldn't last long.*

ABOVE *Young family Sheene, Iris with Barry and Maggie.*

LEFT *A Sheene family wedding in 1959. Iris and eight-year-old Barry are flanked by uncle and aunt John and Joyce Sheene. Barry's maternal grandmother (second right) has Frank's sister Marjorie alongside.*

21

Barry, meanwhile, thrived in Spain's warm sunshine. Once he'd had his plaster cast cut off he was in and out of the water, able for the first time to swim without fear of asthma. Swimming was the only physical sport he ever enjoyed. Already, he had a knack of making friends and getting involved; now he showed another trait that would serve him well, a gift for languages. Spanish would become the first of five languages that he learned, including a workaday smattering of Japanese. And of course he was all over the motorbikes.

The second curse to Sheene's childhood was school. In his first autobiography, *The Story So Far*, he said: 'School was like a bad dream. Every minute of every day was murder.' Iris insisted on good church schools, and Barry made his way through St George the Martyr Church of England Primary School (still going in John's Mews, London WC1, catering nowadays mainly to a polyglot immigrant group, only one in ten of whom has English as a first language). Thence to the now departed St Martin's in the Field School.

According to his family, some of the teachers recognised that Sheene had an exceptional brain. 'The headmaster told me Barry could have been top boy at the school if he'd tried,' Iris would recall. But aside from metalwork and technical drawing (and, oddly, religious instruction) Sheene's interest was very firmly elsewhere. Mainly on motorbikes, increasingly also on girls, and definitely almost always on mischief. He was a professional pest. He had started smoking at nine, and was soon a heavy smoker, continuing until less than ten years before the cancer struck and took his life. He preferred dark French tobacco: Gauloises or Gitanes, with the filter broken off. Later he would tell of nobbling the ignition of a hated master's car by using silver paper

Frank's Bultacos, lined up outside the Spanish factory. In the late Sixties, as Bultaco's racing importer, Frank got a consignment of new 125 and 250 'works' racers each season.

At Queen Square, outside the workshop doors, teenage Barry shows off his new Bultaco trials bike. Grant Gibson, who rode for Frank, is in the middle.

from his fag packet; and of another in a series of canings after making a cocktail out of his father's drinks cupboard and persuading a schoolmate to drink it. The boy required a stomach pump, and Iris was mortified when, in Frank's absence, she was called in front of the head with her son. Later, when it was Frank's turn to face the irate head, he stood there in his boiler suit 'dropping fag ash all over the carpet' and when the tirade was over replied quite simply, 'well, boys will be boys, and that's all there is to it.'

Barry Sheene was certainly a boy when it came to girls. He told how he lost his virginity at the age of 14, in a crypt beneath a local church; he never looked back. Conquest was his aim, tireless persistence and powerful personal charisma his weapons. This was to be a lifelong pursuit.

But it was the motorbikes that dominated, and the racing. Almost every weekend would see the Sheene family setting off to some race-track or other. They were

a fixture, part of a hierarchy: Maggie adorning paddock and pits, Iris presiding over cups of tea, Frank – a senior figure to the smaller classes – tinkering with the Sheene Bultacos, and Barry dashing around, getting in everybody's hair, always up to something. Phil Read later told me how in 1961 he was riding Frank Sheene's bikes at the Isle of Man. Ten-year-old Barry 'spent all his time with the bikes. He was all over them … like a rash. He always seemed to be in the way. I still have a toolbox that had my name stencilled on: Phillip Read. Barry painted over it, to make it Phil Read.'

Read would go on to win eight World Championships in a long career, and eventually find Barry alongside him on the grid as a rival. Now he was a rising star, however, one of several within the extensive Sheene orbit. Another was Londoner Bill Ivy, a close friend of the family, and a future World Champion.

Another in the mix was South African racer Ian Byrne, and Barry was recruited as an informal helper to

his rather ramshackle effort – driving an old Jaguar converted to a 'woody' estate car to carry the bikes, inherited from another South African racer, Paddy Driver. Byrne was a dashing driver on the road, and on one occasion was spotted speeding by the police. After a lengthy chase across much of the south-east of England, they managed to get the Jag unseen into Frank's yard where it lay doggo for a while until the fuss died down. Although only the junior party, this was typical Barry, and typical bike racing.

Except for the favoured few, bike racing then (as now) was largely an amateur affair. There were a number of races and championships up to national level and, for the top riders, money races abroad … in the streets of Holland, Spain or Italy. The national scene was thriving, and the Sheene family was to become an increasingly important part of it. This was at a time when long journeys seldom had the benefit of motorways – the first stretch of the pioneering M1 had only been opened in 1959. Races would involve starting at dawn, or camping overnight at the circuits.

Barry made an impact even as a pre-teenager. This was to become a hallmark – years later, before and after his death, his companions would marvel at his presence, at the impact his arrival would make on a crowded room. Others in the hierarchy, like Andrea Coleman (*née* Williams, daughter of Matchless stalwart Jack Williams and sister to fine racer Peter Williams), recall a cheeky, spotty kid; an adjective that comes up time and again is 'precocious'. Other stalwart families included the Mortimers and the Boddices.

Barry loved it – and also showed fine technical flair, mechanical sympathy and an understanding of how all the different parts of an engine would work together. He never did suffer from shyness, and was happy to volunteer an opinion to anyone looking puzzled in the pits. Irritatingly enough from a young teenager, most of the time he'd be right … at least that's how Frank fondly remembered it, years later.

Wednesday afternoons were bike days down at Brands Hatch, the Kentish circuit that was closest to home. Barry's asthma came in handy: on a regular visit to the clinic he managed to lay hands on a pile of appointment slips, all stamped and signed, but with the dates blank. He had doctor's appointments most Wednesdays after that. It was enough for him to be hands-on with the bikes; he had no idea he might become a professional racer. But he was practising for it all the same, at 13 belting round the fields surrounding the race-tracks on a

LEFT *Smile on, eye to the main chance – Barry Sheene at Brands Hatch in 1968, just turned 18.*

OPPOSITE *Sheene's style is already evident – and his boot already scraped – in this photograph, testing one of Frank's Bultacos at Brands Hatch on 17 February 1968. It is thought to be his first ride at the track.*

100cc Triumph Tiger Cub, and playing with his mini-bike and an old Austin Ten that Frank had bought so he could learn to drive.

The following year Frank bought him a Bultaco Sherpa trials bike, and for a spell he enjoyed club-level mud-plugging in Kent. Trials are demanding, severely testing the niceties of machine control, weight distribution and traction – feathering the clutch, flying the front wheel, carefully measuring the power. Barry, his contemporaries recall, was extremely good … the finesse came naturally, but the sport bored him, and he would lose points trying to do sections at breakneck speed or on the back wheel.

The light two-stroke Bultaco racers were very competitive machines; Frank's bikes were one step down from the full factory stuff, but handy all the same, and also improving year by year. He would pass them to one rider or another – Mike O'Rourke and Fred Hardy rode Sheene Bultacos in the early 1960s, the former winning the Brands Hatch Shield in the 125 class. Grant Gibson bought that bike, and it was the first time he came into the Queen Square orbit. Two years later, after he had won a couple of national races, he came back, to buy one of the new six-speed water-cooled Bultaco 125s.

*In his first racing
season, Barry was
already practising
victory wheelies. Or
maybe just showing off.
This is the Snetterton
paddock in 1968.*

It was now that Frank started to enter Gibbo, as well as Martin Carney, 'spasmodically', as Gibson, now a successful financial consultant, remembers.

'I was one of quite a few people hanging round Frank's yard hoping for a ride. You were always trying to get Frank to put your engine in the vice next. There'd be vans parked outside in the square, and I'd go in there any time of the day, and he always seemed to be working on the bikes.' He remembers Barry, in his mid teens, as having 'a little bit of a stroppy side', and then, choosing the word carefully and emphasising it, he adds: 'He was pretty precocious.'

As Barry grew older, always with the bikes and the racing scene now, he started socialising with the riders. This was a somewhat wild affair, motorcycle racers tending to go out to the edge in all things. Gibson recalls: 'Ian Byrne and me and some others would take Barry out. We'd lead him astray. Any of Barry's vices in later life, we've got a lot to answer for.' They'd haunt the clubs … Café des Artistes in Earls Court, or the Bali Hai in Streatham, and they ran a contest for new female conquests over the year. 'It was called "upping your score". The low 20s was the best, as I remember. Barry liked the idea of that.' Years later, Gibson was at a Suzuki function when Barry was already World Champion. 'He sidled over to me, and said: "Hey, Gibbo. Eighty-seven. And it's only October."' Sheene was still keeping score.

Barry's entry into racing as itinerant mechanic to a number of riders included a first foray into the Grands Prix, very different then from the slick commercial operation of MotoGP, and primitive even by the standards that would prevail at the height of Sheene's fame. With £15 subsistence cash from Frank and permission from his school, Barry went with promising American rider Tony Woodman on the long drive in his Thames van out to the Salzburgring in the foothills of the Alps for a non-championship race, then to Solitude for the West German GP. Barry was in his element, helping prepare the G50 Matchless and 7R AJS for the 500 and 350 classes (a relatively simple task), and tasting the paddock lifestyle for the first time on his own. Later that year the teenager was badly shocked when Woodman crashed heavily at the North West 200, held on an ultra-fast public-roads circuit between Coleraine and Portrush in Northern Ireland. The news that spinal injuries would leave the New Jersey rider in a wheelchair precipitated the return of a serious asthma attack. Racing was more dangerous in those days, but this was one of the first tragedies to somebody close.

Barry had left school when he turned 15, a total failure as far as the education system was concerned. He drifted into more-or-less casual jobs – a few weeks in a nearby Ford spare parts warehouse; some motorcycle courier work for an advertising agency (Alexander Butterfield & Ayres), riding a BSA Bantam; then helping out in a posh car showroom run by a Queen Square friend Dave Buxton. At 17, Barry could now and then take his pick from the second-hand stock for a weekend swanning about. He had no thoughts at the time of racing for a career … or doing anything for a career, really. He was just for having fun, in that headlong way of his.

But the racing was always there.

Sheene's own tale of how his career began seems to have been somewhat packaged into a media-friendly yarn. It was a sort of epiphany. He'd been on the track only once before, he said, for a few terrifying practice-day laps on a weedy 50cc Derbi, in among all the big 500s and so on. A week later, dad asked him to run in the new Bultacos he'd just received for the forthcoming 1968 season – and observers at Brands Hatch were so struck by his speed and his smooth style that they persuaded Frank to give him a go at actually racing.

His companions of the time remember it rather differently. Chas Mortimer, later a GP winner but now a year or so ahead of Barry, had started riding Frank's smaller Bultacos. He insists that Barry already had a lot of laps under his belt, because running in the race bikes had been his task for some time; Grant Gibson is sure that Barry had actually raced already, without showing either much interest or much in the way of results.

Either way, both had to stand aside, over the course of 1968. The new bikes that Barry referred to were 125, 250 and the new 350cc Bultaco – actually an over-sized 250 that Barry and Gibbo had already taken out in the van to Hendon aerodrome, got through a hole in the fence and blasted up and down the runway. 'I was more or less in line to ride the new bike, then Barry came to Brands Hatch to run it in.' That was the turning point. After this 'Frank said to me: "I think my boy's going to have to ride it." I thought: "The little shit." Because at the time I thought he was a bit of a waster.'

That first club race at Brands Hatch in March 1968 ended with a crash. Barry said the 125 Bultaco had seized. Nothing daunted, he jumped onto the 250 and finished third. It was the start of something big.

CHAPTER TWO

A STAR IS BORN

London was officially very Swinging by 1968. The Beatles and the Rolling Stones had conquered pop, Carnaby Street was the height of hippy boutique fashion, the Kings Road the heart of swank. The baby boomers had found a spirit of freedom that was a release for a whole post-rationing generation. At 17, Barry was just the right age to feel its power. From Harold Macmillan's 'never had it so good' of 1959 to the 'never had it so often' era of permissiveness and hedonism, a world of pleasure was laid open. Now earning a living cleaning, preparing (and sometimes driving home for the weekend) flash cars for Dave Buxton, Barry loved every minute of it.

Especially now he was a motorcycle racer.

The start was gradual. Barry's autobiography may have exaggerated when he recalled winning a club race in only his second meeting at Brands, after telling Frank excitedly: 'I can beat half these blokes.' But the need and the hunger weren't really there yet, and soon afterwards came a long break when he enlisted as mechanic with British rider Lewis Young, spending most of the summer abroad at GPs or international races. He also visited the Isle of Man, spannering for Chas Mortimer at the Southern 100 road races at Castletown, on a shorter road circuit. 'Barry was racing then,' recalls Mortimer, 'but these were national races, and he didn't have a national licence. I was riding one of Frank's bikes. He wanted to have a look at the TT circuit, I'd done a

Barry at Spa-Francorchamps in 1971 on the way to his first Grand Prix win. The bike is his prize purchase – the ex-Stuart Graham Suzuki 125.

couple of races there by then. We drove round, and he was saying: "It doesn't look that difficult. There's plenty of straight bits." But all Barry was interested in was pulling. He discovered there was a well-to-do girls' school quite near to the circuit. We were in a tent or a van or something, and he had this string of young girls. He was always cock crazy.'

In this way, even if you're not a rider, racing is very demanding of time, and Barry soon faced his first and last major career choice when Buxton gave him an ultimatum. He chose racing, and from then on supported himself with casual jobs, including driving a furniture lorry for Bourne & Hollingsworth. At the end of 1968, Barry re-embarked on a racing career that for

several years would be nothing less than meteoric. 'One minute Barry Sheene wasn't racing. The next he was winning everything.' This was a common comment, and if it was a slight exaggeration, that's the feeling Barry engendered, especially in retrospect.

In the later events of that year, Barry would trail around England in a beat-up Thames van … Cadwell, Mallory and Oulton Park, Snetterton and Brands Hatch, Croft. His natural riding talent was obvious, the Sheene Bultacos were clearly a help. Barry added that confidence and persistent flair for getting noticed, and soon outstripped any of his racing peers in publicity. The weekly *Motor Cycle News* printed the first story, a short piece in the 20 November edition: 'Barry

Pudding basin helmet already adorned with the Donald Duck motif, Sheene rounds Druids hairpin at Brands Hatch on a Bultaco.

Sheene is a born natural … following in his father's footsteps.'

Barry's timing was typically right. Domestic British bike racing was in a lively condition, but a spell of domination at Grand Prix level was drawing to a close. Mike Hailwood had retired with nine championships at the end of 1967. The legendary battles between Yamaha team-mates Bill Ivy and Phil Read reached a height of bitter rivalry in 1968 when the latter won both 250 and 125 crowns. Only Read would continue, and there was something of a vacuum to be filled.

Both Read and Ivy had in their early days been part of Frank Sheene's loose-knit group, and Ivy had remained close, visiting Queen Square on Christmas Day in 1968. A fast-talking little Londoner with a dazzling talent and a taste for fast cars and posh birds, Ivy had for years been a hero and role model to Barry. You can be sure Bill spoke about his anger that Read had reneged on the Yamaha team agreement, and snitched the 125 title that should rightly have been his. You can be sure also that Barry immediately knew whose side he was on. And when Barry was on your side, you had a fierce and tireless champion. In a couple of years, Barry would find himself racing against Phil …

Ivy's tragedy was round the corner. Disgruntled and dispossessed, he tried his hand at car racing, where he made a big if short-lived impression, then returned to bikes on an elaborate new Jawa, a V4 built to challenge the now dominant Japanese. The bike seized on his first practice lap of the Sachsenring and Bill, who is thought not to have fastened his helmet securely, suffered fatal injuries. Barry was devastated: Iris recalled him sobbing in anguish until stricken with an asthma attack. He thought of quitting racing. As is often the case, he returned stronger and more committed.

The 1969 season was spent in a headlong crash course in increasingly high-level racing almost every weekend. More time would be spent with the three Bultacos – 125, 250 and 350 (now up to 302cc) – on the road in the old van than on the track, for on a Bank Holiday weekend Barry might easily do three different meetings. Straight in at national level, he was up against none other than Chas Mortimer, for whom he had

Sheene tops world 125s

BRITAIN'S world championship hope Barry Sheene won his first ever grand prix on Sunday in the fastest race he ridden.

...ore than 110 mph on his Suzuki twin, Sheene burst ...he 125 cc world champion-...h a sparkling victory in the ...d prix during his first ever

... works rider Angel Nieto ... seized engine on the second ...s no one to challenge the 20-...kney, who smashed both race ...cords on his way to victory. ...to wait for a protest to be heard ...ecame the official victor. ...ne, after Morbidelli's claim that ...s gearbox contained more than ...d six cogs, had been dashed: "We ...l all and the protests. I'm so

...e reigning 125 British champion ...lights set on greater things. "Of ...m going to have a go for the world ...nship. It would be a marvellous ...ny first season of classic racing." ...e, already one of racing's most ...l characters, grabbed the acclaim ...crowd as he lifted his arm in joyous ...and engulfed all the girls he met ...e winner's rostrum in fond embrace. ...win was certainly a record breaker ...senses, for he knocked almost seven ...ls off Dieter Braun's 1969 lap record ...lipped just about 3 mph off the pre-...best race average set by Dave Sim-

...was a really good day for Britain's ...ng lions, for as Barry moved to the top ...the table Charles Mortimer, now down ...be a regular rider of the works 125 ...maha, moved into second place after a ...arkling fifth place ride.

THE Weekend PAGE

Sheene aims for Mallory gold

BARRY SHEENE, at 20 the country's youngest professional road racer, aims to start the 1971 season at Mallory Park on Sunday in the same way as he started last year at Mallory—by winning two finals.

He has entered four bikes —the ex-Stuart Graham 125 Suzuki, a 500 Suzuki, and two new "B" versions of the TR2 and TD2 Yamahas, which he hopes will arrive before those of the opposition, and in time for the Mallory season-opener.

Said Barry: "I hope I can at least repeat last year's performance when I won the 125 and 250 finals and a 500cc heat. Paul Smart and I tested the 500 Suzuki at Brands Hatch on Wednesday. It is great in a straight line, but handles like a camel. Paul agrees that it's the worst handling bike he's ridden."

With Smart on his way to Daytona and stars like John Cooper and Peter Williams cutting down on appearances in nationals, the field is wide open.

For several stars, it's debut day on ... on a 350 ...

by NORRIE WHYTE

Barry Sheene on the ex-works 125 Suzuki ... be takina to M...

BRITISH ROAD RACING CHAMPIONSHIPS

SHEENE CLIMBS THE TITLE TABLE

BARRY Sheene moved up and Derek Chatterton slipped down in the see-saw struggle for points in the British road racing championships in the fourth round at Brands Hatch on Friday.

Sheene climbed to the top of the 250cc table, just one point clear of reigning champion Steve Machin, after finishing second in the 250 race at Brands, where Machin was fourth.

But a broken gear lever cost Chatterton the lead in the 350cc table. The reigning class champion, he started first in the race, but he retired almost immediately when the lever dropped off.

There is no change at the top of the 500 and 750cc tables. Brian Kemp kept his 500cc lead with a third place at Brands, and Percy Tait stays in the lead of the 750cc table, with a second place in the 750cc race. But race winner Charlie Sanby is now only two points behind.

250cc
1 B Sheene (Yahama) 34
2 S Machin (Yamaha) 33

3 D Chatterton (Chat-Yamaha) 26
4 B Kemp (Yamaha) 23
5 T. Dickie (Yamaha) 22
6 P. Mahoney (Yamaha) 18
350cc
1 T Rutter (Yamaha) 43
2 D Chatterton (Chat-Yamaha) 37
3 B Ditchburn (Broad Yamaha) 31
4 K Redfern (Yamsel) 16
5 B Sheene (Yamaha) 15
6 J. Curry (Honda) 14
500cc
1 B Kemp (Higley Seeley) 42

2 C. Sanby (Kuhn Seeley) 37
3 A Barnett (Aermacchi) 27
4 J Harvey (Kirby Metisse) 16
5 D Croxford (Seeley) 15, P M... (Petty Norton) 15, J. Tay... (Seeley) 15
750cc
1 P Tait (Triumph) 47
2 C Sanby (Kuhn Norton) 35
3B Adams (Rickman-Manx) 26
4 B Ditchburn (Triumph) 24 Jefferies (Triumph) 24
6 M Grant (Lee Norton) 15.

Grabbing the headlines – by 1971 Sheene was already big news in the motorcycle papers.

spannered the year before, until Mortimer made a tactical withdrawal from the Sheene team when it became obvious that Barry would from now on be the top rider. 'I could see a conflict of interest, and I had other offers,' he said.

Mortimer, riding an Italian Villa, took the British 125 title, only – he now says – because he had a good start to the year, then went off to do his first few GPs, while Barry finished the year strongly. Barry's natural gifts of mechanical sympathy, bike control, courage and understanding all shone through, and his progress was rapid. Major successes during 1969 were fourth on his 250 at the Hutchinson 100 at Brands Hatch, and second (to Cliff Carr) in the 350 Race of Aces at Snetterton. The Brands ride earned him the adjective 'inspired' in the *Motor Cycle Weekly* of 13 August, and was accomplished on an interesting hybrid. Cheshire enthusiast Gerald Brown had given Sheene a TD250 Yamaha twin-cylinder engine, more powerful than the single-cylinder Bultaco. Frank had shoehorned it into the Bultaco chassis, to make a machine similar to one put together by future 250 World Champion Rod Gould.

If it was not now, it was soon afterwards that Barry showed he had an understanding of another element of

racing often ignored by other riders … the fans. And the power that the fans could give, both financial and otherwise. This was the start of a life-long love affair, perhaps the most important one of his life. And Barry paid initial court to those fans as he would continue to do, giving maximum effort and generously of his time. Until his death, Barry would make sure the fans never felt that he'd broken faith.

First, of course, he had to be noticed. He was one of the first, possibly the first, to have his name emblazoned in bold white on the back of his black helmet. Others had adopted helmet motifs – like John Cooper's famous 'Moon Eyes' – but Barry's choice was wackier than most: a perplexed-looking Donald Duck. (All-white leathers would come in the following year, and he had yet to adopt the number 'seven'.) His ability and a high level of machinery meant these trademarks were generally to be seen up at the sharp end. Within a very few years, they would become international icons. As Barry wrote, way back in the mid-Seventies: 'It helped to be noticed if there were sponsorship rewards going.'

At the start of 1970, Barry was still racing pretty much on his own resources, with Frank right alongside – by now more widely known as Franko, Barry's nickname. Barry learned his fierce loyalty from his father. As far as Franko was concerned, Barry could do no wrong. Given his status in the national paddocks and the level of his machinery, Frank added powerful impetus, and Barry lined up for his second full national season fired with ambition.

It was a year of rapid and important development, of his first national title – the British 125 – and his first races abroad. In 1970, Barry rode a wide variety of machines in all sorts of competitions. At home he was becoming a formidable force. Don Mackay, a family friend and occasional race entrant who used Frank's services to prepare his machine for other riders, told me how 'when the Sheenes turned up, the other blokes would say they might as well go home now.' A partisan view, perhaps: confirmed bachelor Mackay would become a firm ally and soon join Barry as his first mechanic.

The Sheene stable at the start of the year comprised replacements for the three Bultacos – 125, 250 and 350, which could also be run over-bored at 362cc in 500 races. He clinched the smallest title with a devastating early run of success, and quickly learned in the biggest class that running underpowered is no way to a brighter future.

In June, Barry made one of the most important purchases of his life – an ex-factory 125cc Suzuki racer. The RT67 may have been four years old, but it was technologically streets ahead of the single-cylinder Bultaco, for all its water cooling and six-speed gearbox. The Suzuki had two cylinders, ten gears and factory race-shop provenance, along with an impressive 35 horsepower from its disc-valve engine.

This was one of a handful of Japanese factory bikes that had escaped captivity – like the Kawasaki of Dave Simmonds. It had a fair history. This bike had beaten Bill Ivy at the Finnish GP in 1967, and finished second at the TT, at Brno and in Japan, all in the hands of Stuart Graham, son of first 500cc World Champion Les Graham.

Stuart was third in the world, behind the Yamahas of Ivy and Read. The Cheshire rider kept the little bike and continued to race it. Now it was up for sale. Barry scraped together what he could and borrowed the rest from Frank to make up the £2,000 purchase price.

Two days after collecting the bike, Barry found himself up against reigning World Champion Simmonds on the Kawasaki at Mallory Park. He beat him. The omens of the complex little Suzuki were good. For one thing, this was the first of a marque on which he would achieve greatness. After he retired Barry made the bike the centrepiece of his collection out in Australia.

Barry treated the bike with care, having only a limited supply of spare parts. This was why he stuck to the

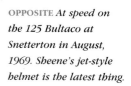

OPPOSITE *At speed on the 125 Bultaco at Snetterton in August, 1969. Sheene's jet-style helmet is the latest thing.*

LEFT *A crestfallen Sheene pushes the three-cylinder 500 Kawasaki of the Read Brothers back to the pits, the handlebar snapped. In his first and last endurance race, the Thruxton 500-miler, he and co-pilot Dave Croxford were leading when he threw it away.*

Bultaco for the British championships, though he claimed it was for sporting reasons. Mackay, now pretty much Barry's full-time spanner man, told me that Barry would never let him touch the Suzuki's engine. Only he and Franko ever saw the inside. 'He wouldn't trust anybody else with it ... he'd paid too much for it.'

The little factory racer was saved for special occasions ... like an important national meeting at Brands Hatch, where two senior Suzuki GB men were present. One was the racing team manager Rex White; another was sales (later managing) director Maurice Knight. White: 'I'd seen Barry on the Bultacos. Now, on the ex-Graham Suzuki at Brands, he broke the throttle cable, and he actually won the race, pulling the carbs open with the cable wound round his hand. I said to Maurice, that's the sort of bloke we want on our team, if he's that determined.' White remembered it wrong ... in fact he was beaten that day by Simmonds, but the point was made, and Maurice Knight later wandered over to the Sheene family in the paddock. 'Franko was sitting smoking on a wooden stool outside an old van and Barry was playing about with the bike out front. They were just like dozens of others there. I said I was Suzuki, that I was pleased with the way he had run the race. That's where the acquaintance started.'

Both sides would benefit hugely in the years to come – and Barry would start working on that almost at once.

The Suzuki GB headquarters were in Surrey, at Beddington Lane, between Croydon and Mitcham on the south-west border of London. Soon after the Brands meeting, Frank and Barry drove across the Thames and out through the suburbs to renew their contact with Knight. They were looking to buy another Suzuki.

This was also a factory machine, and 500cc. But the TR500 – code-named XR05 – was very different from the 125. That was a purpose-built little jewel; this was by comparison a lash-up. The bike also had a history – a dark and evil history ... having ended two distinguished racing careers without achieving any success.

Built by the factory race department for the Daytona 200-mile race, it married a modified air-cooled 500cc twin-cylinder two-stroke engine from the roadgoing T500 Titan with a specially built racing frame. It then passed to Suzuki GB, who entered it for the TT for the experienced former winner Stuart Graham (again). After a few practice laps, he parked it, declared it lethal, and promptly retired from bike racing (to Barry's benefit in terms of the 125). The 500 was passed straight on to

No mistaking the intent ... Sheene looks to his future in his first ride on a 500. This is the twin-cylinder Suzuki he and Franko rescued.

successful Welsh racer Malcolm Uphill, who retired from the TT, also complaining of bad handling. After some modifications, Uphill then raced the bike in Ireland at the Ulster GP, where he crashed heavily, breaking his thigh. He also never raced again. Two top riders …

'It was lying in our workshop in a more-than-critical state,' Maurice Knight told me, 'when Frank and Barry arrived, looked at it, and asked if I would let them have it. I said they couldn't *have* it. They said, at least let us repair it and race it. It won't cost you much.' Knight let them take the wreck away to Holborn. The repair bill was £36, and 'they'd turned it into a new motorcycle.'

The engine was strong by the standards of the time, but the machine was all wrong. Short in the wheelbase, the engine carried high, the handling was skittish and overly prone to pulling wheelies at a time when everyone was trying not to. Rex White recalled first tests at Snetterton, with Barry and Paul Smart. 'Unfortunately they'd put the engine together with the pistons reversed, and the damn thing seized up. They sorted that out, then they both had a go on it, and generally decided it was a heap.' It needed a new chassis, and after Barry had raced it just once at the Snetterton Race of Aces (it broke down twice), the bike went off to

former sidecar champion and now chassis constructor Colin Seeley, who had gained a reputation making frames for 'Yamsel' Yamahas.

Barry, meantime, had smaller fish to fry – a foray to Spain with the little Suzuki, and his first Grand Prix. Barry had raced against the leading riders like Dieter Braun and Dave Simmonds at international events in Britain. The week before the Spanish GP, the final round of 1970, there was a street race where Sheene surprised himself by defeating rising Spanish star Angel Nieto. A week later, the future tiddler superstar (ultimately 13 times champion in the smallest classes) turned the tables at Montjuich Park. Barry was eight seconds adrift, handsomely far ahead of Swede Börje Jansson's Maico and new World Champion Dieter Braun's own Suzuki. Nieto's Derbi factory promptly protested that his Suzuki's ten-speed gearbox was against the new rules. Barry was able to show he was running a special six-speed gear cluster.

Nothing could spoil the moment, or the significance. In his first ever World Championship Grand Prix, Barry had finished on the rostrum. All the sweeter that it was at the same track where he and Frank had made their first contact with Don Paco Bulto, all those years ago.

OPPOSITE *Barry sizes up the Isle of Man TT circuit. He hated it. Above, he is practising on his 125 Suzuki; below, he is first away, firing up before Gunther Bartusch on the factory MZ. Sheene crashed on the second lap, and never returned.*

BELOW *First GP, in Spain in 1970, and Sheene is heading towards third.*

Back home, the rewards awaited. Barry won the 125 British title, and was awarded the gigantic Castrol Challenge Trophy and a £250 prize to boot. Silverware on the mantelshelf, and it was larks aplenty with Paul Smart, a rising racer now a regular at the house for the simple reason that he had fallen in love with the pert and elfin Maggie Sheene. The family relationship would complicate the rivalry between two racers of roughly equivalent ability, but they would remain friends to the end.

The Sixties were now over, numerically and in all sorts of other ways. Events in music tell the story of lost innocence. In 1970 the Beatles split. So did the contemporary Dave Clark Five, and the imitative Monkees. In 1971, Doors singer Jim Morrison was found dead in the bathtub in Paris, aged 27. The hedonism of the Sixties remained, but now there was a cynical edge. A disillusioned world was ready for more human heroes. And certainly ready for a different kind of motorcyclist from the Hells Angels who had stabbed a fan to death at a US Rolling Stones concert at Altamont in 1969. A child of his time, with extraordinary abilities and charisma, and with his usual impeccable timing, Barry Sheene was ready and able to oblige.

There was still the small matter of getting famous first, but already it was becoming clear that fame would follow Barry like a faithful dog. Through fame and through success (Barry was riding better all the time), this would be the last of Barry's happy-go-lucky carefree years in racing. By the end of 1971, things were getting serious.

The racing went really well. According to jealous rivals (ie, all of them), Barry did get good cards. In most cases, he had made his own luck, in the sense of seeing opportunities early, then using his charm to get his own way. But while often in his career he would leave his rivals feeling dispossessed, nobody could say he did not play his cards well.

In 1971, in terms of machinery, this meant the still-competitive little 125 Suzuki, and the rebuilt ex-Uphill 500 Suzuki – feisty air-cooled twin-cylinder engine now housed in a frame built by Colin Seeley. On the first, he would make a strong challenge for the 125 World Championship, winning three GPs; on the big bike he would get the occasional chance to mix it with the still-dominant MV Agusta four-stroke GP bikes, and the up-and-coming 750 Superbikes – Triumph and BSA triples, and the Norton twins. Barry also rode sundry Yamahas

and Yamsels. And he made his debut at that hallowed sanctuary of motorcycle racing, the Isle of Man.

This was a pivotal moment for one old institution, and for a new racing phenomenon.

Since 1907 the Isle of Man had been the senior moment of motorcycle racing. This cornerstone of racing was already long established when the modern World Championship was founded in 1949. Running on a 37.75-mile public roads track round the Island, the various classes (in 1971, 125cc, 250cc, 350cc, 500cc and sidecar – plus a new production-based class, Formula 750) took up a full week of racing. Unique and revered, TT week was a natural part of the World Championship calendar. Always had been. And always would be. Surely.

Standards were very different in those days, and the very notion of racing safety in its infancy. Barry was just one of the nation's racers who happily tackled Brands Hatch the wrong way round, for the Hutchinson 100, which shows how much attention was paid to run-off area and safety zones. In either direction. Of 11 tracks on the 1970 Grand Prix calendar, only five were purpose-built circuits rather than closed public roads – Hockenheim, Salzburgring, Anderstorp, Monza and

Jarama. Of these, the first alternated with the formidably long and dangerous old Nürburgring, while Anderstorp's main straight was also a rural landing strip. Some of the remainder were highly dangerous – seaside Opatija in Yugoslavia, Ireland's ultra-fast Dundrod, and the even-faster tree-lined Spa-Francorchamps. But the Isle of Man was uniquely long, also extremely fast, and where it was not lined with stone walls, it might have been a lamp-post, a bus stop, a telephone booth or even at one corner a graveyard. Then, as now, it was the Everest of motorcycle racing, with a death toll to match. Today, it is a voluntary challenge, taken willingly by a new generation of racers. Back in those days, however, it was different. The TT was a World Championship round, and serious contenders really didn't have much choice but to attend, whether they liked the track or not.

Barry was one of them. While he was steeped in as much Island history as anyone, he was not full of reverence. This year, the weather started poor, and gradually worsened over the week. Barry was appalled. He rode a 250cc Suzuki prepared by Cumbrian dealer Eddie Crookes in the Production event – mainly to get some miles up for the 125 race – and was happy to retire when the bumps started shaking the bike to pieces

during the race. The 125 race was in streaming rain, making it the slowest since 1953. It was won by Barry's pal Chas Mortimer, who had pulled out a 32-second lead over Barry in the first lap. Early on the second, Barry famously slid off at Quarter Bridge, and was delighted not to continue. Not in that race, and not in any others on such a ridiculous circuit. He told Frank as they returned to the paddock: 'That's it. Never again. I was following Chas over the mountain in such thick mist I didn't know where I was going or what I was doing.'

Sheene may have been thinking of his own safety first, but his opposition to the TT put him at the forefront of a growing fashion for dissent, and as his status increased he played a powerful part in the pressure that eventually got the Isle of Man taken off the GP calendar in 1977. Sheene's stance was unequivocal and has doubtless helped to save many lives, but it made him some enemies among the English racing establishment.

No score at the TT hardly changed his championship prospects as his main rival for the 125 crown, Angel Nieto, did not score there either. And, aged 20 in his first full season, Barry's prospects were extremely good. The old Suzuki took him to third in the opening round

Previously unpublished photos by French journalist and friend Jacques Bussillet from the 1970s. Sheene and (bottom left) Franko in the Queen Square workshop; Barry in his faithful van; and (centre) Barry's girlfriend Lesley Shepherd with brother-in-law Paul Smart.

in Austria, to second in round four, the Dutch TT at Assen, then to his first GP win at Spa-Francorchamps. Barry's average of 110.310mph put him almost ten seconds clear of German Gert Bender, with Braun a distant third. Nieto did not score. Barry was second to Nieto's Derbi in the next round in East Germany, third to Nieto and Jansson at Brno, and won again in Sweden and in Finland. Now he led on aggregate points (this year's system took only the best six results into account), with two rounds left. By the time he got to Monza, however, he'd fractured a wrist and chipped his ankle in a money race at Hengelo in Holland, and he took third behind Parlotti's Morbidelli and Nieto's Derbi with his wrist strapped up.

Another heavy smack into the bank at Mallory Park, chasing Agostini's MV and John Cooper's BSA triple on the 500 Suzuki, did further damage before the final round, at Jarama outside Madrid at the end of September. Diagnosed with bad bruising, he went to Spain and, riding in the earlier 50cc event for Kreidler, he retired when the pain suddenly got worse. A broken rib had twanged out of place. Barry forced it back in, taped himself up, and ran an ordeal of a 125 race, to third place. Nieto won it, and the title, with Chas second. Nieto was champion, by just eight points.

The Kreidler Van Veen was just another string to Sheene's bow. He'd been asked to race the machine at Brno, to help out rider Jan de Vries in his world title quest. To his surprise, first time in the class and in the rain on the long open-roads loop, he won. Barry was also enlisted by Derbi to race their new V-twin 250, a bike that made up in clever design what it lacked in reliability. It was his first 'works' bike. He told me later: 'We called it the non-works, because it broke down all the time.' Sixth in East Germany gave Barry his first 250 points, but he switched to a Yamaha later in the year.

At home, Sheene was riding the wave. First in the 125 championship and second (to Steve Machin) in the

BULTACO WORKS RIDER

Barry Sheene

Telephone:
01-837 5112

8, QUEEN SQUARE,
LONDON W.C.1

Classes: 125, 250, 350

Date: 11th January, 1970.

1968

BRANDS HATCH
1st, 1st, 1st, 1st, 1st,
2nd, 2nd, 4th, 5th

SNETTERTON
1st, 1st, 2nd, 5th, 6th

1969 Successes to Date

CRYSTAL PALACE
2nd

OULTON PARK
3rd, 6th

MALLORY PARK
4th, 6th

WALLASEY,
NEW BRIGHTON
1st, 1st, 1st, 1st, 1st 1st, 1st

SNETTERTON
2nd, 2nd, 3rd, 4th

BRANDS HATCH
1st, 1st, 1st, 1st, 2nd,
2nd, 4th, 5th

THRUXTON
1st, 7th

Dear Benny,

Re our telephone conversation a few weeks back I wonder if it is possible for you to acquire entry forms and regulations for the Tubbergren Road Races on the 18th, May.

During our conversation we spoke of start money that I would require, the sum being £140. for four starts should the regulations allow this.

Hoping that you could be of assistance by putting this forward to the Committee when they next meet.

Hoping to see you soon.

Yours sincerely,

B. Sheene.

B. Pinner Esq.,
Amelosestraat No.4,
Tubbergren,
HOLLAND.

Sheene's slightly misspelled letter of entry for his first-ever race outside Britain – the Tubbergen Road Races.

Growing trophy collection; unloading the van in a typical 1970s paddock; racers spent hours on the road.

250, it was in the well-supported international meetings that Barry really shone. Based with Frank and Iris in one of the first caravans in the paddock, and riding one or other of the Suzukis, he was a major presence at meetings that included such world luminaries as Giacomo Agostini and Phil Read, as well as the top national riders. Barry wore his hair long, a fag permanently in his mouth, and his all-white leathers unzipped to the waist. The fan base was growing fast.

It was on the big bike – quick and agile, though not particularly fast on any long straights – that Sheene proved the most. Firstly, that he could ride big bikes as well as small ones. In the June post-TT meeting at Mallory Park he hounded Agostini's MV all the way; and again in August at the so-called 'British Grand Prix' at Silverstone. At that same meeting, Barry won the 125 race, then defeated World Champion Rod Gould, Paul Smart and brilliant Finnish newcomer Jarno Saarinen in a photo-finish 250 race. A few weeks earlier, he'd won twice on the big Suzuki at the reverse-direction Hutchinson 100 meeting. Then came fateful Mallory, with that heavy crash while battling with Agostini. As a rider, Barry was maturing fast.

Close friends noticed a change in Barry during this time. One was Don Mackay, who had enlisted as mechanic for the GP foray with the Suzuki. As much a friend as mechanic, he was a passenger on the Sheene roller-coaster – pranks in the van included leaking diesel on the track at Spa, setting fire to the archaic and foul lavatories in Finland, lots of travel and not much luxury and, for Barry, lots of girls. Lots and lots of girls. And he was Jack the Lad. By the Finnish race at the start of August, Mackay had had enough. 'When he realised he was good, he started to get big-headed. He used to tell everybody how good he was, and how many birds he'd had.' In the van on the way back from Imatra, Don spoke up. 'Do you honestly believe people want to hear about your escapades? Everybody thinks you're a big-headed little prat. They don't want to know. Can't you understand this – I tell you as a friend.' They argued all the way back to Queen Square, where Mackay got out and walked away, his mechanic days over for more than a year.

They say failure matures a rider even faster than success. Maybe 1972 was the proof of it, for Barry. He had ended 1971 on the crest of a wave. Back at the

OPPOSITE *Showman Sheene was working on his image in 1970 – the white leathers medallion-man phase. In the foreground, the Suzuki 500 shows its Seeley frame.*

BELOW *Sheene spent an unhappy 1972 riding for Yamaha. This is the TZ250, at Mallory Park.*

RIGHT *Two World Champions, and one for the future. Rising star Sheene clowns with Rodney Gould at Phil Read's Premier Helmets stand at the 1972 Sporting Motorcycle Show.*

OPPOSITE *Actor Jon Pertwee, famous for his role as Dr Who, was one of many celebrities happy to pose with Britain's new biking hero.*

BELOW *King of Brands, and American racing legend Dick Mann hands the crowned Sheene a carriage clock for his collection.*

start of that year, *Motor Cycle News* had already made him 'Young Lion Number Two' in a series, saying he had 'moved into the classic scene like a breath of fresh air on a humid evening'. By the end of 1971, Barry Sheene was getting many more column inches for losing the 125 title than Phil Read got for winning his fifth, as a privateer in the 250 class.

The next year should have been good, and on paper it looked as though it would be. Barry had offers aplenty … to ride the British Suzuki again, the Derbi 250 in GPs, and both Triumph and Ducati wanted him for their big four-strokes. There were others, but Barry turned them all down in favour of his first ride for a Japanese factory. Yamaha were making a cautious return, via distributor teams, with a new water-cooled 250. Barry was to have this for the GPs, plus a handful of air-cooled 250, 350 and 354 machines for the home races. It had to be the right decision.

For another in the same position, it was. Saarinen went on to win the World Championship on his water-cooled bike. It worked out very differently for Sheene.

The year began with some sun, fun and racing. Paul Smart and Maggie Sheene had married secretly on the last day of 1971 at the Maidstone Register Office in Kent, eschewing a big family affair. Maggie had also forfeited a honeymoon … because Paul had a date to go racing in South Africa straight away, and Barry was going too. On hearing this news, the South African organisers immediately flew Maggie out to join them, and the Queen Square coterie had a fine old time, generally raising mayhem … like tipping oil in the swimming pool of the posh Kyalami Ranch hotel after being evicted for refusing to obey the dress code. Barry rode his Suzuki 500 to second at Pietermaritzburg's Roy Hesketh circuit to Agostini's MV Agusta. Paul rode the new water-cooled Yamaha there and Barry had it at Kyalami the next weekend. Both found the bike fast but clumsy. This was a bad omen.

Barry won OK at home, as was now expected – at Mallory, Oulton and Brands Hatch, where he gained his first King of Brands title. His GP season was the reverse: crashing in pre-season testing, and racking up non-finishes before a disappointing fourth in Austria, behind a year-old private Yamaha ridden by John Dodds. Over the Alps to Imola, and in practice Barry had his worst crash ever, after yet another engine seizure on the factory 250. He smashed his left collarbone, gashed his stomach, and was severely concussed. The collarbone required the first metalwork in what would become something approaching a lattice over much of his body.

The rest of the year availed little, and he split with Yamaha on bad terms, after they told him that while Saarinen would have the expected new 500 bike for the following 1973 season, Sheene would have to wait until at least the middle of the year. The problem was not so much Barry's discontent with the motorcycle, but that he was so public. Yamaha racing staff would in time be promoted in the company, and their memories were long. For this reason, if no other, Barry never would get anything but second best from Yamaha.

He did not shrink from criticism, and his voice was becoming exceedingly loud – 1972 saw *Motor Cycle Weekly* run the first of a series of columns that he used as a mouthpiece for many years to come. In March of the same year, the Barry Sheene Fan Club had been founded.

Looking back, this was the first proof that Barry Sheene was more than just a fine, strong racer, and a dashing hero for his times. In terms of results, 1972 had been relatively barren, but Barry's fame and popularity turned out to have more to do with his personality than his results. Sheene was a natural star, and he was just beginning to shine.

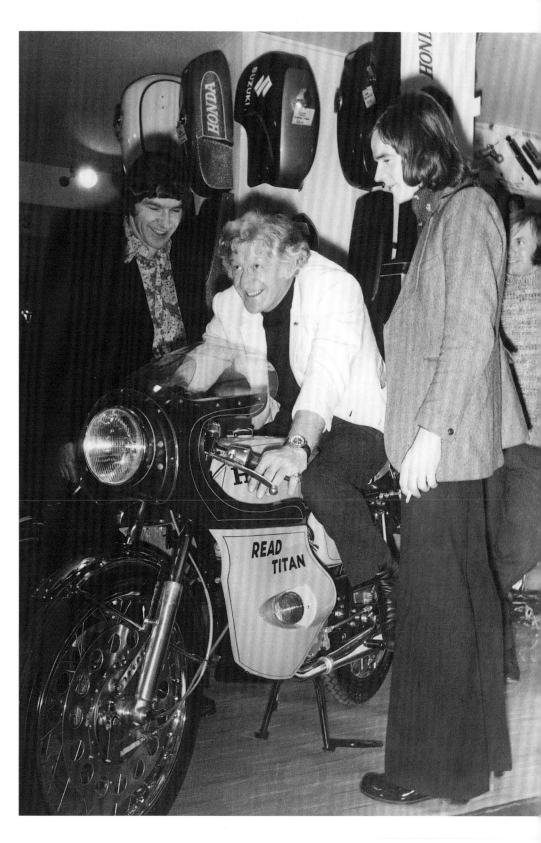

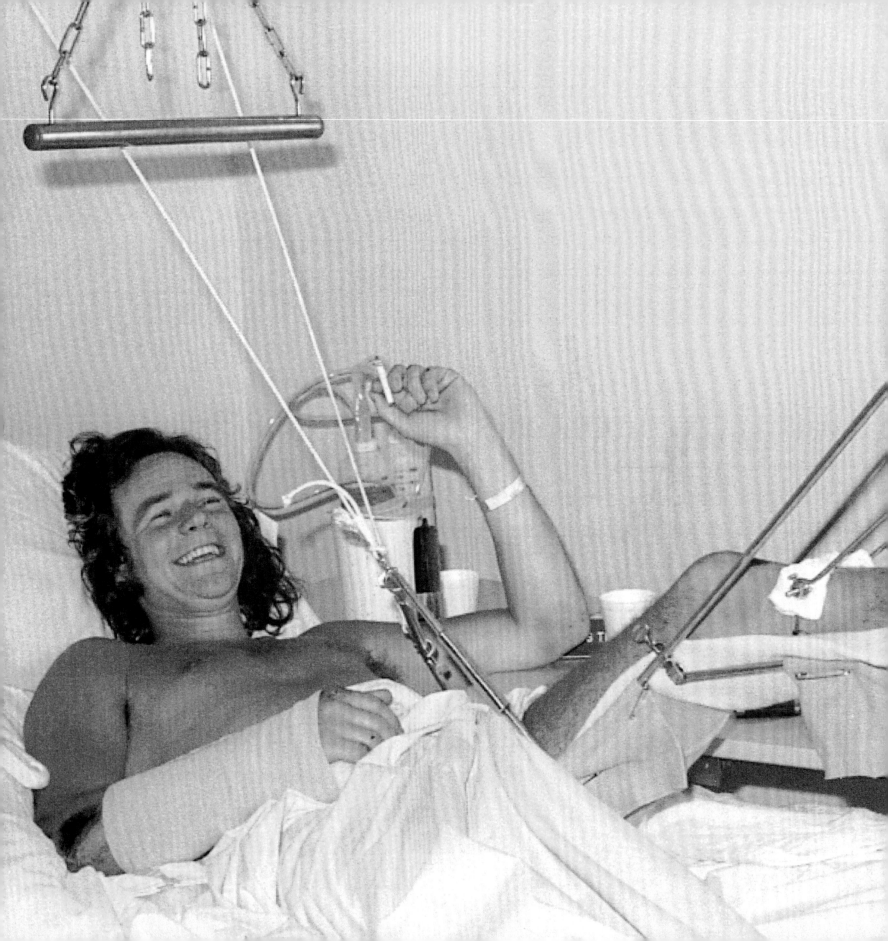

CHAPTER THREE

FAME THROUGH PAIN

Nobody would make it his life's ambition to achieve fame through getting injured. For Barry Sheene, however, the first of two near-fatal accidents was a brilliant career move. This crash, early in 1975, in a pre-race training run at Daytona's famous speed bowl, set several milestones. It was one of the fastest ever motorcycle crashes, at almost 180mph. Secondly, the cause was controversial. Thirdly, the victim made a recovery so courageous that he immediately joined the ranks of the world's natural heroes.

Most importantly, it was all recorded on film.

After his retirement in 1984, Barry co-hosted a Yorkshire Television show – *Just Amazing* – a Saturday prime-time clunker, showing daft stunts and lucky escapes. But none could hold a torch to award-winning documentary maker Frank Cvitanovich's sequence for Thames Television, being filmed at Daytona that day.

The film shows the big Suzuki at high speed on the banking. For a heart-stopping instant it slews sideways in a ball of smoke, then a jumble of flying objects hurtles past the camera. Barry came to rest in a crumpled heap 300 yards further on, still conscious, his left leg snapped at the thigh and folded behind him. He thought at first

Sheene made his reputation for his courageous response to injury. Look at the size of his smile, as he enjoys a fag after his record-speed Daytona crash in 1975.

he had lost it completely. You can't see this in the long shot, but he tries to open his visor, to discover that his right arm is also broken. Then the big American ambulance rushes to the scene, way down the track, at the entry to Turn One.

Sheene recalled, the year before he died, how he came to, 'completely compos mentis in every way. I just wanted them to take my helmet off, give me a cigarette, and leave me alone to settle down. None of which they did.'

Cameras rolling, treatment began almost at once … not before Barry had cheerfully reeled off his list of injuries – broken left femur and right arm, compression fractures to several vertebrae, broken ribs and extensive road rash on his back – adding impishly: 'Apart from that – I'm fine.' Later, he would say: 'I lost enough skin to cover a sofa' and as tellingly: 'If I'd been a race-horse, they would have shot me.'

Instead, they put an 18-inch pin to reattach his left femur, and seven weeks later he was back on a racing motorcycle. His fans were overwhelmed with admiration. His stature in racing was hugely reinforced. But it went much further than that.

This single incident – detailed in 'Disaster at Daytona' on pages 64-65 – more than any other propelled Barry from the sports pages to the news pages, and onto TV. Until then he'd been just a clever youngster with a cockney accent and long hair, wearing leathers, who had a reliable quip before or after any race, and a tendency to the win most of them. The crash marked Barry's transcendence from sports star to rock star. He was more than ready to make the most of it.

After the disappointment of 1972, Barry's career had turned right back around again in 1973. He was lucky to get his old job back with Suzuki GB, having dumped them for Yamaha the year before. Barry's exhausting persistence persuaded Rex White to intercede on his behalf with directors Peter Agg and Maurice Knight. 'I told them that, whatever else, Sheene was still the best rider in England.'

The early 1970s was an interesting time in motorcycle racing. The previous decade the Japanese manufacturers had come in like a rising tide, through the smaller classes. Honda excepted, this meant two-strokes – a new generation of ear-splitting heretics, with the power and speed to sweep away the four-stroke old-guard. For technical reasons, this was easier to do with smaller engines, and the breakthrough in the 500 class was

awaited with trepidation by MV Agusta, last defenders of a long-standing faith.

But there was a pincer movement, via the new Formula 750 class, originally created in Europe mainly to find a role for production-based racers developed from the likes of Triumph's three-cylinder 750 Trident and Norton's bored-out-twin Commando. By now, the Japanese were making their own big street bikes – Honda's seminal 750 Four had appeared in 1969. The big bikes were three-cylinder two-strokes, in the case of Kawasaki and Suzuki. The Kawasaki was a rapid but more erratic machine. The Suzuki had a special edge … it was water-cooled, meaning much more reliable power at racing speeds. Until something more specialised came along, Suzuki's 'kettle' made the foundation for a highly effective racer. Especially since it was also undergoing constant development racing in the US, where European road-racing had been discovered in their own lively 750 series, and where English racer Cliff Carr – and, from 1974, also Paul Smart – had a flourishing career. This brain drain across the Atlantic would soon be going the other way.

Sheene got one of these machines for 1973, as well as a much newer version of the air-cooled 500. This, however, was a stop-gap, because Suzuki had already started to draw up their own full-race 500-class challenger. It was the square-four RG500, which would have a long and glorious career in Grand Prix racing, including seven manufacturers' championships, and four individual riders' titles. The first two would go to Barry Sheene.

In fact, the Suzuki GB team was down the pecking order, and the bikes had a taint of hand-me-down and surplus-to-requirements. Sheene visited Beddington Lane to take first pick from a batch of 12 good 500cc race engines; but the 750 motors were distinctly tired. Seeley frames were commissioned for both the 500 and 750. Colin Seeley also built an experimental monocoque chassis for the 500, but Barry rode this only once, and it was shelved.

His 1973 racing year was two-fold. At home he contested the MCN Superbike Championship on the 750, and the Shellsport 500 series; abroad, he took on the new FIM Formula 750 series, a World Championship in all but name. Don Mackay rejoined the party, Stan Woods was Barry's new team-mate. Life with the sharp and cheeky Londoner was to be an eye-opening experience for the matter-of-fact Cheshire rider.

The Suzuki 750, with almost 100 horsepower delivered to over-stretched tyres by a frame at the limit of its strength, was a seriously fast and powerful racing motorcycle. Any doubts that the spindly 22-year-old would be able to handle a big bike were swept away. Barry was a big-bike natural. And his riding was getting better and better.

Woods, looking back after retirement, told me: 'I sussed the job out quickly in 1973 – that if one was going to beat Barry Sheene, one was going to have to live very close to the line. I was married, and I had a youngster, and I just wasn't prepared to do that.'

Their first international together was a bit harem-scarem. Barry liked to explore short cuts and, on the way over the Alps to Imola in the van with Stan Woods, they'd run into some heavy snow and had to use their stock of spare chains as impromptu tyre chains. At least that's how Stan remembered it. The upshot was that neither finished the race … chain trouble!

The rest of the campaign was better considered. Sheene won round two at Clermont-Ferrand, his first foreign win on a big motorcycle; in Sweden he was third, behind veteran Australian Jack Findlay, famously the world's most successful privateer, and team-mate Woods. Barry switched to the lighter 500 twin for the Finnish round at the tight Hameenlinna circuit, taking second. Then came Silverstone, with Paul Smart in attendance

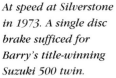

At speed at Silverstone in 1973. A single disc brake sufficed for Barry's title-winning Suzuki 500 twin.

with his US Suzuki machine. Smarty won, Barry was fourth overall after switching to his 500 at the last minute when the 750 blew a head gasket while it was being warmed up for the second leg. Three weeks later … sensation: Sheene was disqualified for effectively changing bikes mid-race. Jack Findlay moved into the championship lead.

The head gaskets were a continuing problem, and led to trouble at the next round in Germany. Stan Woods's machine, with a standard chassis, was running well, but Barry's bike kept blowing that gasket on the long wide-open straights through the Hockenheim forests. Given his championship position (not to mention his personality) Sheene went straight to team manager Rex White. 'He said he must have Stan's bike, or at least Stan's engine. I was right in the middle. I'd spend five minutes in Barry's caravan and five minutes in Stan's.' Advice from Maurice Knight back in Britain was to do whatever was best, but that Barry must take priority. 'It was difficult, because Stan was extremely loath to give up anything.' At the 11th hour, White said: 'I decided that each would ride his own bike.'

Woods's blood was up after this to and fro. 'I was upset, and I made an all-out effort to win the race.

Flared trousers and feline friends, as Iris joins Barry for a photocall at his new Wisbech home early in 1974. The motorcycle is a three-cylinder Suzuki GT550, complete with Ram Air cooling!

Which is exactly what I did.' Sheene's gasket trouble struck again, and he was fourth overall.

It would come down to the final round, where Barry was second to John Dodds. Findlay was out of the results, and Sheene took his first major world title by ten points.

This was achievement enough to prove his career had regained impetus. But it was in Britain that Barry had the world at his feet during 1973 – in spite of a couple of costly crashes. The first came after winning the King of Brands title at his home circuit at the start of the season – in a later race, he took several toenails off after a front tyre deflated. The second crash was testing at Silverstone. Painful, but not enough to stop Sheene proving his dominance with both the Superbike and the Shellsport 500 titles.

Sheene's sharp features, flowing hair and lippy comments were instantly recognisable throughout motorcycling by now, and increasingly beyond the sport as well. Among the faithful, he was rewarded by a landslide win in the reader's poll for the MCN Man of the Year. He had carried all before him in 1973 and wiped away doubts about his talent and the depth of his commitment. He would add another dimension in 1974.

The oil crisis had struck late in 1973. As 1974 began, there were still queues and rationing systems for fuel in Europe and the USA where drivers were trying to get used to the idea of a gas-saving national 55mph speed limit. Motorsport was out of favour as a consequence, and somewhat apologetic: the season-opening Daytona 200-mile race was cut to 180 miles, to save fuel too!

Motorcycle sport was booming all the same, and Sheene's career with it. His star was in the ascendant at Suzuki. He retained his Suzuki GB contract for the 750 and 500 races at home and in Europe, and signed up with Suzuki USA for Daytona, plus a handful of other well-paid US races. Most significantly for his future, there was a third contract, direct with the Suzuki factory in Japan. This was to develop and race their formidable new 500-class racer, and the Grand Prix adventure is described later in the book.

Away from the GPs, his busy year started at Daytona, for the shortened '200'. It was Barry's first time there, and his first time on the daunting flat-out banking at the Florida tri-oval, more famous for NASCAR events, but a major fixture on the international motorcycle calendar, ranking with the Isle of Man in importance to the Japanese factories. He was up to fourth in the race

The Sheenes' Queen Square workshop was transplanted to Wisbech in 1972. Here Frank and Barry fettle the Seeley Suzuki 750 (with victory stars on the fairing) and 500.

when he retired. There was a sensational winner, however ... multiple World Champion and Italian idol Giacomo Agostini, giving the new 700cc Yamaha TZ750 a dream debut, after his own headline-grabbing switch from MV Agusta to the Japanese company.

This was the first time Barry used the racing number '7' that would become his trademark. It was available in the US because of the retirement of dirt-track superstar Mert Lawill, and Barry liked it enough to make it his own. In this, he was unwittingly following racing driver Stirling Moss.

Agostini's new Yamaha TZ750 was the bike that would unseat the Suzuki and Kawasaki triples from their domination of Formula 750 – a pure racer built in sufficient quantities (200 models) to qualify for a class intended for production-based bikes. It would give Barry quite a lot of trouble. Especially when ridden by the maverick leader of a new wave coming from America, where growing interest in road-racing had unearthed a seam of hard-riding talent from the dirt tracks. The maverick was Kenny Roberts. His first visit to Britain, for the 1974 Transatlantic Challenge series (*aka* the Easter Match Races) brought him five wins in six races. Kenny's Yamaha triumphed at Brands Hatch, Mallory Park and

ABOVE *Slightly pebble-dashed, the Sheene 750 was well used. This was in Italy, for the Imola 200 of 1974.*

LEFT *Seminal moment: Sheene takes his trade-mark number 7 for the first time, in his first race in America. The full US Suzuki team for the 1974 Daytona, from right: Sheene, Gary Nixon, Cliff Carr, Paul Smart and factory tester Ken Araoka.*

once at Oulton Park. Barry beat him in the other race.
The writing was clearly on the wall. Sheene might
arguably be the best rider in Britain, but there was a
greater challenge to come.

Barry's next escapade with Kenny was at Imola, the
first round of the F750 series. It involved a rentacar,
another American rider, Gene Romero, and three
worse-for-drink racers sharing all the controls, Barry
on the handbrake. The car ended up inverted in the
canal and sinking – by luck all escaped unhurt. Barry
finished fifth in the race, but defence of his title was put
on the back burner. Suzuki had something much more
important … a year of fast-forward development to
their new square four.

It was during his GP campaign that Barry had another
big crash – at Imola, when the gearbox locked up.
Heavily concussed, he broke a bone in his foot and
sported a horrendously bloodshot eye from an internal
haemorrhage. He was fit enough to ride in the King of
Brands meeting a week later, but was on crutches, lifted
on and off his bike, and wearing film-star shades to hide
his horror-movie eye. The crowds and the press loved it.
Many rivals would comment rather sourly that Barry did
make a lot of his injuries, and there was truth in this.
Mick Grant recalled how different was his own approach.
'If Barry had a broken leg, or a broken arm, or whatever
he had, he made a big shout about it. And I didn't. I was
more terrified of people saying you can't race. But
because Barry was Barry, I don't think people had the
bottle to tell him he couldn't race. At the TT in 1979, I'd
broken my hip, my pelvis and my ribs, and I was being
lifted on and off the bike – I just told everyone to fuck
off and leave me alone. I could have made great mileage
out of it, but I thought: bloody hell, if I don't do this
race, I lose my start money. I think Barry would have
exploited it.'

Anyway, another rival – Barry Ditchburn – took the
King of Brands title, but Barry got all the headlines.

For once, Barry didn't win the MCN readers' poll –
the 1974 Man of the Year title went to Phil Read, who
had defeated Yamaha-mounted Agostini to win his
second successive 500cc title, and MV Agusta's last. Barry
had ruled supreme at home, defeating Grant and Peter
Williams in the MCN Superbike series, with race wins at
Cadwell Park, Mallory Park, Olivers Mount and twice at
Brands Hatch. For the second of these, he was again on
crutches, following a crash at the Swedish GP. He beat
Read's MV at two home internationals – Mallory Park's
Race of the Year and the Silverstone curtain-raiser for the

F750 round. Barry also retained his Shellsport 500 crown, riding the old twin (now water-cooled) rather than the GP machine.

That year ended with a trip to Japan with Phil and Madeleine Read – by now good friends with Sheene – to test the next year's 500 machine. They nearly became team-mates. Read later told me his decision to stay with MV Agusta rather than join Suzuki with Sheene had been 'the biggest mistake of my career'. Their friendship, already tinged for Barry with memories of Bill Ivy, would not last much longer. During 1975, in Read's words, 'we became unfriends'. There were sundry reasons … one being that Read suspected Sheene of having an affair with his then wife Madeleine. Much later, there was a heated exchange of revelations between the now deadly rivals, Read in the *Sunday People*, Sheene in the *News of the World*. Sheene admitted there had been some sex-play between them, adding uncharitably that she hadn't been particularly good at it. Madeleine later took her own life.

A more trenchant argument concerned an alleged bribe during the season, for Sheene to help Read in a late-season race, when the MV rider was still in the running for the championship. Read admitted to me

ABOVE *It's 1974, and Barry has just won Mallory Park's major international Race of the Year. Lesley Shepherd, his first long-term girlfriend, shares the moment.*

LEFT *Five's a crowd, on a 900cc BMW. Sheene takes fellow competitors round Mallory. From left, Dave Croxford, Paul Smart and Peter Williams, with Phil Read on the front mudguard.*

OPPOSITE *If Barry flaunted his courage, it was because he had plenty to spare. A week after a 100mph crash at Imola, he raced in the King of Brands meeting at his home circuit. He didn't win the race, but he took all the headlines.*

ABOVE *Moment of truth. The rear wheel locks solid at more than 175mph. The camera recorded every moment of the fastest racing motorcycle crash.*

March, 1975: The late-afternoon sun casts long shadows on the steep banking of the Daytona speed bowl. This was a week before the big 200-miler – a race Barry had every hope of winning. He and US Suzuki team-mate Gary Nixon were at private Suzuki tests which were going well, and coming to an end.

Dunlop motorcycle tyre technical manager Tony Mills was one of the small party in the pits. They watched as Sheene rounded the final banking, swooping down to gain extra speed on the home straight, fastest part of the ultra-fast course.

'Barry had run a number of laps, and I was monitoring the tyre all the time. It looked perfectly all right. Barry went out with the intention of doing three or four hot laps.

'I was watching him pass a couple of laps later, then just as he was more or less crossing the finish line, all hell broke loose. The bike went into an almighty out-of-control situation.'

The first to reach the crumpled figure was US Suzuki team manager Merv Wright. It was a shocking sight. They all feared the worst. Amazingly, Barry moved. Groaned. Then the ambulance arrived and he was rushed to the nearby Halifax Hospital.

Barry's major treatment was the insertion of an 18-inch pin in his left femur. The other injuries would only need time. Barry was reluctant to give them any. He was obsessed with getting back onto a bike. As he said: 'I knew it hadn't been my fault.'

But whose fault was it?

There is no doubt that the crash was caused by a mechanical failure – the rear wheel locked. Barry's explanation, repeated many times, and once again to me in February 2003, was plain and simple. The tyre had delaminated at speed. Something similar had happened to another rider, Henk Claessens, later that week.

Dunlop had acknowledged this to Sheene, he confirmed, in a private visit to his Wisbech home. Had they settled out of court? 'In that they gave me a wedge of cash, yes.'

I was able to verify these details unofficially with sources close to Dunlop, where an engineer told me: 'There wasn't much doubt it was a tyre failure. They were experimental days, with the first use of aramid fibres … Kevlar.'

But it was equally easy to find persistent dark rumours of a long-standing cover-up, in which for some reason Dunlop took the rap for a failure triggered by something on the bike breaking first. When Barry died, almost exactly 28 years after that afternoon in Florida, many still suspected a conspiracy of silence.

Memories of the incident differ, while the machine is well beyond detailed investigation.

Sheene's first words to his Japanese mechanic had been: 'The transmission seized.' As he told me shortly before his death, it was an easy first impression. 'I knew the rear wheel had locked, and I declutched and it was still solid, so I assumed it was the gearbox.'

Investigating the crash scene, Dunlop's Tony Mills and the Suzuki

RIGHT *Help was immediately at hand, but they all thought at first the crumpled figure must surely be dead.*

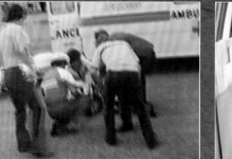

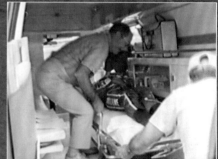

team found intermittent skid marks leading to the final black smear. The terminal rear-wheel lock-up had been preceded by a series of brief chirrups, increasing in duration.

The tyre was more or less in bits, with witnesses contradicting one another on whether the remains were still inflated, 'to about 30psi,' according to one contemporary report. Mills casts doubt on this. 'Straight after the crash, Suzuki's Mitsuo Itoh came up to me with some pieces of tread. Quite small pieces.'

Mills confirmed this was a very early use of Kevlar. 'Dunlop were the first. At that time tyre problems were beginning to emerge at Daytona. In '72 our triangular profile tyre had given a lot of problems, and we developed a flatter, wider profile. It was all in its infancy at that time. We never found out exactly why the tyre failed.'

There was a suggestion that a new chain tensioner might have shifted and fouled the tyre. This did not explain the intermittent lock-ups, and was denied by Sheene himself, who told me: 'As soon as I saw the chain adjuster, I had it taken off my bike.'

A stronger possibility lay in a small design detail of the bike – the amount of clearance between the centre of the tyre and the suspension. Speeds were rising constantly, and the amount of tyre fling (half an inch or more added to the diameter) at more than 175mph may not have been fully catered for. Even if the tyre crown was only brushing lightly against the metal, it would have been very destructive to the tyre.

This was more consistent with the pre-crash skids, and also reflects the relative lack of knowledge at a time of rapid tyre and engine development, with horsepower and top speed playing leapfrog year by year.

A third theory took into account the fact that one of the rear wheel adjusters had disintegrated, and the rear wheel was severely skewed in the swing-arm. This, however, was more likely to be the result than the cause of the crash.

Almost 30 years later, another insider rumour surfaced – that Barry was testing an experimental six-speed gearbox, with specially slim gears inside the five-speed casing. The suggestion was that at full speed, fifth and sixth had become intermittently engaged at the same time, causing the chirrups, and eventually the terminal seize. When the bike had come to rest, the gears freed up again. This is contradicted by the report of the

Suzuki team mechanics, who had found both engine and gearbox in perfect working order when they stripped the bike.

In the months before his death, Sheene also ruled it out. 'That's rubbish. We'd been using a six-speed gearbox since October or so of the previous year.

'It was caused by the tyre delaminating, and anyone who says anything different doesn't know what he's talking about.'

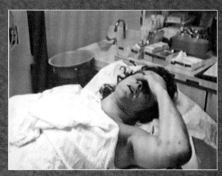

LEFT Sheene's career as a famous X-ray pin-up began here. 'If I was a race-horse, I would have been shot.'

later that he had made this request and considered it to be reasonable – it being better for Suzuki if MV were to triumph than Yamaha, and also on the grounds of past friendship. He denied offering money, though he said: 'I don't know if MV might have made an offer.' Sheene took great offence, and the friendship was firmly over.

The Daytona injuries dented the start of a busy year, and another injury was to bracket his British season. In between, the pace would have been frenetic even had he not started out as a recuperating invalid. As well as the GP effort, Barry managed a full-scale attempt at the F750 title again, plus the home series, riding for Suzuki GB in a reconstituted team. Woods was his team-mate again, White back as manager – the previous year a budget cut meant both riders had run independently.

The latest three-cylinder Suzukis had staged something of a comeback in the Formula 750 series. Sheene won three of the first six rounds and, as the season drew to a close, was narrowly ahead of old rival Findlay when injuries at home meant he had to sit out the final round. Suzuki drafted in John Williams to aid Newbold and Woods in an attempt to retain Sheene's lead. He needed Findlay to finish lower than third.

'Willie' did well, finishing second, but the other two were unable to prevent Findlay from claiming the championship. Barry openly blamed them for not trying hard enough. His popularity among fellow riders took another blow. Many fans inevitably sided with Barry.

The fresh injury was really rotten luck. Barry's home season had gone well, and he was disputing the MCN Superbike title hard with Mick Grant. The late-season Mallory Park Race of the Year (still Britain's biggest pay-day for riders) saw Sheene's Suzuki take the bacon, ahead of Read's MV and Kenny Roberts on the 750 Yamaha. During that race, Sheene had clouted his right knee on a kerb while cutting inside a slow and dozy backmarker. Protected by little more than an extra layer of leather – there were no knee protectors or sliders in those days – it was acutely sore, but nothing seemed broken. His left leg was still pinned and painful; now his other leg was also injured.

A week later, he was defending his Superbike title at Cadwell. He'd borrowed wheelie king Dave Taylor's Bultaco trials bike to nip over to the organisers' office. Racers are almost all unable to resist the temptation to show off and on his way back, when he spotted a fan with a camera, he pulled an obliging wheelie. It went

OPPOSITE *A word to the wise. Sheene shares a confidence with 1974 World Champion Phil Read, the man he would depose as top British racer.*

LEFT *Sheene on the new square-four 500cc Grand Prix Suzuki: he took a second successive win in Mallory Park's Race of the Year, but hurt his knee on the kerb.*

Barry's first international win after the Daytona crash was the French F750 round at Magny-Cours.

too far, as sometimes happens, and Barry simply stepped off. His right leg buckled under him.

Sheene insisted on being taken to London on the back seat of his Rolls and, as rival Mick Grant took the MCN Superbike title, his kneecap and the top of his shin were screwed and wired together. His medical record was becoming increasingly bionic; his gait on crutches increasingly familiar.

Didn't stop him enjoying himself – starting with another new Rolls-Royce as soon as he came out of hospital, at a cost of £16,543. Now almost permanently at his posh pal Piers Forester's Chelsea flat, Barry would later talk about how he had trouble stopping the girls from bumping into one another on the stairs. He moved in the fast set; his name was linked with Pammie Townley, daughter of a Naval officer, and Irene Durnford, a fashionable beauty.

Sheene was already a superstar at home. Like Valentino Rossi in Italy in the early years of his career, his name was getting around. He was always in the papers, and revelling in it. In 1973, he'd posed wearing underpants with a skimpy model for the *Sun*, been photographed for *Vogue* by David Bailey, had a page interview by Ian Wooldridge in the *Daily Mail*. His circle of friends included Formula One driver James Hunt and team owner Lord Hesketh, and his name was linked with a possible move to cars with the lord's F1 team. Or, reported elsewhere, Ford rally cars. Cuttings and rumours galore.

One night, soon after leaving hospital, he was perforce sitting out the dance-floor action at Tramps – Springsteen's 'Born To Run' on the turntable, or maybe something from the new Supertramp album – when he met the latest elegant blonde in his life. Her name was Stephanie McLean. Mrs Stephanie McLean. And when she asked him the following week if she could borrow a pair of his racing leathers for a photo shoot, Barry Sheene's life crossed a watershed.

SUZUKI

KGO 599N

OPPOSITE *Breakfast of champions included the all-important cuppa and a fag.*

LEFT *She is Page Three glamour model Jilly Johnson, he is patched-up motorcycle superstar Barry Sheene. Barry's pin-up potential peaked with this underwear ad.*

CHAPTER FOUR

SQUARE FOUR

The noise was something new. It was busy and, like all the unsilenced two-strokes of the time, ear-damagingly shrill, but with a deeper cadence – four single-cylinder 125cc motorcycle engines fused into one. The Doppler effect meant the sound waves piled up on one another, falsely treble. A small party of Suzuki-uniformed technicians looked down the track at the approaching machine. It was weaving visibly at speed, Barry Sheene's Donald Duck helmet tucked down behind the screen. Simultaneously, they stabbed at their stopwatches.

A new record. That day, early in 1974, Barry Sheene had taken 1.5 seconds off the best ever time round the 6.5km private Suzuki test circuit at Ryuyo. And if he was wide-eyed when he pulled in after that hot lap, it was not so surprising. Ryuyo is more than just a tongue-twister for westerners. It's also dauntingly fast, and lined with unforgiving trees. And the new 500cc Suzuki, their fastest-yet racing motorcycle, was still a raw-edged and unrefined little monster.

Sheene spoke about it later. 'It was very fast, and a bit lethal. The prototype was more powerful than the bike I won the title on two years later. It had the power band of a 125.' Barry awaited the next encounter with both excitement and trepidation.

Suzuki, and Barry Sheene, were going for the ultimate prize, the senior title in motorcycle racing.

Classic Grand Prix motorcycle racing at its finest.
Massive Belgian GP crowd shares the drama in 1975, as
Sheene's two-stroke Suzuki pursues the last-ditch four-
stroke MVs of Bonera and Read through Eau Rouge.

The premier class was at a watershed. Four-strokes had ruled since before its inception in 1949, and the howling four- and three-cylinder MV Agustas had been supreme since 1958, during which time they had narrowly fought off a challenge from Honda. Now the two-strokes were coming.

In 1973, Phil Read had claimed another title for the glamorous Italian 'fire engines', much to the chagrin of his team-mate Agostini, who had won it for the previous seven years straight. The patrician marque had been favoured by some dark luck. Yamaha had come in fighting, and the legendary Finnish racer Jarno Saarinen had won the opening two rounds on the two-stroke. Then came tragedy at Monza, when Saarinen was killed, along with Italian Renzo Pasolini, in a multiple pile-up on the first lap of the 250 race, a championship he was also leading. Yamaha withdrew for the rest of the year out of respect. MV won effectively unopposed, but the four-stroke's days were numbered in Grand Prix racing, until they were brought back with new MotoGP regulations some 30 years later.

Barry's class entry had been a cheeky few practice laps on a 360 Bultaco at the 1971 Spanish GP. During 1973, he had a second and more serious outing on the Suzuki 500 twin in Finland – and retired.

The new Suzuki was the real thing, and Barry's first encounter was with Paul Smart and fellow Briton Cliff Carr, now racing in the USA, when they flew out to Japan to test the prototype. Riding the new bike in freezing conditions, all were impressed by its enormous speed. Maybe the cold, Smart now recalls, is why there were no major technical failures at the tests. 'It was a frightening thing, really, because one thing the Japanese didn't do then was build chassis. It was bloody fast … I think we were doing 180mph down that long straight. All trees. Funnily enough it wasn't breaking too much when we were there. But then again it was really cold. I remember them moaning about my weight, but drive was the problem – it had spoked wheels and little tiny tyres. In fact I was faster through the speed traps because I didn't get so much wheelspin! It was the first genuine 100-horsepower 500.'

Unseen photographs taken at the first RG500 tests in Japan.

THIS PAGE From top: flimsy frame of blindingly fast new prototype; pheasant damage to the screen of Sheene's machine; Ryuyo's long, long straights.

OPPOSITE From top: Cliff Carr and Barry with RG500; Suzuki man humbly presents Sheene with the remains of the pheasant that smashed his screen.

The Suzuki RG500 XR14 was the prototype of what would set the two-stroke standard for the 500 class, winning four riders' and seven manufacturers' championships between 1976 and 1982. For Barry Sheene, it represented the next big opportunity. The compact racer, in blue and white and with a funny little mock Kamm-tail aerodynamic seat, was his ticket to domination on the track. He would use that as the springboard for even greater fame. The Suzuki carried on winning long after Barry's results on it had faded and he had left the company. But his close involvement in its development meant this was to a large his extent his baby. 'I used to think of it as my bike,' he said.

Suzuki had adapted a design previously used in the 125 class: two twin-cylinder two-stroke engines fused together in a square four. This configuration, suitably splayed, would evolve into the V4s that came to dominate the 500cc class. The Suzuki, however, was more like four separate single-cylinder engines, since each cylinder had its own crankshaft – the gearing together of these would cause many teething problems. Even relatively detuned as it developed, it was extremely powerful by the standards of the day. More importantly, it was a more compact engine design than the in-line-four Yamaha, and the disc valves (carburettors on the sides) gave a crucial edge in performance and control.

The first XR14 version had a weight-saving open frame, lacking the usual bottom loops, and claimed 95 horsepower in a 290-pound package, setting new standards for its time both in performance and in wayward handling. The chassis gained full loop design during the year, the handling improved gradually.

The engine had several teething problems, including a tendency to seize abruptly. Nipping up the pistons was a worrying side effect in two-strokes, leading riders to keep their hands over the clutch lever at all times, to give them a chance to declutch rapidly before the otherwise almost inevitable crash. The Suzuki also suffered transmission failures, which are even more terminal … if the gearbox seizes, no amount of declutching will free up a locked back wheel.

Smart: 'Every part of it broke, to start with … everything. The big gears joining the crankshafts, piston seizures … I remember the first race we went to, the Grand Prix at Clermont-Ferrand. Mine did 300 yards – first, second, third, locked solid, with all the pack behind me. And Barry completed the race. And that's how it was … for the first six or seven races.

Mine seized up every time I got on it. It never ever finished … and Barry's finished races.' The team blamed Smart's riding, so there was some perverse satisfaction when they swopped bikes at Imola during practice. True to form, Sheene's bike gave Smart an easy outing, but Smart's bike locked solid within hearing of the pits, throwing Sheene off, without injury. 'He comes back with all bits of grass sticking out, and I said: "That's the best thing you could have done for me."'

For the first season, Suzuki signed up Sheene, Smart, and veteran Jack Findlay, Barry's old sparring partner. Smarty had an awful year, marred by injury early and again late in the season; the other two would

OPPOSITE *Brand new, and set to be hugely influential. Sheene lines up for the new Suzuki's first race – the French GP at Clermont-Ferrand.*

BELOW *The bike's new levels of horsepower were hard work for the racing tyres, especially in the days before treadless slicks.*

apply their very different approaches. Barry got better results, but Findlay's greater consistency meant he finished one place higher in the championship. That was, however, only fifth, for although the square four was highly competitive, it was very hit or miss.

For Sheene, this was the first machine that he couldn't really get his hands onto, which was a novelty. Suzuki ran their GP effort out of Belgium, the Japanese mechanics meeting the riders at the tracks, and handling all the work themselves. This reflected the higher level he had reached. It would have been the same had he taken another tempting offer for that year, to join MV Agusta. It got no further than a brief run in the paddock at Imola, and a formal invitation from Count Agusta, which Barry refused. He could see that Japan held the future.

The 1974 GP trail brought Barry's first full season in the top class, back to many familiar tracks with the all-new Suzuki. It started well in France – Sheene second to Read and ahead of Gianfranco Bonera on the second MV. A week later in Germany Sheene was just one of the top riders to withdraw when the organisers declined to add extra straw bales to the daunting Nürburgring, an early taste of rider politics. Another weekend later it was

Austria, and Sheene third. To his embarrassment, however, he had been lapped by winner Agostini and second-placed Bonera's MV. It was an unwelcome career first.

The season was shorter then, but intensive. Just one weekend off before the Italian round at Imola. After crashing in practice, Barry was lying third when a gearbox seizure sent him looping off for another visit to the circuit's scrubbing-brush nuns in the local hospital. Badly concussed, confused and battered, he had broken a bone in his foot, bloodied one eye, and had a huge graze on his back. His sister, Maggie, went with him to hospital. 'All he did for hours was say: "What happened, Mags?" I'd tell him, and he'd say: "Oh yeah. I remember." As he finished saying it, he'd start again. "What happened, Mags?"'

Findlay qualified the new Suzuki fastest for the Isle of Man TT, but did not finish. This was a race that Sheene had long since foresworn and which would be dropped from the calendar after 1976, at least partly due to his unswerving criticism.

The next outing was at Assen, the Dutch TT. By now, Barry was thoroughly nervous of the fast but fragile racer because, since his own lock-up and crash at Imola, there'd been another serious crash triggered by a seized piston.

The victim had been American hard nut Gary Nixon – the two had been friends since they'd met at the Transatlantic series of 1971. Nixon told me, 'Barry was the one British rider who showed us Americans a good time', and both Nixon and Sheene were notoriously fond of having a good time. Sheene also much admired Nixon's talent, honed on the mile and half-mile dirt tracks, and in the rough and tumble of US 750 Superbikes (Nixon was twice Grand National Champion). He persuaded Suzuki to give the American a test on the GP bike, with the plan of racing at Assen. Nixon, fresh from winning at Loudon, had suffered a piston seizure on his first lap of the Ryuyo circuit, bringing himself and following factory test rider Ken Araoke down at high speed, and suffering serious arm injuries among a comprehensive list. Barry blamed himself, since he had arranged the test, and told Nixon: 'If you'd been killed, I'd have given up racing.'

With this in his mind, when his gearbox started to make graunching noises at Assen, Barry was happy to (as he put it) 'make my excuses and leave'. A simpler problem – the gearshift coming adrift – put him out of

the Belgian GP; then a different mechanical failure triggered another high-speed crash at Anderstorp in Sweden. This time it was the water pump, and as he went flying high into a catch-fence, Agostini also fell trying to avoid him. That effectively handed the title to Read and the MV, and Ago was full of angry criticism in the Italian press, blaming Sheene, with Sheene in turn protesting his innocence.

Fourth at the final round at Brno meant that hopes of winning a GP in its first season came to nothing for the Suzuki, but Barry had given the Japanese something to celebrate with a hard-fought last-lap win over Read's MV Agusta at the non-championship 'British Grand Prix' at Silverstone.

Clearly the RG500 was a competitive design. At the same time, the Suzuki factory race department had learned a lot during the year – not only fixing reliability problems, but also designing a full-loop frame with an aluminium swing-arm for 1975, with horsepower up by five to reach the magic 100 – a level of 200 horsepower per litre. It was this bike that Barry went to test at the end of 1974, only to crash and suffer concussion at the Ryuyo circuit outside Hamamatsu.

Flying out to join him was none other than title

In 1974, his first 500-class year, Sheene already played a leading role in rider politics. Here, at the Nürburgring for the German GP, he discusses rebellion with Agostini. The top riders refused to race, for safety reasons.

ABOVE *Franko sets the pace, as Barry pounds the punishing path to fitness after the Daytona crash.*

RIGHT *Barry helps Iris with the family washing at Wisbech, by only spattering mud in the other direction.*

winner Read – also invited to tests. They were still pals at this stage. Read later told me how he'd arrived with Madeleine to find post-crash Barry much down in the dumps. They took him out for dinner and a few drinks. Back at the hotel lobby, a British journalist called. 'You would have thought Barry was in the intensive care ward, the way he played up his injuries. We'd just been out, and he was fine.'

There was no need to play up the injuries sustained on the big 750 at Daytona at the start of 1975. Sheene, never a willing patient, was an awe-inspiring spectacle to his inner circle when recovering from that 180mph crash on the banking – driving himself insistently into the pain and beyond, forcing injured joints and damaged muscles into action again. He allowed himself at least one big treat – his first Rolls-Royce, with the plate 4BSR. There was not much luxury otherwise. Barry would push himself physically to a degree few could understand, let alone tolerate. This, the deepest confirmation of Sheene's courage and genuine heroism, was something the fans never saw.

Seven weeks after the crash, he was ready to ride again – and entered for the opening MCN Superbike

ABOVE *Sheene wanted*
to race at the Austrian
GP, barely two months
after his big crash in
1975. He argued to the
bitter end to be
allowed a push-starter
from the back of the
grid, but was denied at
the very last minute.

OPPOSITE *With his*
usual casual air,
Barry waits for the
start of the Belgian
GP of 1975.

race at Cadwell Park. He let few people see how nervous
he was about getting back on a bike. One was Don
Mackay, returned to the team and handling the big 750
at the private test on the back loop of Cadwell. 'He said
to me he felt he was going to be a spastic, but he had to
prove it to himself. He was going so slow at first. He
stopped and said: "How am I doing?" I said: "Hmmm,
not too well." He said: "Well give me a chance."

'After about 20 or 30 laps, he was going as fast as he
usually did. He came in with a big grin on his face. He
said: "OK, pack the bike up. I know I can still beat
the bastards."'

His main rival for the home series was Mick Grant, on
the Kawasaki, and a fierce rival too. Grant, asked now
what of all their races he remembers most, picks that
Cadwell Park return. 'It was just a few weeks after his
crash. I mucked up the start, and most of the grid had
gone. At that time it was either going to be me or Barry
winning the races, though with his injuries it wasn't
going to be him that day. But as I came through the
field, the hardest guy to pass all the way was Barry. He
got a lot of respect from me for that. He wasn't well, and
the bones weren't mended. Had he fallen, he'd have
been in bits again.'

Mackay recalls Barry pitting after leading, barely able
to stop the bike. He'd exercised all of his body, but
neglected his hands and simply run out of strength
there. 'He was a physical wreck … just a blob of jelly.'
Sheene didn't make that mistake again. I recall visiting
him at Charlwood after his other big crash, at
Silverstone in 1982. In his study, as well as an exercise
bike that his legs were not yet strong enough to use, he
had rigged up a pulley system, operated by twisting a
steel tube, the width of a handlebar, with rubber grips
on each end. He challenged me to twist this, lifting up
a weight. I managed a couple of goes; Barry laid his
sticks to one side and hoisted the weight skyward at
record speed.

Barry's focus for recovery was the GP series, and the
injury spoiled his chances in what transpired to be the
swansong of MV Agusta, and to claim the first 500 title
for a two-stroke. Phil Read had turned down the Suzuki
offer to partner Sheene, deciding to stay with MV
Agusta, with Bonera again, and a new team-mate
Armando Toracca. Yamaha had Agostini once more, and
Japanese rider Hideo Kanaya.

Suzuki had enlisted Finn Teuvo 'Tepi' Länsivuori as

GITANES
ESSO
UNIROYAL
Gulf
Shell
MICHELIN
Castrol
BARRY SHEENE
SUZUKI
12
SUZUKI
KING
HELMETS
12
CHAMPION
MICHELIN
Castrol

Sheene's team-mate for the 1975 GP season. Stan Woods and John Newbold were also to have occasional rides.

The rest of the field comprised mainly enlarged (at least nominally) 350cc Yamahas, privateers who were effectively in a different race.

Barry missed the French GP, but returned for the Austrian round on 4 May, only to be ruled unfit on the start line, to his great distress, having raced at Cadwell the weekend before. He had produced medical certificates declaring his fitness, and demonstrated to officials that he could bump-start the Suzuki. Not to their satisfaction, however, and he went home fuming.

Mechanical problems put him out in Germany (over-jetting caused an insoluble misfire) and Italy (transmission failure again, but luckily no seize). Then came Assen, the cathedral of motorcycle racing. Serendipity selected the best of showcases for Sheene's and the Suzuki's first win.

It was over no less a rival than Agostini on the Yamaha, by mere millimetres, after a neat tactical double-bluff on the last lap. Sheene had qualified on pole position for the first time – a fine achievement that showed how he was reaching a peak of riding skills. It was only his third visit to the difficult old long circuit, then at 4.787 miles, where the banked public-roads track zig-zagged at high speed through the flat countryside. Accuracy, delicacy of touch and courage are all required at Assen. Remember, this was barely three months after that Daytona smash.

The old master and the young pretender had battled throughout the 16-lap race, and Sheene's victory – the narrowest in history – fully demonstrated not only that he was fast, but also clever. He had feinted a couple of dummy attacks on the veteran, then on the last lap went steaming past on the other side. They crossed the line almost abreast, but the photo finish gave the race to Sheene.

Sheene would go on to win 18 of his 19 wins on the RG500; the machine would win a total of 52 GPs.

Sheene was now finding his level. 'There couldn't have been a more confident 24-year-old,' he said a couple of years later. At Spa the next week he qualified on pole again, and was duelling with Read's MV, lining him up for a last-lap pass, when he felt something rough, and – fearful of another seize – retired. It was a failed bolt in a primary-drive shaft. Within a week, Suzuki had made new one-piece parts – a pace of

development and response that the current GP team would dearly love to see.

One more Grand Prix triumph remained, at the next round at Sweden. Barry was undiverted by a row over starting money for the F750 race he was also taking part in – the Swedish organisers planned to pay just once for both appearances. Barry threatened to pull out of the whole meeting, but told team manager Rex White: 'Don't worry, I'll ride, no matter what happens.' His contract meant he had to, but the race organisers didn't know that, and coughed up.

Pole again for the race at the rough-and-ready Anderstorp circuit, with its landing-strip main straight, and a start-to-finish win that left Read's MV trailing by nine seconds.

The remaining races were disappointing. Over-rich mixture meant a misfire and a retirement in Finland; a transmission rumble at the final round at the Czech GP meant another precautionary pull-in. Barry was sixth overall; Länsivuori had actually out-pointed him without winning a race, placing fourth. The champion, with four race wins, was Giacomo Agostini, giving Yamaha the honour of the first-ever two-stroke 500-class World Championship.

OPPOSITE *Sheene's growing fame outside motorcycling meant he became a face around town, and moved up the social ladder. He revelled in it, as here, at the 1975 Sportsman of the Year lunch.*

LEFT *Bits and pieces: Sheene's RG500 stripped on the ground in Brno's primitive paddock. It now has a full loop frame.*

CHAPTER FIVE

THE GLORY YEARS

There were two years, 1976 and 1977, when Barry Sheene forged his name and identity into a global presence. He did this primarily with a sweeping, dominant performance in the World Championships. With his easy, natural riding style, flowing yet forceful, and with the best of the factory Suzukis, he was more or less unbeatable. He made it look easy too, adding credence to his later claim that 'I never had to ride more than seven-tenths of my capacity'. His relative lack of accidents and injuries reinforced the point. Barry continued to endear himself to an ever-growing fan base quite effortlessly and, for once, painlessly too.

For British motorsport, 1976 was a marvellous year.

It was the year that James Hunt, the long-haired devil-may-care Formula One driver, triumphed over the valiant injury victim Niki Lauda to become World Champion – a Sunday afternoon hero for everyman. Hunt, a public school rebel, was feted and admired. But his own success was enhanced by the other winner that year.

Barry Sheene was the perfect complement, the Cockney working-class hero for alternate weekends, and on Saturday's *World of Sport* in the home races. His return from the injury of the previous year was still very

Landmark moment at La Source, Spa-Francorchamps, 1977: Sheene at the slowest corner of the fastest motorcycle race in history. He averaged 135.067mph.

fresh in the public mind; his cheeky crooked-tooth grin ever-present, as he figure-headed advertising campaigns for Texaco and Fabergé. Barry was the man for that moment. He never looked back.

Other riders envied, and still envy, Barry's gifts for self-promotion. There was plenty of aggression within the Suzuki team as well – from the start, he viewed it as Team Sheene, and never rested in making sure that's how it worked. Outspoken Barry, with his financial awareness and consequent demands, made enemies within British racing. He also charmed many more legions of fans, internationally.

But for those two golden years, let nobody underestimate the pure talent of his motorcycle racing. Barry's performances and his results stood out as much as did his black helmet with the bold number '7' on the side, among all the pedestrian striped designs. He was equal to every challenge.

It all nearly came off the rails before it began. Suzuki, least pecunious of the big three Japanese manufacturers, had committed a huge budget to the development of their first four-stroke road motorcycle, the GS750. This left a shortfall in their racing budget. Reluctant to compete at world level at anything less than full stretch, they announced they were to pull out instead. In any case, the project was in a way completed. For 1976, they had made production versions of the RG500, Barry's bike, and these were selling rapidly, both for Grand Prix hopefuls and to national riders all over the world. The bike had become instantly a great racing standard, and would remain so for many years.

Suzuki GB were appalled. Sheene was on the brink of domination, everything was set to go, sponsors lined up … It took the intervention of Gerald Ronson, head of the entire Heron Group, as well as investment from the importer group's chairman Peter Agg, to convince the Japanese factory to continue to supply them with works bikes. Suzuki GB would run the team at their own expense – and Sheene's expertise at finding, and then at pleasing, sponsors would be of huge value.

Sheene had been to Japan on his own account, testing the latest version of the machine, which had already been developed prior to the decision to withdraw. The main difference was a new engine configuration, square cylinder dimensions (54 x 54mm) instead of the oversquare 56 x 50.5 of the 1975 and new production bikes. He found then that the production version, the machine anyone could buy, was barely any slower, but reached an agreement with the factory that the new bikes were to be only for him. As well as having slightly better mid-range power, the factory machine was also somewhat lighter.

Suzuki GB assembled their newly independent Texaco Heron Suzuki Team. At Sheene's recommendation, Merv Wright was brought in as manager. They'd got on well when Wright was in the same role with the US Suzuki team. During the forthcoming year, however, the two men would turn out to have very different conceptions about how the team should be structured. Wright envisaged Team Suzuki, with three riders on equal equipment; Sheene envisaged what Wright would call 'Team Sheene'. Maurice Knight confirmed to me that Barry had the backing of the factory in this, but the fighting reached a peak by the home races at the end of the season, with Sheene storming out of the team caravan at Silverstone saying to former manager Rex White: 'Either I go, or he goes.' Obviously, it was Wright who went.

Barry's hapless team-mates were fellow Englishmen John Williams and John Newbold. There was friction here too, especially with Williams, who many rated as the more talented rider. By the end of the year Williams would give a bitter interview to *Motor Cycle Weekly*, complaining of unfair treatment, second-rate equipment and sundry skulduggery, even accusing Sheene of deliberately colliding with Newbold. When he'd signed for Suzuki, 'the deal was for equal opportunities, that never came my way,' he said, adding prophetically enough: 'I'll not race in the same team as Sheene.' By a twist of fate, Williams was talking about the man who had only recently saved his life. In practice for the Swedish GP, Williams had crashed heavily. First on the scene, Barry had removed his helmet, cleared the unconscious rider's mouth of sand and grass, then retrieved his swallowed tongue to restart his breathing. Sadly, Williams perished in 1978, after an accident at the public-roads North-West 200 race in Ireland. 'Noddy' Newbold was killed in 1982 at the same event.

Barry re-assembled the Queen Square nucleus around him, choosing as mechanics Franko – his father – and Don Mackay. At the end of the next two years, they would be firmly moved aside by Suzuki, to be replaced with professionally trained engineers. Nevertheless, it was the old family firm that won the championship for two years straight.

Barry, by hook or by crook, secured all three of the latest Suzukis. This was a constant source of dismay for Williams and Newbold. One was Barry's GP machine, the

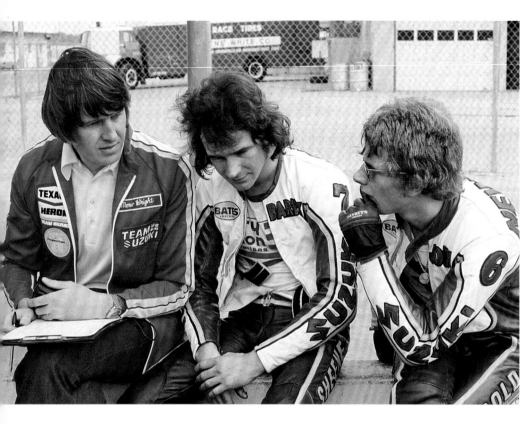

ABOVE *Sheene with Suzuki team manager Merv Wright and fellow-rider John Newbold. Everyone but Barry thought they were equal. His results proved him right.*

RIGHT *Sheene and long-time ally Don Mackay fiddle with the 750 Suzuki in 1976. He's about to test the new Goodyear slick tyres.*

second was for racing in Britain, the third was reserved as his 'international' bike. The team-mates had 1975 machines of varying vintages and with sundry updates, but not the latest cylinder dimensions. It is hard to say how much of a penalty this was, since Sheene kept the new bikes firmly to himself and comparisons could not be made, but it certainly set the friction rubbing.

The team had a hectic schedule, contesting not only the GPs, but also Daytona in the USA, the home rounds of the MCN Superbike and Shellsport 500 series, and selected rounds of the F750 series, on the now obsolete three-cylinder machines. By mid-year, this would take a back seat; but the British 750 class, the MCN Superbike series, ran under different rules. Franko and Don made a special big-bore version for these races – using the longer-stroke of Barry's new motors with the bigger pistons and cylinders of the older version, to arrive at 532cc.

It hardly mattered that Barry's bike might have had a small edge in mid-range performance: he was flying anyway. His Grand Prix racing record alone tells it all.

There were ten GPs that year, although no obligation to do each one as only the best six results counted to the final points. Factory team status meant Barry and

the Texaco Suzukis were able to pick and choose races. This was a big change from Barry's debut year of 1971, when entries were negotiated race by race, and even successful riders had no guarantee they would be able to enter the next GP. Thus Barry shunned the Isle of Man TT, in its last year as a championship round. In any case he preferred the big payday of the annual international race at Chimay in Belgium. This caused further friction in the team, with a serious squabble between Sheene and Merv Wright over spare parts for the crucial week.

MV Agusta had officially withdrawn, and Agostini was back as a semi-private entry on the nostalgic four-strokes; Yamaha had also pulled back from direct factory support – although Johnny Cecotto's machine was in every other way a works bike. The Venezuelan boy wonder, a new friend of Sheene's, had won the 350 title the previous year. And there were any number of private Suzukis, including one for Phil Read, as well as for rising young Italian Marco Lucchinelli, the well-regarded French rider Michel Rougerie, American newcomer Pat Hennen and (after the first couple of races) Agostini himself, having found the MV embarrassing.

The Grand Prix campaign started in France. It was cold and windy at Le Mans. Pole qualifier Barry's leg injuries were aching, and the uphill push start worried him. He requested a pusher, and to start from the back, but was denied. Slow away, he forged through to the front, to catch and ultimately pass Cecotto.

Sheene was on pole again at Austria, where he'd been refused a start the year before, and took fine revenge with another clear victory; Cecotto crashed trying to keep up, Lucchinelli was a distant second, Read third. Maximum points after two rounds.

Race three was at the then-new track of Mugello, and the layout – one of the most popular today – did not find favour. Sheene described it as 'a dusty bumpy track in the middle of nowhere', adding that it was 'both uninteresting and dangerous'. The atmosphere was marred by two fatalities in the smaller classes. Sheene's third win in a row, however, was a classic, tooth and nail with Read all the way. The two best British racers were inches apart over the line, but Sheene's slingshot tactics at the long last curve had suckered Read into an outbraking move on a bad entry line. Sheene was earlier on the power, and ahead over the finish line.

The TT was won by Irishman Tom Herron on a 351cc Yamaha after John Williams's Suzuki suffered a variety of maladies while leading.

Franko stands behind pole qualifier Sheene on the warm-up grid for the French GP, first round of 1976. He has Lucchinelli alongside, then Cecotto and Christian Estrosi (24). Row two comprises Agostini (1), John Williams (5) and Read (2).

RIGHT *Sheene and increasingly threatening American rival Kenny Roberts pose with the John Player girls at the 1976 Transatlantic Trophy races. Barry found promotional duties like this far from onerous.*

OPPOSITE *Heading for victory at Anderstorp, to clinch his first World Championship. It was the second of six consecutive Swedish GP wins.*

Meantime, Sheene's 750 campaign got off badly, a non-finish in Venezuela followed by third at Imola, then two more non-finishes in France and Belgium.

Back at a circuit he was happy to race, Sheene did it all again at Assen, starting from pole position, and setting fastest lap as he claimed yet another (effectively) successive win, his fourth. Sheene was notably the fittest finisher on a day when heat stroke nearly claimed the life of one sidecar competitor, and overcame several others; Pat Hennen's Suzuki was an impressive second. Barry didn't know it at the time, but there was trouble on the way.

A week later, in the forests of Spa, came a weekend that was pivotal for many reasons. Victory for Barry would have tied up the title with four rounds remaining; instead he came second. The axis was within the team, and an unexpected event in practice. Sheene lent Michel Rougerie his spare factory machine – that supposed team-mates Williams and Newbold had yet to ride. Sheene said this was on 'instructions from the Japanese', but Wright recalled firmly insisting that he should not have the bike for the race. With Sheene on pole, Rougerie had qualified fourth, ahead of both the other Texaco Heron Suzuki teamsters.

An increasingly angry John Williams was determined to prove he could beat Suzuki's big star. His intention was to lead to the last lap, then slow before the finish line, to demonstrate he was letting Barry win. The plan went well … until, on the final lap, Barry wasn't there any more. Suffering from fuel vaporisation, a limping Sheene was far from sure he could reach the finish line. Willy waited and waited, almost coasting round the final hairpin looking back up the track, before crossing the finish line a reluctant winner, still almost ten seconds ahead of his team-mate. It was his only GP win. (This race marked the end of Phil Read's GP career – the mercurial multiple champion, seeing the kid's dominance, decided the game wasn't worth the candle and went home abruptly halfway through practice. One less rival for Barry.)

Barry had to do one more race … in Sweden, and he need finish no better than third to be sure of his first World Championship. That is not, however, the style of a champion – a view shared by current racing giant Valentino Rossi. Barry did it with another fine win, shaking off all challengers to finish streets ahead. It was still only July; Hunt would have to wait until the end of October before adding the Formula One crown to Britain's tally for the year.

Barry's home season was triumphant too, in that he swept to victory in the MCN Superbike and Shellsport 500 classes, and won the readers' poll MCN Man of the Year award hands down.

It was on home ground rather than on the GP tracks that he would also feel the cold wind of the future on the back of his neck. It was coming from America. Kenny Roberts he knew about; Pat Hennen was becoming a force too, but at the Easter Anglo-American Match races, by now a major international fixture, yet another of the breed had arrived ... the weedy and bespectacled Stevie Baker, who took four wins to one each by Roberts and Sheene. Baker returned later in the year for the Mallory Park Race of the Year, and again beat Sheene.

Sheene's second successive championship year was achieved with equivalent on-track authority; the intervening winter had been busy in all sorts of ways.

Sheene and Stephanie McLean had been together now since early in 1976, and at the end of that year, after a welcome operation (filmed, of course) to remove the 18-inch pin in his left thigh, there since the Daytona crash, they left for three blissful Bahama weeks on Treasure Cay in the Abaco Island chain. At home, speculation about his future was taking over from the celebration of his success. Much more easily able to commandeer sponsorship on his own account than any of the Japanese factories, he openly debated options. Only when he returned, and after he had visited Suzuki to see their new machine for 1977, did he sign to stay put.

His own squad remained unchanged; but he got two new team-mates. One was his best mate now and for all the years to come, Steve Parrish, a rising rider in his own right – though the subsequent many times European Truck Champion, and now BBC MotoGP commentator, happily admits he was always 'in Barry's slipstream'. Perhaps that's why, out of all Sheene's team-mates, 'Stavros' was the only one with whom there was any cordial relationship.

The same could not be said of the other addition to the team. It was Pat Hennen. Barry started the ball rolling in one of his columns in the motoring press. 'If you pay peanuts,' he said, 'you get a monkey.' Barry was used to being outspoken, and used to having his every word quoted in all the papers that any of his rivals might read, and he used his criticism as a weapon. But, as Parrish told me later: 'Some monkey. This one turned out to have horns.'

And then there was Stephanie. Sheene and Steph after his Dutch TT win in 1976; posing on a Suzuki GS750 at the Earls Court Motorcycle Show; and clowning for the cameras for a London Evening Standard feature.

Sheene explained to me that his antipathy dated from the previous year. He felt the young Californian had taken advantage of old mate Nixon's injuries to get his place at Suzuki. Others believed that Hennen's clear threat was as much responsible for rubbing Sheene up the wrong way. Because Hennen was definitely tough. He not only thought very analytically about his riding, he also embodied that other quality that was to power a wave of American talent in the years to come. Schooled on dirt-tracks, he didn't mind if the wheels weren't necessarily always neatly in line. Compared with Sheene's classic slow-in/fast-out approach, with smooth fluidity, his style was both very untidy and extremely fast. 'There's no need for all that stupidity, stuffing it up the inside of somebody in a corner, so if you go down you take them with you,' ranted Barry.

This came later, after he had swept to a second dominant World Championship, simply sustaining the impetus from one GP season to the next. There were 11 rounds in 1977, and the scoring system had been changed, specifically to encourage big stars like Sheene to attend every race. From now, every round counted.

Sheene faced Baker on the Yamaha four, plus Cecotto and Agostini again (rather part-time), similarly mounted. Plus his team-mates, and the Suzuki hordes. Nor was his factory Suzuki vastly superior to the latest production machines. Barry bought one and lent it to Paul Smart, and after some careful work with his engineer Bob Rourke, spark-eroding the ports and fitting an oil pump which also lubricated the disc valves, this bike was faster than Sheene's. 'I went out with Barry, and I wasn't going to beat him, but I could sit behind him, and pass him any time I wanted,' said Smart.

This was a time of plenty for Grand Prix race organisers, if not for the lower orders of riders, with often more entries than places on the grid. There were no fewer than 45 starters at Hockenheim for the German GP, and either 30 or 36 at most other races, a sharp contrast to today, when there are fewer than 20 in 2006 MotoGP racing.

It was not so, however, at Venezuela. For the first GP there, held at San Carlos, 160 miles from Caracas and out in the humid hinterland, there were just 14 starters in the 500 class, backed by 350, 250 and 125 classes. Barry had already stolen a march. *Motocourse* of that year described San Carlos as a 'flea-bitten, one-horse town … no tourist trap', with hotels to 'bring a smile to Clint Eastwood's lips'. Sheene's friendship with Venezuelan racer and fixer Roberto Pietri meant that he and Stavros

were sorted out in the only decent hotel for miles around. Franko and the mechanics, meantime, dossed down in the local fire station, having been adopted by the brigade.

It was a fine race. Barry was slow away, his left leg still weak from the operation. But he cut through, his fitness in high heat paying dividends, to catch, stalk and then narrowly defeat Baker's Yamaha. Hennen did the same, a little way back, to Cecotto's Yamaha.

Austria was next, and a debacle. Most of the 500 riders withdrew in protest after a multiple pile-up in the opening 350cc race, triggered when Franco Uncini fell at the head of a pack and cart-wheeled back across the track amongst them. Former champions Dieter Braun and Johnny Cecotto were also brought down and badly hurt, as was Patrick Fernandez. The marshals struggled to cope and when, with no warning given, the following riders ploughed into the wreckage, Swiss rider Hans Stadelman suffered fatal injuries.

Sheene, Baker and Swiss rider Philippe Coulon sped to the organisers at the start line, pleading with them for the race to be stopped, but it still took an amazing eight laps before the red flags were shown, by which time the wreckage and the victims had been cleared. The 125cc riders staged a sit-down protest on the grid; most of the 500 riders followed the lead set by Sheene and his two cohorts and withdrew from the 500 race.

It was almost a clean sweep in Germany, Sheene dominant in first, Hennen second; but Parrish on the third Suzuki had dropped to fourth behind Baker's Yamaha, after leading on the first lap of the fast Hockenheimring.

Barry was on pole at Imola, but again slowly away, finishing the first lap only 14th. As Hennen finally had the big crash that Sheene had been predicting, lucky to escape only bruised, Barry once again stamped his authority on the year, just fast enough to shade local heroes Virginio Ferrari and Armando Toracco, with Baker beaten back to fourth.

The 500cc two-strokes, having taken over the top class, were gaining sophistication. Yamaha were persevering with their in-line four and, with piston-port induction (as against the Suzuki's more user-friendly disc valves), it was snappish on the throttle, with a fiercer power band, but rapid. Sheene's claims that the Yamaha was faster were born out at the long Mistral straight of the Paul Ricard circuit at the next French GP, where Baker narrowly claimed pole. Sheene was the winner of a heroic race, however, Baker's hopes

The 1977 season started with another winning streak. This is the second win, at the Hockenheimring in Germany.

Lining up at Spa-Francorchamps, Belgium, for the fastest race of all time. Sheene's '7' is prominent as always; likewise Steve Baker (2), Giacomo Agostini (1) and Pat Hennen (3).

thwarted by a fuel leak contaminating his rear tyre, letting Agostini through to second on his Yamaha.

Sheene was actually only second in Holland, but the Assen victor was Wil Hartog, no title threat, and this was achieved in iffy half-wet conditions. No momentum was lost, and then it was directly off over the border to a landmark race in Belgium.

This was the penultimate year the long Spa-Francorchamps circuit was used, and the old public-roads track measured almost nine miles, adding Malmedy and Stavelot to the shorter loop used today, linked by the fearsome Masta straight. Much of the track was taken absolutely flat-out, a severe test of courage and commitment.

Sheene missed pole to Coulon by half-a-second, and was strongly placed in a fierce six-bike battle over the early laps. By half distance he and Rougerie had broken away, and both were beating the record in their quest, Sheene tucked into the Frenchman's Suzuki's slipstream.

As the year before, Barry ran into fuel starvation problems that slowed his final lap, but by then Rougerie had gone, with a piston failure. And in spite of that handicap and the fact that the track also has one very slow hairpin, Sheene's race average speed was 135.067mph. The fastest motorcycle race of all time.

Old mate Johnny Cecotto was back for the next round in Sweden, after his Austrian GP injuries, and gave Barry a good run for his money. But it was Sheene on pole, the lap record and, ultimately, the race winner by three seconds. Baker, still his closest title rival, was third, but the points gap yawned: Barry had amassed 102, Baker 68, with Hennen next on 44. If Baker won all three remaining rounds, it would put him on 113. The next round was at Imatra in Finland, a track Barry didn't like for its combination of speed and danger – on public roads, it crossed a railway line twice, once at high speed. Barry needed to come second to secure the title, assuming it was Baker ahead.

It wasn't. Nor was it Barry. Both had machine trouble, Baker dropping back to 12th, out of the points. Barry had every intention of another win from pole position, but by the time Cecotto took to the front, on a fearsome charge, Barry was already glancing anxiously at the temperature gauge, his bike overheating. He nursed it home, fully aware of Baker's plight, and on the last lap waved Stavros through to fifth to improve his mate's championship chances.

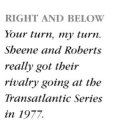

OPPOSITE *Classic Spa shot shows Sheene's utter dominance in his record race. He's already climbing the hill, with second-placed Baker yet to come into sight round the distant hairpin.*

RIGHT AND BELOW *Your turn, my turn. Sheene and Roberts really got their rivalry going at the Transatlantic Series in 1977.*

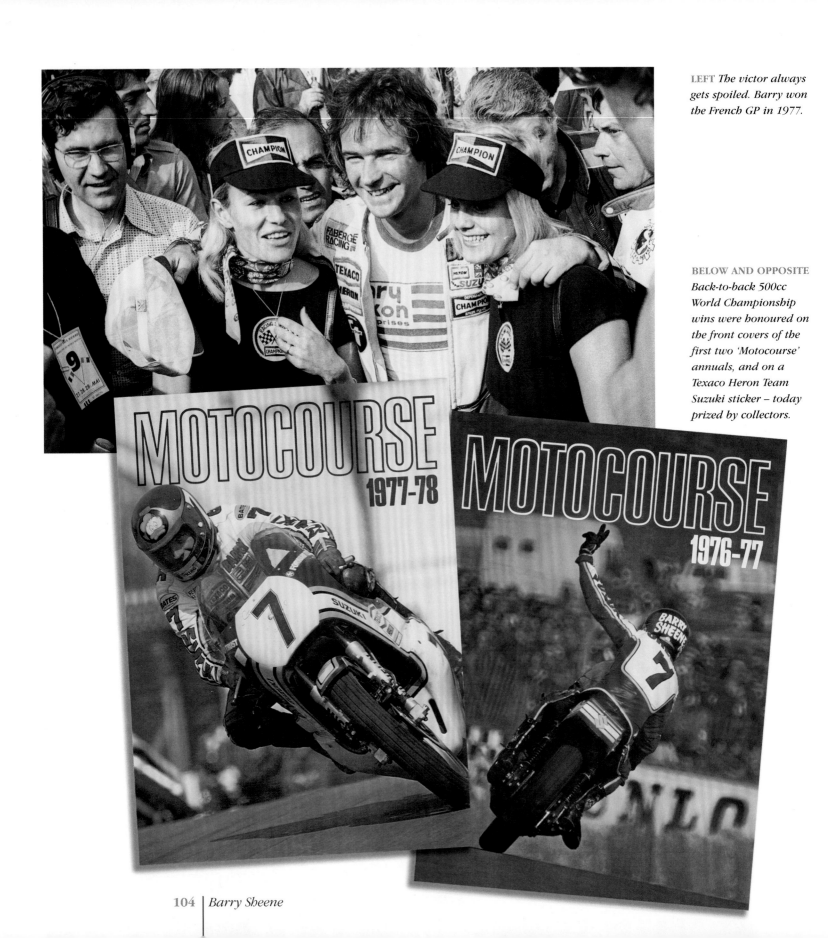

LEFT *The victor always gets spoiled. Barry won the French GP in 1977.*

BELOW AND OPPOSITE *Back-to-back 500cc World Championship wins were honoured on the front covers of the first two 'Motocourse' annuals, and on a Texaco Heron Team Suzuki sticker – today prized by collectors.*

MOTOCOURSE 1977-78

MOTOCOURSE 1976-77

Barry had done it again, in dominant style. He thankfully missed the next round at Brno's road track, but returned for the final round, the inaugural British GP, at Silverstone, intent on giving his loyal home fans something to remember.

This was not to be. He had to borrow Parrish's bike to set pole, his own giving head gasket problems that continued into the race. Never really in contention, he eventually retired, his visor so steamed by his boiling radiator that he crashed into the pit wall. For a while this handed the lead to Parrish: Barry leaned over the pit wall with a chalked message: 'Gas It, Wanker'. It was enough to tip the inexperienced rider over the edge, and he too fell on the tricky damp circuit, handing the maiden British win to Pat Hennen, the first American to win a Grand Prix.

Sheene won the major home titles too, in a somewhat difficult season with one big lucky escape … at the Snetterton Race of Aces before the Swedish GP, when a mechanic's error with a misplaced retaining clip left him brakeless at high speed, crashing heavily into the bank. He also had an even clearer warning of the imminent American invasion, at the Easter Match Races. An American team including Kenny Roberts and GP stars Baker and Hennen trounced the British team. Roberts won five out of six races, but broke down in the last one; Sheene fought hard and salvaged some pride by taking the victory, but he had been outpointed in individual results by Hennen and Baker.

Barry retained his British Shellsport 500 title, only because some racing licence irregularity meant Hennen was docked points; and also his MCN Superbike title, though Hennen outpointed him handsomely in the final five rounds. Pat was just one of several riders who were becoming exceedingly troublesome.

If the head wearing the crown was uneasy, however, he didn't let it show.

TEXACO HERON TEAM SUZUKI

BARRY SHEENE

1976 1977

500cc WORLD CHAMPION

CHAPTER SIX

THE PLAYBOY

Barry Sheene had a remarkable rise from the pesky, pasty kid in the Queen Square workshop. By the time he was 25 he was not only hob-nobbing with high society and big business, he was running rings around many of them. By the time he left Britain in 1987, he had even been to Buckingham Palace.

It goes without saying that he never lost the common touch.

Barry was a racer before he was a businessman, but he may have been better as a businessman. Considering he was twice World Champion, this put him in the big league. The role of racing's first millionaire had already been taken by Giacomo Agostini, while Mike Hailwood was at that level anyway by inheritance – but Sheene's scale of fees set new standards, those of a self-made man on the way up. It was without question Sheene who paved the way to the multi-million-dollar rider contracts of today. He did it leading by example. No contemporary rider had as clear a vision as Barry Sheene about the true value of the entertainment he was providing; and if anyone did, then nobody had the intelligence, persistence and negotiating skills.

The experience of Mick Grant, a rival, was typical. 'I was in the shadow of Barry quite a bit … but he got so much publicity that he brought publicity with him. That's swings and roundabouts – in terms of earnings, everybody else followed along.

Sheene and Stephanie. The image was exactly right for the times.

'I won the MCN Superbike Championship in 1975, then I was runner-up for the next two or three years. And I used to think: fucking hell, if it hadn't been for Barry! But if it hadn't have been for Barry, none of us would have been paid so much. And if it hadn't have been for Barry, Suzuki wouldn't have put so much into it, and Kawasaki wouldn't have followed suit.

'If it hadn't have been for Barry a lot of things would have been different, with the net result not as good as with him being there. But you've not got to make a mistake with Barry. He did a tremendous amount for the sport. But it was purely coincidental. Barry was a natural survivor. He was looking after himself.'

Barry's first jobs had been to support his racing – cleaning cars, delivering messages, or furniture. Within a couple of years the racing was self-supporting and more, and the business side started to get serious even before he joined Yamaha in 1972. Barry took the best financial advice he could get, then often as not improved upon it. As early as 1971 Barry was racing as a private company. Within four years he had an accountant to handle his affairs, a lawyer to handle his three companies, and an agency to handle sponsorship contracts and press relations. But he still did an amazing amount himself.

ABOVE *The Shakespearean and the Suzuki. Actor Sir Ralph Richardson (a motorcyclist himself) tries the 500 for size. They were fellow guests on 'Parkinson', host Michael on the left.*

RIGHT *'This Is Your Life' – Eamonn Andrews surprises Barry with the famous Big Red Book.*

He would negotiate on his own behalf, and was an expert at finding sponsorship – the Fabergé 'Brut' deal of 1977, sponsoring the Suzuki team as well as the rider, was all Barry's. ('He cut Suzuki in on that deal, for which all credit to him,' said Maurice Knight.) Fixing vans, working on the bikes, he was always pushing, always looking for the angle, imagining the possible, seeking the advantage to himself, then making it happen that way.

One typical Barry story concerned Mashe jeans. In 1976 (actually for a lot longer) he had a private sponsorship deal with the French fashion house. He wore their clothing in public, carried their logo on his leathers, and also on the motorcycle on which he won the championship – unless Suzuki team manager Merv Wright got there first. There was a constant battle, stickers going onto and off the bikes.

Barry still astounds for his PR nous. Master of the sound-bite long before the term was invented, he was also master of the mention. Interviewed on radio, for instance, he would slip in the name of his sponsor so seamlessly that it would be part of a quip or an anecdote, sounding perfectly natural. After winning the championship twice, among the accolades he received was to appear on two major British television

programmes that were both mirrors and even arbiters of public taste. One was Thames TV's *This Is Your Life*, on 25 January 1978. Among the guests were Senor Francesco Bulto and George Harrison. Other stars featured that year included presenter Terry Wogan and news magnate Rupert Murdoch. In November, Barry appeared on the BBC prime-time Saturday evening chat show *Parkinson*. Barry's fellow guest was veteran Shakespearean actor Sir Ralph Richardson (also a motorcyclist … they got along famously). Asked about the negative image of motorcyclists, he managed to slip the name Fabergé quite naturally into an answer that had the audience hooting with laughter as he spoke about 'the mods and rockers thing, roaring down to Brighton on bikes and pinching Granny's handbag'.

Another signal of his acceptance by the establishment was an invitation to appear on the august and revered radio show *Desert Island Discs*, with founder-presenter Roy Plomley. Barry charmed the audience as ever, though his choice of music might have disappointed anyone expecting the usual rather self-consciously highbrow symphonies and arcane arias. Barry's favourites displayed no pretentiousness: 'Crackerbox Palace' (George Harrison), 'In The Mood' (Glenn Miller),

LEFT *Stephanie and Iris by his side at the show's climax. Guests include famous racers Paul Smart (behind Stephanie), Giacomo Agostini (with Sheene) and Mike Hailwood. And, looming like a dark horse on the right, Beatle George Harrison.*

'If You Leave Me Now' (Chicago), 'Do You Know The Way To San José' (Dionne Warwick), 'New Kid In Town' (The Eagles), 'Don't Let The Sun Catch You Crying' (José Feliciano), 'Sunshine After The Rain' (Elkie Brooks) and 'Nights On Broadway' (Candi Staton).

With Barry, sponsors knew they would get value. They also knew they would have to pay well for it. His knack of going straight to the top in all his dealings eased the way to the big numbers. Nothing in his education or background would have suggested this flair, but he was very, very astute, and a bold negotiator.

Even before he was a full factory rider, Barry was in a position to make money out of racing. The GPs were not profitable; you often had to bargain hard just to get a start, especially in the smaller classes. But in those days, and for many years to come, the World Championship formed a relatively small percentage of a top rider's year; the season was filled by a number of well-paid international races in Britain and Europe, and soon also the USA. A successful rider could make a good profit back in the early Seventies. Chas Mortimer, on much the same trail as Sheene, recalls: 'There was start money, prize money, and bonuses on results from the tyre companies, technical suppliers, the clothing and helmet people. We always did one meeting a weekend, sometimes two, on occasions more. For about four years the Finnish GP was on the Sunday, then we'd race at a place called Kammela outside Helsinki, on Tuesday or Wednesday night. Then you'd do Alderbrook on Saturday, Brands Hatch on Sunday. And you could come away with £4,000 quite easily over those four meetings … and that was a hell of a lot of money in those days.' Not to mention a hell of a lot of miles in the ubiquitous Ford Transit vans.

Barry's landmark year was 1975, when he passed £100,000 for the first time. In 2006 terms, that equates to somewhere approaching three quarters of a million pounds – small beer compared with the four or five million commanded by Valentino Rossi, but it was to a large extent Barry who started the trend.

At the start of that year, he bought his first Rolls-Royce Silver Shadow, a reward after the big Daytona crash. It was also the classic symbol of Cockney pride; and an up-yours to Phil Read, who already drove one. Barry owned two more Rollers before later switching to Mercedes-Benz in 1980; a big 500SE saloon with a bumper sticker on the back reading: 'Helicopter Pilots Get It Up Quicker'. Because by then his toys, and his status symbols, were onto another level.

Another day, another TV documentary. Sheene's second Rolls-Royce is the prop for a man at the height of his fame. He had a gift for making interviewers – and thence viewers – feel special.

Whenever there were two or more pretty girls, Barry would usually find a way to squeeze in somewhere. On the left, two Penthouse Pets; opposite Miss World contestants the Misses United Kingdom (left) and United States.

Barry never let up his quest for money, and he was quick, ruthless and persistent. Later Suzuki team manager Garry Taylor was constantly exposed. 'Barry tended to view anybody else on the team as taking money away that could have been his,' he told me. Many is the team functionary who has been called 'a parasite' (an epithet vouchsafed also to this author, after writing an 'unauthorised' biography that did not include a percentage for the subject). And he explained his attitude to *Guardian* journalist Adrianne Blue in a 1978 interview, referring to his preference for doing his own business, rather than relying on agents or middle-men. 'Why have someone spongeing off your success? Rather than have someone pilfering so many percent here and so many percent there, I'd rather not have it at all. Why the bloody hell should I have someone else living off my back?'

Barry's upward move through society was as accomplished, as rapid and as considered as his racing success. The London high life was ready for him, indeed welcomed him with open arms. 'A lot of those people from Eton and Sandhurst ... that was what they were craving.' So says Chas Mortimer, who straddled the two worlds, having been public school educated while also brought up in racing, and in long-term close contact with Queen Square. Barry's friendship with Mortimer gave him an entrée into grand society; Barry's magnetic charm meant that the toffs and nobs were very soon glad to see him.

Mortimer and Sheene were racing companions rather than friends, and Mortimer divines a hidden agenda. 'Barry and I never got on particularly well. In the early years I was the only other young British rider doing anything in the Grand Prix scene.' (Mortimer ran consecutive and improving top five finishes in the 125 World Championship, ending as runner-up to the title in 1973.) 'There's a natural rivalry anyway between two riders.

'Barry was very, very smart. He knew the circles he mixed in, he was never going to get good sponsorship or good contacts. He needed to move into Chelsea and Kensington. I had a friend called Piers Forester, and I introduced Barry to Piers, and Piers was able to introduce him – at a lot of these parties in 1969 to 1971 – to really influential people, who were able to pave the way for him into society circles.

'Even then, he had a tremendous charisma about him. We'd mix with the likes of Patrick Lichfield. I had

RIGHT *Barry and James Hunt: World Champions, good pals, and rebel darlings of the fast set on two or four wheels.*

OPPOSITE *Barry and George – the biker and the Beatle met at a Formula One race, and were friends for life.*

a better education than Barry, but I couldn't greet him by saying "Oh 'Ullo Patrick, how the fuck are you?" the same as Barry could. But those people loved that.'

Piers Edric Weld-Forester was very well connected indeed. Of an old and noble line, he was a royal equerry, and fancied himself as a royal suitor as well. Princess Anne was his target. Piers loved cars and bikes, racing a Ford GT40 at Le Mans and Daytona 24-hour races in 1969 and 1970. Friendship with Barry would see him try his hand at racing bikes as well. And another thing they had in common … a dedicated application to the high life. Mortimer calls Forester's flat 'Piers's den of iniquity'; and if there wasn't a serious drug scene in racing at that time, there certainly was at Piers's parties – amyl nitrate, cocaine, the sweet waft of hashish, and plenty to drink. All part of the innocent adventures in the early 1970s.

Was it the new company he was keeping that meant Barry now felt the beckoning of the country squire lifestyle? Or was it just an astute property move? Either way, at the end of 1971, he bought a rambling ten-bedroom farmhouse, Ashwood Hall, at Walton Highway outside Wisbech, due north of Cambridge, well up towards the windswept shallows of The Wash. It needed plenty of work, with Frank and Iris taking early

retirement to move in and supervise – a big step after so long at Queen Square, and another indication of their devotion to him. It was soon ready, and Barry moved out of London for a first try at country life.

This was, he discovered, as dull as the water in the numerous ditches in the fenland levels. At least, that's how he felt after living it up in London. However, it was now that he formed a friendship with Steve Parrish, who lived relatively nearby. They rollicked about the countryside in somewhat legendary fashion. One of Barry's escapades ended in a collision on a narrow bridge. Barry scarpered – later claiming he had shards of glass in his eye and wanted urgent attention – but found the constabulary awaiting his arrival. He failed the breath test, and was banned for 18 months.

Soon he was back as Piers's flatmate, having trouble (he would later brag) keeping girlfriends from bumping into one another as they trooped in and out. A clubland regular, Barry's haunts now included fashionable night spots like Tramps in Jermyn Street, where he enjoyed handing a flunkey the keys of his Rolls, for parking, and Annabel's in Mayfair. This was a far cry from the Bali Hai in Streatham, though equally packed with nubile opportunities for Barry to keep

upping his score. The accents were a bit smarter. The clientele of Annabel's at the time included the cream of London's fashionable society, among them the young royals – Prince Charles and his paramour (and later second wife), then Camilla Shand. Sheene's associates of the time included society photographers Patrick Lichfield (the Queen's cousin) and David Bailey, as well as Lord Hesketh, the spend-happy motor racing peer, and his driver James Hunt, who won the F1 title after switching teams to McLaren. Lord Hesketh continued with a costly and ill-fated attempt to build a British road motorcycle bearing his own name, and after the turn of the century sold the ancient family seat at Easton Neston.

In the matter of name-dropping, which by the late Seventies was going both ways, Sheene outranked all his Grand Prix peers when he brought along a Beatle to the French and Spanish GPs. Barry and car-racing fan George Harrison had met in 1977 at Long Beach, where Sheene was taking part in an unusual experiment for F1, a bike race on the eve of the GP. Sheene headlined it, and enjoyed mixing with the car crowd; George was there with fiancée Olivia, wandering through the paddock incognito. Barry recognised him, and vice versa, and they hit it off immediately. Through Barry, Harrison took a mild interest in motorbikes for a while, and attended several races. It was with George that Barry reconnoitred Australia before the family moved there in the Eighties. They remained good friends until George died of cancer in 2001.

His friendship with Piers Forester, however, came to a tragically early end. Piers had bought himself a TZ750 Yamaha, a big handful of power for a relative novice bike racer. In the late-season Race of the South at Brands Hatch, Piers crashed coming onto the main straight, and suffered fatal injuries after he hit the top of the barrier. It goes without saying that for Sheene, this was yet another very dark moment in a life otherwise blessed.

Barry had no trouble making the transition from Cockney chancer to Kensington dandy, and did so without having to change in any way, and without ever betraying his roots. His personality was big enough to fill both roles, often to overflowing. Rejoining Suzuki in 1973 had marked the start of the golden years, and the foundation of a popularity far beyond motorcycling. The accident at Daytona, the courageous recovery, and then two world titles in a row sealed his status. He was more than a sports star. Barry Sheene had become a folk hero, and a worldwide household name.

Stephanie McLean has a special quality – always did. Her willowy good looks are plain to see, but she adds an air of … not distance, exactly, or detachment, but perhaps of composure or self-containment. Paul Smart, Barry's brother-in-law, believes this is what captivated Barry, and kept him captivated. 'Barry liked to have total control … and he never had control over Steph, ever. I think that was his challenge in life.'

Daughter of a warrant officer in the British Army, Stephanie had grown up mainly in Malaysia. Back in Britain, by the time Barry met her in 1975, Steph was already a successful glamour model, star of *Penthouse* magazine, where she took the cover of the April 1970 issue in a pink shirt open to the waist, and was Pet of the Month. A subsequent 'Penthouse Pet Play-off' in the May '71 issue was followed by more photographs in September, when she was on the cover once again as Pet of the Year. She also modelled for *Mayfair*, and (switching attention further north) was the *Daily Mirror* 'Face of 1973'.

She was also a married woman – to glamour photographer Clive McLean – and a mother, of their son Roman. And then she met Barry.

It happened at Tramps at the end of 1975. Barry – a committed bopper – was obliged to sit out the action with his year-end injuries. Stephanie later joked that her eye had been caught by the glint of disco lights off his walking stick. The next contact came almost directly afterwards, when Stephanie asked to borrow a set of Barry's racing leathers for a photo shoot. Their relationship quickly became unstoppable.

At first, Barry later insisted, their friendship was chaste. He became friendly with the whole family. But by Daytona in March, it was love letters across the Atlantic, and by 25 April Stephanie had joined Barry at the French GP. A week later, at the Austrian GP, the British press were onto them. 'We had nothing to hide,' said Barry, as they both freely admitted the affair, but the *Daily Express* reported that Clive was keeping 'a round-the-clock vigil on his son Roman'. The day before, Barry's loyal mother Iris had been quoted: 'It couldn't be all his fault – I'm sure she's as much to blame as my son.'

Divorce proceedings followed directly; within six months, on 22 October 1976, a year since they had first met, the *Daily Mail* reported that the marriage was over and Stephanie free, quoting Clive McLean: 'It was an amicable divorce after seven years of marriage.'

Stephanie was now a fixture in the Sheene camp at

THIS PAGE *Fleet Street sensation – Barry and Stephanie made the main lead of 'The Sun', and headlines everywhere.*

OPPOSITE *Domestic animal: Sheene and Stephanie kept putting off the wedding – not that it made any difference.*

the races. Andrea Coleman (then married to Tom Herron, now head of the Riders for Health MotoGP charity) recalls trying to teach her how to manage the rack of three manual stopwatches used at the time. 'I said to Tom: "I don't think she'll ever learn". Then I realised that I'd been doing these things all my life, they were second nature to me.' Stephanie did learn … to the extent that there was at least one occasion when her own lap charts were used to settle disputes with official race timers.

The couple planned to marry at the end of that year, and had even set a date for a quiet register office wedding. Then, the way Barry told it, his new bikes arrived from Suzuki, needing urgent testing – so they agreed to put it off. Later, he spoke more frankly of how he had shied away, persuading Stephanie that formalising their love was irrelevant, that his commitment needed no rubber stamp. They continued to put it off for another eight years, waiting until 1984. Nine months and three days later, their daughter Sidonie was born.

The new relationship meant a change in Barry's living arrangements. With typical astuteness, he saw the chance to take significant steps up the property ladder. He had retained the Wisbech property, where Frank and Iris still lived, but had added to the portfolio a four-bedroom London town house in fashionable riverside Putney.

Another move was coming up soon, however. Barry's next and last property in Britain was at Charlwood on the Surrey-Sussex borders, a five-minute drive from Gatwick airport. This was of special relevance for several reasons, not the least being Barry's growing interest in flying.

Some of the 30-plus rooms in this magnificent manor house dated back to the 12th century. It had an open view over the land, and a sizeable duck pond. The main house included a comfortable self-contained separate wing for Frank and Iris; the outbuildings were big enough for the workshops and storage for the racing teams of Barry's later independent GP years. There was even room, in the meadows out the back, to land the helicopter he would soon adopt as his chosen transport. It was Queen Square, recreated at the opposite end of the social and financial scale.

Sheene sold both his Wisbech and Putney properties and paid £100,000 in cash for Charlwood. The property's value today would be several millions; Barry took full profit from the rise in its value during his six-year residency. He moved in during 1978. Double World Champion and Lord of the Manor.

The house was carefully refurbished, with a surprisingly sympathetic eye. The builders unearthed a bricked-in old inglenook fireplace, for instance; Barry had this authentically restored to its original glory. Like the beams throughout, the huge refectory table they bought with the property, and the well-stocked wine racks, everything in here was the real thing.

Barry had a work-out room upstairs; in the study downstairs, the room with the fireplace, he would entertain business visitors and guests, Steph passing through regularly to change ashtrays and bring mugs of coffee. The phone would ring frequently, even constantly; the answer machine would field every call: 'This is Barry. I'm out and about. This machine's on 24 hours a day, so leave your number and I'll call you back.' If it was someone important, he would pounce on the receiver.

The Sheene family remained at the manor house until they quit England en masse for Australia in 1987.

Blue-jean believers and lords of the Manor House. The new house at Charlwood had more than 30 rooms, and you had to duck to get into some of them. There was also space to run a racing team and land a helicopter.

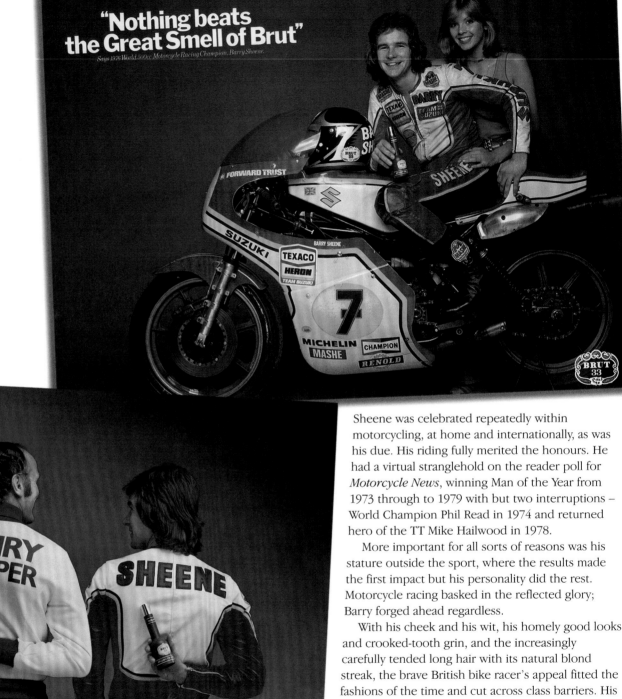

"Nothing beats
the Great Smell of Brut"

Says 1976 World 500cc Motorcycle Racing Champion, Barry Sheene.

*Splash it on all over!
Teamed with British
heavyweight boxer and
sporting legend Henry
Cooper, 'Our 'Enery',
Sheene quickly became
'Our Barry' to the
public at large. The
famous Brut ads are
from 1976 (right) and
1977. Opposite, a
handshake on the
starting grid in Britain
in 1976.*

HENRY
COOPER
SHEENE
Behind every great man
BRUT 33
BRUT 33

Sheene was celebrated repeatedly within motorcycling, at home and internationally, as was his due. His riding fully merited the honours. He had a virtual stranglehold on the reader poll for *Motorcycle News*, winning Man of the Year from 1973 through to 1979 with but two interruptions – World Champion Phil Read in 1974 and returned hero of the TT Mike Hailwood in 1978.

More important for all sorts of reasons was his stature outside the sport, where the results made the first impact but his personality did the rest. Motorcycle racing basked in the reflected glory; Barry forged ahead regardless.

With his cheek and his wit, his homely good looks and crooked-tooth grin, and the increasingly carefully tended long hair with its natural blond streak, the brave British bike racer's appeal fitted the fashions of the time and cut across class barriers. His ability to enjoy and exploit his two world titles were the foundation of his status as folk hero. When the fortunes of racing went the other way, it mattered not a jot to the stature of Sheene the Superstar.

This made him, in retrospect, an obvious choice for Fabergé. They were selling an aftershave called Brut –

a mass-market fragrance for the flare-trousered medallion-flaunting disco-flouncing peacock males of the age. Fabergé had already secured massive popular appeal with everybody's favourite heavyweight boxer Henry Cooper heading the campaign, but 'Our 'Enery' lacked youth appeal. Not so Barry. The series of TV and print ads they made together had a catch-phrase that passed into contemporary folklore, recounted in Barry's distinctive Cockney twang: 'Splash it on all over.' For Barry, as a boost to his fame, nothing – not even the life-size cardboard cut-outs at Texaco service stations, and the TV ads he did for them with actor Michael Crawford – beat the great smell of Brut.

Popularity on this scale certainly didn't hurt his chances. Even so, it was sporting achievements that gave the depth to his vast and ever-growing public appeal. One measure of this came from the professional journalists who cover everything from football to snooker, the Sports Writers Association. In 1978, he beat the popular middle-distance runner, Olympic gold medalist Steve Ovett, by 470 to 436 points to be their Sportsman of the Year.

Barry was everywhere in the late 1970s; and after making direct contact with Formula One at the Long Beach race (and with the friendship and support of barefoot jeans-clad friend James Hunt) there was a flurry of interest in moving this ready-made publicity-friendly star in the footsteps of his predecessor John Surtees, still in 2006 the only man to have won World Championships on two and four wheels. There was an echo – at the time of writing – with Valentino Rossi, a thoroughly modern bike racing superstar whose move to F1 with Ferrari was thought to be imminent.

Barry's own F1 career never got quite so serious – scuppered by a lack of backing and too many other commitments. But it was quite close for a while. He tested for none other than John Surtees, now a team owner, at Brands Hatch in August 1977. This was a private affair (George Harrison was the only outsider present), where he impressed with his steady progress, ultimate speed, and only one spin over 50 laps. He was reported as being within three seconds of the lap record. Next was a plan for a bit more, when Arrows offered Barry a further test with a view to competing in the Aurora F1 series in 1979. His first outing, in September at Donington Park, lasted only eight laps before he spun and hit the wall; a second, at Silverstone at the start of December, went more smoothly, but without spectacular lap times. The

Born for publicity, Barry's face seemed to be everywhere in the later 1970s.

OPPOSITE The Sheene sandwich adds excitement to low-alcohol lager.

THIS PAGE Increasingly famous page by page, Sheene advertised everything from a bang-up-to-date TV game (includes tennis) to Michelin, Texaco and Champion.

enterprise founded on the rather surprising inability to find the generous funding Sheene was demanding, and Barry's affair with open-wheel racing was over.

The ultimate recognition of this golden period came right at the end of his second title year, 31 December, when it was announced that Barry Sheene was one of four MBEs for sporting achievements. His fellow winners were yachtswoman Clare Francis, rugby hero Phil Bennett and cricketer Mike Brearley. There was a small contretemps over who would attend the investiture, with only two guests allowed; Stephanie stepped aside to let Frank and Iris take the reserved seats at Buckingham Palace.

'Do be careful,' the Queen was reported to have said to him. Did Barry really raise a royal titter with the reply: 'It's no more dangerous, Ma'am, than your horses.' Only Her Majesty knows for sure.

BARRY SHEENE TO FORMULA ONE? The headlines were as big then as for Valentino Rossi in 2006. In April 1978 Barry privately tested a Surtees Formula One car at Brands Hatch. Motorcycle and car World Champion John Surtees played host also to interested spectator George Harrison.

CHAPTER SEVEN

INTO THE DOLDRUMS

Of course, it wasn't really a failure. Sheene wasn't doing anything different, and he was riding as well as ever. Better, say some, even if he was taken by surprise at the level of the competition. He insisted that it was a mystery virus that spoiled his 1978 season, and he almost fought back to win. From then on circumstances (and indeed Barry himself) seemed to conspire against him – all the way from 1978 to the second major crash of his career, in the middle of 1982.

And it wasn't only Kenny Roberts. Just mostly. Because when Kenny arrived, it was with the avowed intention of ousting Barry Sheene, the reigning king; and even before the maverick American's debut-season title win, he had become Barry's major rival. The two inspired one another, in the same way as Wayne Rainey and Kevin Schwantz would in years to come. In each case, it led to a golden age of racing.

There had been some omens. Sheene was already aware that people, especially British sports fans, grow tired of serial success, and turn on their heroes. His popularity, the size of his fan base, had transcended the boundaries of bike racing but, within the sport, a rising tide of disenchantment had begun by the end of his second title year. Always high visibility, Sheene enjoyed being star of the show. He liked to keep his rivals waiting on the grid, for instance, knowing the organisers would never start the race without him. He was an outspoken

Barry's German GP was symbolic of his 1979 season – qualified on pole, broke down. Note fashionable new fairing 'winglets', an inconclusive aerodynamic experiment.

OPPOSITE *'And this is the clutch.' Sheene tries Mike Hailwood's 1978 Isle of Man TT-winning Ducati, as the great racing legend looks on.*

RIGHT *Cockney racer and winsome actor/crooner: Barry Sheene and David Essex could each have entered for the other's look-alike contest.*

RIGHT *Tarnished hero? The once adoring fans turned nasty at the Brands Hatch Transatlantic meeting.*

columnist in the specialist papers, never slow to cast aspersions and slurs. To many, the Rolls-Royces, the social snobbery, the gossip-column inches and the superstar style didn't sit well with the general idea of a motorbike racer – particularly up north, homeland of Mick Grant, flame-haired son of a coal miner and until now Barry's greatest British rival.

Once, at Oliver's Mount – a scary parkland circuit at Scarborough that Barry attended regularly which, while swelling his coffers, somewhat undermined his safety stance against road circuits like the Isle of Man – he had stopped out on the track with his engine seized. Instead of friendly waves, he faced jeers and catcalls. 'They wanted me to kill myself,' he told the *Northern Daily Mail*. Worse would follow: some of the fans took to pelting him with drinks cans on victory laps, while on the other side of the country, at Oulton Park in Cheshire, he was confronted with a hanged effigy of himself. 'Rip-off Sheene', they called him.

'Rip-off' was a bit strong, unless it referred to the fact that there often wasn't much left for the other riders. Barry charged top dollar, but gave top value. He raced good and proper, to win, and frequently did so. He would spend hours in the paddock signing autographs,

and cheerfully overstayed at fan sessions or sponsor events. But the criticism put him on the back foot. Barry, as Garry Taylor discovered in his years running the Suzuki team, had a simple view of matters: 'You were either for him, or you were the enemy.'

I was editing *SuperBike* magazine at a time when the bike press was falling at Barry's feet, and we ran a rather puerile satire of this adulation. That it included an interview with Barry Sheene's toothbrush defines the level, but it was all meant in fun. It became clear, when we met by chance at Suzuki's Beddington Lane headquarters early in 1978, that Barry hadn't seen the joke. Working all hours as usual, Barry was fitting out his van, and needed someone to hold a spanner on the outside of the bodywork while he screwed a nut on inside. He berated me through the sheet metal: 'Oh yeah, that's the magazine that's always working my case,' he said. He was not the target, I pointed out, but it fell on deaf ears, and there followed a tirade on how much he had personally done for motorcycling in Britain.

But if the fans on the dark side, those throwing the beer cans, had him on the back foot, he responded with typical self-confidence, hanging a photo on his study wall of a kid wearing a T-shirt with the legend: 'Sheene Is A Wanker'. It was in his rogue's gallery, right next to a lurid picture cut from a men's magazine, proclaiming 'Arsehole of the Month', into which he had montaged the face of Vernon Cooper, boss of the ACU, Britain's sanctioning body, with whom Barry often found himself at odds.

The challenge that stretched him more came on the track. Roberts and his increasingly numerous American cohorts were only part of it. Ironically enough, the bike that Suzuki had built around Barry would go on and take a pair of Italian riders, Marco Lucchinelli and Franco Uncini, to victory over Sheene, long after the old RG500's supposed sell-by date. Barry had by then turned his back on Suzuki, staging a public burning of the bridges at the end of 1979 when he went to pick up his MCN Man of the Year award – wearing a Yamaha T-shirt. Barry thought it a great joke; Suzuki's Maurice Knight, who happened to bump into Barry and his party at a restaurant prior to the event, had a different view. Both knew by then that his contract with Suzuki would not be renewed for 1980, but it still ran to the end of the year. 'I told Barry, if you wear that to the awards, it'll be the most expensive T-shirt you've ever worn.' Barry went ahead anyway. Knight withheld the remaining unpaid £5,000 of his fee as a consequence.

Graduates of the US dirt-track school did have some special gifts. There was the obvious rough-and-tumble willingness to ride handlebar to handlebar, with a special kind of trust between riders. There was the knowledge of how to keep the throttle open when the back tyre was spinning and the bike started to skitter off sideways. And there was the ability to read and adapt to difference surfaces – essential, in a sprint race of only a handful of laps of an oval course that changes its grip levels from lap to lap. This proved useful on tarmac, especially in finding ways to adapt to the tyres – then, even more than today, far from equal to the ever-rising horsepower (now 120bhp-plus) they were called upon to transmit.

It was the sliding that everyone spoke about; a new level of the game, a technique one step further from the knee-out weight shifts pioneered by Smart and stylishly adopted by Sheene – who remained dubious for years afterwards. In Australia in 2001 he said to me: 'Everyone's written about Kenny sliding the bike. Can you show me one picture, just one picture, that shows him doing it?' But, as Smart explains, it wasn't that simple; it wasn't like the languorous rally-car-style power slides of a 2006 MotoGP machine. 'It's a bit of a broad statement to say Kenny used to slide the back wheel. The tyres wouldn't have allowed much sliding in those times. The American riders had a tendency to control the bike once it got out of control, so they didn't worry too much when the wheels got out of line.'

For Sheene, master of the European school of smooth, controlled riding – something he could show to special advantage in wet weather – this meant rivals who pushed him harder than anyone had in the past. He had been able to cruise to his first title riding at 70 percent … he'd said that himself. The Americans were used to giving 100 percent.

Pat Hennen was the most troublesome so far, all the more so because he was a so-called team-mate, riding the same machines. He had finished 1977 with a string of key home-series wins over Sheene, and started 1978 the same way. In the pits, Barry was still engaged in a war of misinformation. He would deliberately note the wrong carburettor jet sizes and tyre choices on the strip of duct tape kept for reference on the seat. According to team manager Rex White, Hennen was probably wise to this, and did a bit of the same back. 'Pat was a very analytical rider, who thought a lot about what he was doing.'

Hennen had outscored Sheene and Roberts at the Easter Transatlantic series; led the Shellsport 500 and MCN Superbike championships; and was ahead of Barry (though not Kenny) in the World Championship when he went to the Isle of Man for a second time. Pat might have said all the right things about the TT tradition, but the real reason for racing there was the money. Sheene's jibe about paying peanuts had been almost literally true: he was on a fraction of Barry's Suzuki sign-up fee. The TT, fighting to maintain popularity after losing Grand Prix status, paid very well for appearance, and even more for success. Pat, riding his GP bike, had just set the first lap under 20 minutes, an average speed of 113.83mph, when he clipped a kerb at Bishop's Court, between Kirkmichael and Ballaugh Bridge, and was thrown at high speed to spin and tumble down the road. He survived, but lay in a coma for three months, before making a slow but almost complete recovery in the years to come.

That left Kenny.

One other thing Paul Smart had observed when racing against Kenny in the USA, where the young ex-dirt-tracker made a habit of following him closely, once telling Smart he'd learned more about racing in one afternoon than ever before: 'Kenny Roberts was totally dedicated.'

Kenny, at 26 one year younger than Sheene, had twice won the AMA Grand National title, on an underpowered Yamaha up against the mighty Harley-Davidson armada. At that time, the title was skewed towards dirt-tracks, with some road racing thrown in. Kenny had already shown Barry and his peers what he could do in the latter department, with crushing performances at the Transatlantic and other international races. Kenny's view was clear enough. 'I was better on smaller bikes, and I could beat Barry on the bigger ones.' He figured the World Championship would be worth a shot. And he said then, still says now, that Barry Sheene was the reason for doing it. And, pretty soon, vice versa.

Kenny had one of only two factory Yamahas, the other going to Cecotto, but in a small two-man team, headed by former 250 World Champion Kel Carruthers. It was very different from the big multi-vehicle three-rider Suzuki team. On top of that, Kenny was also contesting the 250cc class. This was largely to get more practice time on circuits he was seeing for the first time, and didn't last the season. His tyres were different: Kenny uniquely ran American Goodyears. This threw a disturbing unknown into the equation for Sheene. But his biggest problem was quite different. It was that

Barry Sheene and Kenny Roberts: inches – and poles – apart.

infamous mystery virus that struck, he said, on the aircraft home from the Venezuelan GP, where he'd started the year with a win.

Barry was clear enough – it was a lingering ailment that made him listless, sometimes feverish, sometimes giving him pain when breathing. He saw doctor after doctor, but the best they could do was suspect it might be Bornholm Disease, or some related viral infection. This was in the days before the still misunderstood Chronic Fatigue Syndrome, also known as ME (myalgic encephalomyelitis) or 'Yuppie 'Flu' was being discussed; it is likely that a few years later this might have been given the blame.

Either way, the louder Barry protested, the louder grew the chorus of disbelief. 'It's a funny sort of virus,' said some, 'that makes you come third instead of first.' 'It's Hennenitis,' quipped the Italian press, and most thought Sheene's real trouble came from the two Americans, rather than anything medical.

Barry continued to blame ill health, being permanently off colour. He explained it to me thus, some years later: 'The difference between coming first and third is very small, but it makes all the difference.' His assertions were somewhat vindicated by his riding later in the season. He had woken up one morning in June, on Heron boss Gerald Ronson's yacht, and suddenly realised he was better. From Assen onwards, he was a real racer again, regaining almost all his lost momentum. It was lost again, the way he saw it, in one key passage in Finland. This was to be a pivotal moment, not only for the 1978 championship battle between the two new great rivals, but also in Sheene's career with Suzuki.

Suzuki had made a significant change to the square-four for 1978. The RGA500 'stepped' the cylinder pairs, the rear pair higher than the front, the gearbox tucked underneath. This made a more compact engine, and eliminated a gear from the primary drive train. Suzuki had just one factory team, Sheene and Hennen, but other favoured riders also had the RGA, including Dutchman Wil Hartog (or Hot-Dog, as Barry nicknamed him), plus Steve Baker (moved from Yamaha), Frenchman Michel Rougerie, and fast Italians Virginio Ferrari and Marco Lucchinelli. A slew of private or semi-private riders rode production machines, among them Stavros, sacked by Heron, but helped to keep going by Barry and George Harrison.

Compared with the Suzuki, Yamaha's in-line four had a narrower power band, cutting in sharply at higher revs,

LEFT *Factory teams ran out of trucks, tents and caravans in 1978. At Karlskoga, in Sweden, Suzuki's new stepped cylinder design is clearly visible.*

OPPOSITE *Barry declared himself virus-free for France, but it was premature. He leads Hartog and winner Roberts.*

but better top-end performance. Both of these factors were enhanced this year by an ingenious new rotating exhaust 'power valve', which applied a crude but effective variation to the exhaust phasing, akin to a four-stroke's variable valve timing.

Sheene was well-known for his innovation of a smoking hole drilled in the chin-piece of his helmet. At the first round in Venezuela he added a drinking tube and, with his hot-weather stamina, he outdistanced Hennen as Roberts retired.

It was on the flight home, Sheene said, that the debilitating viral infection struck. A month later in Spain he was fifth, as Hennen won from Roberts. At the high-speed Salzburgring in Austria, the Yamahas powered away, Sheene third; in France (where Barry prematurely declared himself fit) Roberts and Hennen beat him; likewise in Italy, where Barry fell back to fifth. It was Hennen's last Grand Prix.

The Sheene camp had a lucky escape themselves in the summer break, at the Chimay race in Belgium, one of Barry's big annual private paydays. In a horrifying crash, a motorcycle cartwheeled down pit lane, killing at least two people there, and hitting Franko, breaking his ankle. Less than a minute before, Stephanie had been standing alongside him. Barry dragged Franko out of the carnage and away from the medics, and flew him straight back to England.

The GP season moved on without Hennen. It was now between Kenny and Barry, the American ahead by just ten points, with six rounds still to go.

At Assen, Barry might have felt he was back to full strength, but the battle was hard and Johnny Cecotto led Roberts and Sheene home. A week later, at Spa in Belgium, Barry was third, with Hartog the winner and Roberts second. Hot-Dog's role had been to help Sheene, but although he had waited as much as he could, it was in vain. This result skewed Suzuki's tactics; if Sheene was going to get beaten to the riders' championship, strength in numbers could at least give them more chance of the manufacturers' crown.

At bumpy Karlskoga in Sweden, Hartog did ride in support, finishing second to Sheene as Roberts, who crashed in practice, fell back to a poor seventh. The points gap was now just three points in the American's favour, with three races to go.

Then came the Finland catastrophe. In practice, Barry later explained, he felt the faint grumble in his motor of a crankshaft main bearing beginning to fail. He even

ABOVE *Friendly but
uneasy Suzuki team-
mates: Barry and
Dutchman Wil Hartog.*

OPPOSITE *Flying
through the Finnish
forests … and then the
main bearing failed.
This was the race that
soured the partnership
with Suzuki.*

identified which one, number four, by faint traces of oil
on the sparking plug, showing the oil seal was getting
pulled out of shape. That's what he said. Suzuki's
Japanese mechanics Tady and Mitsi (Tadao Matsui and
Mitsuru Okamoto) thought differently. 'No, Barry-san,'
said Tady. 'Engine is good.' They declined to make the
engine swap he demanded, weary perhaps of just too
many demands that had turned out to be fruitless or
unnecessary – because Barry never tired of making
technical changes and experiments.

Sure enough, the bearing failed. That Roberts also
broke down meant nothing to Sheene. He could have
won, taking 15 points, and the lead in the championship.
A lead, as it transpired, that would have tipped the title
in his favour. Livid, he let fly as only he could: verbal,
articulate, scathing, and in full public earshot. The
papers next day were full of it.

This was acutely embarrassing for the mechanics, and
equally so for Suzuki. By all means complain, even say
out loud that this mistake cost you the championship.
But behind closed doors, please, Barry-san. Not out
there in the pit lane, the paddock; especially not to all
those eager journalists. Anyway, what about all the other
times Tady and Mitsi hadn't made a mistake and the bike

ran flawlessly? Barry and Suzuki had ridden hand in
hand through the glory years. After this, the relationship
would never be the same again.

Sheene was very vocal again at the next race, and
with good reason. Nor was he alone. The British Grand
Prix, his chance to show everyone he could beat Kenny
and reclaim his title, had been turned into a sorry farce
by the organisers' muddled response to an admittedly
impressive rain storm. Barry's opinion of the lap scorers
resounds still: 'This lot couldn't time an egg!'

Slick tyres were still relatively new, and nobody had
bothered to think out a procedure if a dry race should
turn wet – neither the organisers nor the designers. In
the summer downpour, some riders tiptoed on daintily,
their smooth tyres surfing over the puddles; others
stopped, for mechanics to wrestle with the problem of
making a quick wheel change on a machine not
designed for such an eventuality. Sheene stopped, losing
seven-and-a-half minutes to the procedure; Roberts
likewise, but in less than three minutes. Barry rode like
a demon, unlapping himself twice over Roberts. He
thought he'd won. The lap scorers thought otherwise.
In fact, nobody seemed quite sure. In the end, victory
was awarded to a bemused Roberts, shaking his head;

Sheene was third, behind British national rider Steve Manship, who had gone the whole distance without stopping.

One round remained, at the daunting Nürburgring. As Barry said: 'It's very, very dangerous.' Roberts thought likewise of the 14.189 miles through the Eifel mountain forests and valleys. Barry finished fourth, 36 seconds behind winner Ferrari. If Roberts had failed to finish, he would have been champion. But Kenny was three seconds ahead in third place. The title was lost, and won. It was small consolation that strong form at the end of the season meant Sheene's reign at home continued, winning the Shellsport 500 and MCN Superbike titles. The important part was that he was riding like a potential champion again.

If Barry Sheene had stayed with Suzuki, Kenny Roberts opined recently, he would have won the World Championship again. Barry Sheene didn't stay with Suzuki. The 1979 season would be his last with the factory, and his last year at the cutting edge of factory bike development. But not his last serious attempt at winning the title.

The cracks in the relationship with Suzuki, in retrospect, were visible before the end of 1978, and before the Imatra bust-up. Until then, Barry's force of character meant he'd had his own way in retaining Don Mackay and Franko in his pit, despite the factory's preference for formally trained engineers. Now came the ultimatum. Don was the first to go. Sacking him was an unpalatable task that Barry got his major domo Ken Patterson to do, while he himself was away on holiday in Venezuela. 'We spoke again after that, but he never ever told me why. And I never asked him,' Don told me.

Franko, now approaching 70 and with poor eyesight, lasted into the 1979 season, until an incident at the Austrian GP. A misplaced washer cocked a brake disc out of true, ruining Barry's race. After that, at Suzuki's insistence, Franko was relegated to driving the motorhome.

The clearest sign came at pre-season tests in Japan, attended by Sheene and the latest factory-equipped riders, Hartog and Ferrari. There were two different chassis to try, one distinguished by a nose-mounted radiator. This was the one Barry preferred, more for the way it felt than the placing of the radiator; the other pair chose differently. Suzuki took their advice over that of Sheene. He was more than dismayed when

he suggested that they should have the bike they preferred, and he should have his choice. No, Barry-san – they must be all the same. After six years as their number one rider, this was deeply mortifying. Particularly when, as he wrote at the time: 'After Hartog had fallen off about 15 times and Ferrari said it was a camel, then they sent the frame I had chosen originally.' In fact, he did tests with the front-radiator bike again, but raced mainly with a 1979 chassis until Suzuki's late-season revision arrived.

There was a souring of relations in Britain too. The 'Rip-off Sheene' banners were the result of three weeks of will-he/won't-he headlines in the bike press. These concerned negotiations over appearance money with Motor Circuit Developments, who owned or operated a swathe of tracks – Brands Hatch, Mallory Park, Oulton Park and Snetterton. This year, there was a new rival – the recommissioned Donington Park – which was to play host to a new made-for-TV championship, for ITV's national *World of Sport*. This was founded to a large extent on Sheene's popularity, and he would be paid handsomely for one or two races a day. He was demanding the same sort of treatment from MCD.

Director Chris Lowe explained his side of the story to me. 'Car racing had moved from when Jimmy Clark and Graham Hill would jump from their Formula One cars to do a saloon race, to drivers just doing the one race. Barry was a bit early to try that on with bike racing, but he'd got this one-ride-a-meeting thing.' He was already commanding five-figure fees, continued Lowe, 'but the gates had stopped going through the roof.' Meeting Barry's terms would have meant making other riders suffer. Lowe said no. Barry had gambled, and lost, and so had his fans. At least it lightened his racing work load, but it meant he forfeited any chance to defend the Shellsport 500 and MCN Superbike titles he had held since 1976 (won by Parrish and Dave Potter respectively). British racing was left to the likes of stalwarts Mick Grant and Roger Marshall and the rising Ron Haslam, who were likewise obliged to race each other without the major target being present.

In fact, Barry did race a couple of times on MCD tracks, winning three of the Transatlantic match races in his role as team captain. There was also a one-off gallop on a big 1,000cc four-stroke Suzuki at Oulton Park, where he was beaten by rising star Ron Haslam. Four-strokes, opined Sheene, were 'muck-spreaders'. One wonders what he would make of the latest highly

After changing to treaded tyres, Sheene was easily the fastest man through the inland sea of Silverstone in 1978. The ill-prepared British GP organisers were swamped by the weather; people still argue over who actually won.

evolved four-stroke MotoGP machines. Barry won the inaugural ITV meeting at Donington, and came second in the next (to Hartog); and in September also won the AGV Nations Cup at the same track. Two weeks later, back at Imola for the final of that series, Sheene crashed in practice, breaking his collarbone. Rather surprisingly, it was his first fracture in four years of racing. Sheene was in fact a careful racer whose bad crashes were down to machine failure or bad luck, but he couldn't help but be more famous for his injuries than for his skill.

Hartog and Ferrari were in independent teams for the Grand Prix season of 1979 (Nijmag Suzuki and Nava Olio-Fiat); Heron Suzuki re-employed Stavros, and added forceful Irish rider Tom Herron. Herron had an impish sense of humour, and even managed to turn the tables on Barry, teasing him by feeding him crazy tyre information at Imola, where Barry switched back to Dunlops for the one and only time since the Daytona crash in 1975. Here was a team-mate that Barry seemed to respect in a new way. Nobody would ever know how it might have turned out between them. Herron's GP season had barely got going when he went home to Ireland, with some misgivings and an injured hand, for the North-West 200 road race. He lost control at high speed, and suffered fatal injuries.

The GP year began with Roberts still recovering from a bad crash at Yamaha's test track in the winter. Compressed vertebrae meant he was still in bed, as Sheene showed his customary hot-weather endurance to win the opening round in Venezuela once again. Kenny made his own heroic return five weeks later, with a decisive victory in Austria, while Sheene struggled to 12th and nil points with that cocked brake disc.

Sheene fried a big-end and retired at Germany's Hockenheimring, his season rapidly coming undone. In Italy, on Dunlops, he was fourth behind Herron, as Roberts won from points leader Ferrari. It would be Herron's last Grand Prix finish.

Spain – and Sheene retires after a practice spill and a bike that failed to start; Rijeka in Yugoslavia, and a stone thrown up hits his knee right on one of the screws inserted at the end of 1975, and he retires in agony.

The title now was between Roberts and the Suzuki of Ferrari, and with company loyalty in mind Barry finished one tenth behind the Italian at Assen. That hurt.

Salzburgring, Austria, 1979 – the infamous race with the out-of-true brake disc, blamed on an error by Franko. On lap one, Sheene briefly leads team-mates Tom Herron and Steve Parrish. He is riding a high-radiator version of the RG500.

ABOVE *On tip-toe through Spa's Eau Rouge corner in practice for the 1979 GP. The track's new surface was dangerously slippery; Sheene was a ring-leader of a race boycott.*

OPPOSITE *Smiling through: Barry in 1979.*

The Belgian GP was boycotted by the leading riders (see following chapter); Sheene won convincingly in Sweden, where Roberts regained the points lead with fourth as Ferrari failed to finish. The Yamaha rider drew further ahead with sixth in Finland, Sheene third. Then came the epic British GP, described in detail below. There was just one more race after that – the French GP at Le Mans, where Barry won after a race-long duel with Roberts and newcomer Randy Mamola. Ferrari crashed out, and Roberts was champion for a second year in succession.

It was his last of 18 GP wins on a Suzuki.

Every race fan and every rider has one greatest race lodged in the memory. For many, it was the 1979 British Grand Prix at Silverstone. For once the weather was sunny and warm. And if his home race yet again withheld the ultimate favour from England's greatest racing hero, it was not without giving him the chance to etch an unforgettable image in the mind ... the picture of Sheene, knee out, leaning forward, coming within inches of passing Kenny Roberts on the grass, after having started the last lap a long way behind.

This wasn't just Barry's greatest race. It was one of Kenny's as well. One of the greatest in GP history. The BBC included it as the only motorcycling clip in a series of *Great Sporting Moments* at the end of the old century. It remained breathtaking.

The championship was between Roberts and Ferrari; this race was all about Roberts and Sheene. After a bad season, it was time for Barry to set the record straight, and Silverstone offered the opportunity.

Sheene qualified fifth, behind Roberts, Cecotto, Hartog and Ferrari. He was still fiddling with damper changes right up until morning warm-up, trying to settle the handling.

Hartog led away round the fast airfield circuit, with an average approaching 120mph in the days before chicanes. Ferrari, Sheene and Roberts kept him company. After one-third distance, Roberts upped the pace. Only Sheene could match him.

For the next 13 laps, they tested and probed at each other, alternately raising and lowering the pace, taking turns to play cat and mouse. They even had time to exchange insults – the famous raised middle finger, Sheene insisted afterwards, had been a friendly greeting ... 'a little light relief in a titanic battle'.

The Greatest Race? Sheene lost to Roberts by inches at Silverstone in 1979, after such a heroic come-back lap that the result hardly mattered.

It would be decided on the last lap. Each had a plan.

For Sheene, this was to start close behind, pounce on Roberts halfway round, then use his greater speed through the last sweeping Woodcote corner to stay in front. 'I knew that was one point where I was faster than Kenny, so if I started the last lap within 25 feet or so, I could win the race.'

Roberts recalls it 25 years later. 'From my side, I thought I was the fastest guy. But there was another Silverstone I thought I'd won, and I lost it' (versus Jack Middelburg, in 1981).

'But for the backmarker at the start of the last lap, I'd have done more,' Roberts continued. 'I had the corner before Woodcote wired. I was the only guy I ever saw go through there wide open. I would have used that on the last lap … if you led the last straight into Woodcote, you'd won the race.'

But the backmarker was there, as they powered round Woodcote on the second-last lap. It was national rider George Fogarty, father of four times World Superbike Champion Carl, being lapped for the second time. Roberts went inside him, Sheene was stuck outside … and he started the last lap with a gap more like 150 feet. An unbridgeable chasm.

Or was it?

Sheene had already broken the lap record, but the last lap was his masterpiece. By the end of the 2.9 miles, the Suzuki was right up with the Yamaha again. Into Woodcote, Kenny was relatively slow and tight. Barry went sweeping round on the outside.

For a moment, it seemed he might make it. In fact, Roberts was right. There was no way round. As he eased the power on and drifted out towards the white line, he didn't even see Barry desperately surging up on his left.

Roberts hit the paint; Barry puffed up dust on the other side of it. He crossed the line just 0.03 of a second behind.

Second place was a small reward for one of the greatest rides of his career.

Why did Barry Sheene split with Suzuki? Was it a gamble that went wrong? Was he just too big for his boots? Or did he really envisage a brighter future with Yamaha?

Those involved think it was the failed gamble, that Suzuki called his bluff, after one more example of Barry's greed and brinkmanship. Certainly, for a man who was always planning and scheming, Barry didn't seem to have a fall-back position. Plan B – riding for

Yamaha – had to be hastily put into action, and the reality fell far short of the factory bikes he had dreamed of.

The cracks had been appearing for some time. There had been the Imatra incident in 1978, still very fresh in the memory in Japan. Barry had been complaining also in 1979, with some justification, that the factory Suzukis were no faster than the production models.

What Barry really wanted to do was to gain independence … to run factory Suzukis in his own team, his own way, from his own workshops at the manor house. Cut out the middle-men. All the parasites and hangers-on. He knew he could get the sponsorship required. But he wanted Suzuki to give him the bikes.

Negotiations had been going on for some time during the 1979 season, to little effect. According to Suzuki's Maurice Knight: 'The Japanese were very much against the bikes leaving company premises, except for race meetings.' This was how matters stood, neither side giving way.

In October, Knight was in his office, preparing papers for an imminent meeting. 'It was never Barry's style to ring up or make an appointment. He'd just bang on the door, irrespective of what was going on. I told him I was in a rush, and asked if he had come to a decision. "Yes," he said. "I'm going to ride for Yamaha."'

If the desired effect was to bring Suzuki to its knees, this was a grave miscalculation.

'I asked if he was sure, and he said he was, so I said: "Well, there's nothing more to say. I have a meeting in two minutes, so all I can do is wish you luck and say goodbye."' By all accounts, Barry left the office looking flabbergasted; and later that day Franko arrived at the Suzuki offices, now in Crawley, to 'try and sort this thing out'. It was too late.

Knight remained convinced that Sheene was taken unawares. 'I believe Barry was bluffing, that he really hoped to get Suzukis to run from home,' he told me. 'But what Barry didn't know was that I had the whole Heron board behind me. We'd agreed that if it was going to get difficult, then we weren't going to go into it any longer. I didn't let Barry go on my own.'

Sheene got his wish of being independent. He had the finance – taking most of the Texaco backing with him, and adding other sponsors. Now all he need do was find some motorcycles.

Sheene's lap of honour in an end-of-season home race – always helmet-off – showed how far the relationship with Suzuki had soured. He's riding Ron Haslam's Yamaha.

CHAPTER EIGHT

THE YAMAHA YEARS

The year he turned 30 was both a triumph and a disaster for Barry Sheene. He had proved he could survive without Suzuki, finding plenty of backing to run his own team out of the converted manor house barns at Charlwood. Although he wasn't anywhere near fighting for the championship in 1980, this was only his first year of independence. But he discovered that neither his riding ability nor his unparalleled commercial acumen held any sway with the people he needed most if he was to regain that position – the Japanese factories building the motorcycles. Just one factory, in fact, as he had burned his bridges with Suzuki.

Over at Yamaha, however, it wasn't much better. Japanese factory staff had a job for life back then, and many of the Yamaha racing people Barry had upset during his unhappy Yamaha season of 1972 were not only still with the company, but had risen to positions of greater importance. As he told me ruefully, some years later: 'The people you crap over on the way up, you meet them on the way down again.' Superstar Barry was tailor-made for any marketing man's promotional dreams, and his request for factory

Past trees and houses at Imatra in Finland in 1981.
Sheene was riding as well as ever, but against the odds.

machines was greeted with enthusiasm in England and Europe. But in Japan his entreaties fell on deaf ears.

He went first to the British Yamaha importers, Mitsui Machinery Sales Ltd. There, Robert Jackson was head of the recently formed racing department. He took the proposal to Yamaha's European headquarters in Amsterdam. Once Sheene had convinced them that he had now learned to keep his mouth shut in the event of any machine problems, they too became enthusiastic supporters. At least, the European staff members did.

The Japanese retained their mistrust of a man whose name was in any case so strongly linked with Suzuki. And, as Jackson discovered, 'there were so many of them, and they shut the door all along the line. I'd like a penny, not a pound, for every telex I sent round the world on Barry's behalf ... because Barry does give you a hard time until he gets what he wants. But I would send a telex to one particular person, and get a reply quite mysteriously from somebody quite different.' No motorcycles were forthcoming. Barry, without much choice in the matter, signed up anyway, as he told me, 'in the expectation of supposedly getting works bikes in 1981'.

In January, Barry hired TV presenter Frank Bough to announce his plans and reveal his new machines. He had secured £300,000 sponsorship. Hi-fi manufacturers Akai were supplemented by Texaco, Marlboro and DAF Trucks. The bikes, painted black striped with red, were Yamahas ... but not the exotic factory models of Roberts and Cecotto. Barry had the new production model, the TZ500G, the same as anyone with £8,000 could buy.

The in-line four looked like the works bike, but this was skin-deep. It was some 20 horsepower down, in a flexible tubular-steel frame, with flimsy forks. Many years later, when he was in Australia, I asked Barry what was the worst motorcycle he had ever raced. Without hesitation, he chose this machine.

'I was used to Suzuki, where the production bikes were as good as the factory bikes, and sometimes better. I thought Yamaha would make a good production 500. Their TZ750 was really good. I was wrong. It was the ideal anchor for anybody's boat. The frame was too weak, it didn't have enough power. It was just something they produced and sold on the back of Kenny Roberts winning races.'

Never one to sit around, Sheene got to work pronto, commissioning a new frame from Hertfordshire motorcycle race engineering specialists Harris

Performance Products. This at least addressed the handling issues, but Yamaha were not pleased. 'It wasn't politically correct as far as they were concerned, and with my position that was the end of that,' said Barry. Unusually for him, he kept quiet and kept racing. Paul Butler, nowadays Race Director of MotoGP, was then at Yamaha in Amsterdam, and noted how different the independent Sheene of 1980 was compared with 1972. 'He was very changed, very mature, very professional. He had grown up into the ultimate ambassador for the sport.'

The sport needed ambassadors. During 1979 there had been a fundamental change. It was the stillborn World Series. This had been conceived as a series of races, but rapidly turned into a political movement, and a rallying point for disaffected riders. Ideally, it was nothing less than an alternative World Championship, independently run, and the antidote to years of high-handed management by the Switzerland-based FIM (Fédération Internationale de Motocyclisme) ... to their cavalier attitude towards safety, lack of respect for riders, and mingy rates of pay. Also the series was as an acknowledgement that TV and the sale of TV rights meant a new era for international sport. Kenny Roberts was a prime mover, as was Barry Coleman, then editor of *Motocourse*, later founder of the MotoGP charity 'Riders for Health'. Few appreciated the commercial realities more keenly than Sheene. He was soon a valuable asset.

Proud of his mistrust of authority, Barry had never been slow at coming forward when there were officials to be argued with. There had been countless disputes over the years, frequently to do with money or other interests of his own, but he was quite altruistic when it came to the rights of riders in general, and especially when the problem concerned safety – as in Austria in 1977, where he took the leading role in getting the race stopped.

He and Cecotto also represented the riders to the FIM during 1978, when Sheene's persuasive line of argument won several concessions, including getting the long and ultra-fast Spa-Francorchamps circuit in Belgium taken off the calendar, unless it was significantly shortened. Since the Belgians were doing this anyway in order to regain the lost Formula One car GP, it wasn't much of a concession. Some of the old track was kept; a new loop was added to shorten the lap, and the entire track was resurfaced.

When the bike GP circus arrived to inaugurate the revived Spa circuit in the first week of July, the surface was so new it was exuding oil. It was impossibly treacherous, even after road-scrubbing lorries from Brussels airport had worked through the night. Simply not fit for a World Championship race. Sheene and Roberts led the rebellion, canvassing the riders and dealing with the officials. All requests fell on deaf ears – including Sheene's own suggestion that the race be run as a (voluntary) non-championship event, in which he promised to take part, so the fans would at least have something to watch. Sheene and Roberts then led the general paddock exodus on race eve. It was a turning point in the politics of racing. All the leading riders followed them; all were subsequently fined by the FIM, all refused to pay the fine. If the World Series needed any further encouragement or justification, this was it.

The World Series was attractive to the racers. Teams and riders would get an increased share of the purse; it would be run as an accountable business enterprise, in contrast to the essentially amateur FIM. Several willing circuits, including Donington Park, had been enlisted, and 43 riders signed up. The first official announcement came at the British GP, later in the 1979 season: war with the FIM became open.

Coleman had originally planned to launch the series in 1981, and believes that if they had waited until then, it would have had a much greater chance of success. But racers are by nature impatient. They wanted to go ahead right away, in 1980. This headlong rush was crucial to its failure. The breakaway organisation was not strong enough, nor were arrangements sufficiently well advanced to survive the FIM's resistance. They, via the national federations, had strong-armed the circuit owners. The series was running out of places to race.

Nonetheless, an unprecedented unity had been achieved among the riders, and Coleman was anxious to exploit that power. He called a meeting in Belgium on the eve of his own meeting with the FIM, to explain the gravity of the situation. Most riders attended. Coleman wanted them to sign a letter, refusing to ride at six dangerous venues: Venezuela, Sweden, Imatra in Finland, the Nürburgring, the road circuit at Brno, and Spa-Francorchamps.

Coleman: 'Sheene was the only person as good as Kenny Roberts, in terms of understanding the requirements of the riders, and in comprehending the full situation and all its implications. I was quite startled at the hitherto hidden depths.' Multilingual – at least in a sort of paddock patois – and evangelically persuasive, he commanded the stage.

'Sheene was in a class of his own. His invective was quite brilliant.' When some of the Dutch riders were expressing doubts, Sheene invented a mythical compatriot, Hertz van Rental, to help re-illustrate his points. To no avail in the case of Wil Hartog, who became the first top rider to walk out of the meeting, fearful of otherwise losing his factory contract. Barry called him back, to ask: 'How can you walk, without a spine?'

The series collapsed, but not without changing the ground rules significantly: prize money was increased by up to 500 percent, and within three years most of the blacklisted circuits, including the Nürburgring and Imatra, were off the calendar for good.

Kenny Roberts's third successive World Championship year, 1980, was nothing but a disaster for Barry Sheene. It was left to the new Heron Suzuki riders, Randy Mamola and New Zealander Graeme Crosby, plus Wil Hartog, and the Italian Suzukis of old pal Marco Lucchinelli, Franco Uncini and Valentino's father Graziano Rossi, to provide opposition. Mamola came

the closest, but not especially close, for the first of four runner-up positions in his long career.

The shortage of horsepower was insoluble. Kiwi mechanic Ken Fletcher had come with Barry from Suzuki, and he explained how the motor 'just kept running and running. It's easy to make something reliable when it hasn't got any horsepower.' The handling was the real issue. As Sheene told me: 'It pattered so badly, mainly because the frame was so weak. It seemed to twist around the steering head, and make the front wheel skip.' It was now that Sheene commissioned his own chassis from Harris, with a rising-rate rear suspension linkage like the Suzuki. In fact, Yamaha did let him use this, and it was into this chassis that Fletcher slotted the works engine that Yamaha finally unbent enough to lend Barry for his home GP (it lost power, and he retired).

Barry managed to get more out of the TZ Yamaha than anyone else in the early GPs, but it was nothing like enough. Snowed off in Austria, he was a poor seventh in Italy, and fifth at Jarama in Spain. The next round was at Paul Ricard in France, where Sheene had a rare rush of blood to the head, and a crash that for once was simply his own fault. He was driven to distraction by the sight

OPPOSITE *At his team launch, with Stephanie and young nephew Scott Smart, at the start of 1980.*

LEFT *As an avid water-skier, the introduction of the Wetbike to Britain took his fancy. He figure-headed the official UK launch on the Thames.*

of Crosby on his old Suzuki, faster on the long straight but slower through the corners. 'I was catching him from the end of the straight to the last right-hander before the pits, then he'd piss off and leave me again. I crashed because I was just trying too hard.' The little finger of his left hand, trapped under the handlebar as he went down, got badly mangled.

This relatively trivial injury was to cause Sheene much trouble. He had a long-abiding horror of amputation and, after surgery at Marylebone Hospital in London, where the joint was stitched together with silver wire, it seemed he might escape this fate. A month later, he retired at Assen after qualifying 16th, unable to operate the clutch properly. At the Belgian GP, moved to Zolder, he was timed 38th fastest in practice, unqualified, and though he disputed the timing he was happy, in his condition, to go home. In despondent mood, he was caught speeding the Roller at more than 100mph in Britain, adding another £100 fine to the £200 plus a one-month ban for 113.5mph earlier in the year.

Constant pain meant by now that the dreaded amputation was a welcome alternative, and he missed the Finnish GP as the finger was finally removed. There was little sympathy in the motorcycle press, where one trader offered three-fingered 'Barry Sheene racing gloves' for sale.

Once again, Barry's big comeback was planned for his home GP. The factory bike on loan from Yamaha arrived very late, the Monday of the race, and in not especially good condition. Nor was it the latest version like Kenny's, with the reversed outer cylinders. This was a factory bike, however, with an aluminium frame and an electronic power valve. Barry set to work, but they were short of time, and it came to naught.

It was the non-championship races that made the 1980 season worthwhile for Barry. Yet another breakdown of negotiations with MCD meant his home appearances were as limited as the year before, but when he did race, he frequently won.

Mitsui had given him two each of TZ500 and TZ750 Yamahas, and they were good enough for Barry to win at Cadwell Park, and then the first ITV *World of Sport* race at Donington, as well as an international race in Holland. It was only when the competition got hotter that the bikes showed their weakness. The first time was at the Transatlantic races, where new American rival Freddie Spencer won two of the six races, Roberts won three, and Mamola the other one.

Downbeat debut: Sheene was seventh in the first GP of 1980 in Italy, and first Yamaha privateer ... but miles behind the factory Yamahas of Cecotto and race-winner Roberts.

Sheene was successful also at the back end of the year, winning another *World of Sport* race, adding more wins at Oliver's Mount and Cadwell Park, though he ran second to Mamola in the race of the year at Mallory Park.

In 1980 the most important race, however, was an odd one – in Japan, at Yamaha's annual festivities at Sugo, which always included an invitation race on their private circuit. Mitsui's Jackson nominated Sheene; at first the factory staff were wary. The chance of meeting Yamaha's top brass face to face was too good to miss, however. Sheene and Jackson called in at the factory for talks on the way to Sugo. Jackson said: 'It was obvious that the promises we got were based on what was going to happen in the race.'

To Roberts and the other Westerners, it was a holiday event. But Sheene had brought Ken Fletcher with him, and took the qualifying and set-up time very seriously. Conditions were atrocious on race day … rainy and misty. Barry's bike went onto three cylinders in the first leg, but still he finished second. He was leading the second race when his front tyre deflated suddenly, and he fell at some 130mph, knocking himself out and breaking a bone in his wrist. It was as good, said Jackson, 'as if he'd fallen on his sword'.

When Barry came round in the medical centre, he found Yamaha president Hisaeo Koike looking down at him solicitously. 'You did very well,' he said. The look on the great man's face was enough to assure Sheene that at last he had broken through some of the barriers with Yamaha.

The helicopter flying instructors at Shoreham Airport, on the coast between Brighton and Worthing, were impressed by their latest pupil. He may have been on the older side, but his capacity and willingness to learn, and his possession of that magic understanding between man and machine, put him in the top bracket. 'He could have trained for the air force, or become a commercial pilot,' said Chris Bartlett, one of those who trained Barry Sheene.

Maybe it was something to do with turning 30, maybe a present to himself after a dismal year. Either way, late in 1980 Sheene became the proud owner of a second-hand American Enstrom helicopter, and threw himself headlong into training.

He'd owned a fixed-wing Cessna, and of course could fly it, but had never bothered to get a licence. Helicopters were something different – a real challenge.

Rotary-wing pilots will tell you, their eyes shining, just how much more difficult and involving it is to fly a helicopter than a fixed-wing aircraft. Barry was no different. In automotive terms, a helicopter is a motorcycle, a fixed-wing a dull old car. He started studying with real fervour, and passed the first exams he had ever passed in his whole life, with flying colours.

The crash in Japan was a problem, because his left wrist was weak … the wrist that operates the heavy and all-important collective pitch control, so he was grounded for a while; when he was fit enough he came back and qualified, all within two weeks.

Even before he was flying solo, he was flying wherever and whenever he could, coercing one or another instructor to go with him on weekend trips, so he could log up the hours while covering the miles. By January, he was solo. There was a bit of a scare on an early flight. Soon after take-off he ran into rough weather. He radioed Gatwick for assistance, and they advised him to gain height to improve radio reception. Bad advice. Once he broke out of the weather, he could see nothing but a blanket of white. And he was a relative novice, with no experience of flying on instruments. After some worrying time, another helicopter with an experienced pilot was dispatched from Shoreham to shepherd Barry down to ground level.

Helicopter travel is always exciting, and there are myriad stories about Sheene's escapades. Paul Smart recalled one trip where there was something banging on the helicopter fuselage … surely something broken. After an emergency landing, they discovered it was just a seat belt, hanging out of the closed door. Parrish recalls how they landed once, quite out of the blue, on the front lawn of a posh retirement home. Angry residents melted into admiration when Barry Sheene applied a bit of his distinctive charm. And Gary Nixon recalled a lucky escape. 'He offered me a flip. I said OK, but then he said no, there was too much weight, and I got out. He was going to do a dead engine stick landing. He'd have done that without even telling me – from 10,000ft or whatever. Another time, we were flying back from Mallory Park, and I took a look at the gas gauge, and I thought … we ain't gonna make it. I said to him what happens if we run out of gas. He said … it gets real quiet. He got on the radio, and they finally let us land at a military base and refuel.' Sounds harem-scarem, which is the way Barry liked it; but he would always remind you of his perfect record, and that in fact he was a conscientious pilot. Often adding, for the laugh: 'A good landing is one you walk away from.'

Yamaha's high-level change of heart towards Sheene didn't go all the way for 1981. Mitsui did get the factory machines they had asked for, but these were last year's model, and Barry was one of five riders with the same machines – Dutchman Boet van Dulmen, Swiss Michel Frutschi, and the French pair Christian Sarron and Marc Fontan were similarly equipped. The machine was the final version of the long-serving in-line four design that had taken the first ever two-stroke title with Agostini in 1975, with the reversed outer cylinders. It was the last gasp of an obsolete design.

Kenny Roberts, however, had something different: the all-new OW54. This was virtually a copy of the square-four Suzuki, with similar disc-valve induction, as well as Yamaha's own 'power valve'. Barry badly wanted one.

Mitsui's Jackson was again the liaison man. 'We'd thought at first our problems were solved. When it became clear we weren't going to get the latest bikes, Barry complained bitterly, while still keeping his mouth shut in public. Yamaha always replied that "Kenny Roberts is just testing new machines, and is also having problems. When we have sorted them out, then Barry can have the bikes."'

Barry didn't think much of this plan. In his opinion, nobody could develop a motorcycle as well as he could. Look at the Suzuki RG500, still fully competitive. It had been his baby. This view included a corollary – that Kenny Roberts was very much the wrong man. And this, in the weeks and years to come, was something Sheene was prepared to say in public. The test would come if they were on equal equipment, and that was to happen very seldom during 1981, or indeed the year after that.

Barry was pleased by one addition to the pit – Japanese-American tuner Erv Kanemoto, who had run his friend Nixon's team in the USA, and was coming over for an exploratory GP year, ahead of bringing Freddie Spencer in 1983. The reserved Kanemoto was on a path to glory, in the future winning 500cc and 250cc championships with Spencer, Eddie Lawson, Max Biaggi and Luca Cadalora.

As the GP season got under way, Yamaha found themselves under serious Suzuki pressure, not least because Roberts was indeed having teething problems with the new square four. Sheene was fourth, first Yamaha, at the opening round in Austria, with Roberts retiring. Lack of speed on the long straights of the Hockenheimring in Germany saw Sheene only sixth as

OPPOSITE *Curiosity about the King of Spain's helicopter at Jarama got Barry into trouble with the royal security guards in 1982.*

LEFT *At the controls of his own helicopter, Barry and Stephanie get ready to go home from Donington Park in 1982.*

Roberts won; Kenny triumphed once more in the wet at Monza, with Sheene third. Erv and Ken Fletcher had tried everything to get more speed out of the old straight four … only to run into a familiar barrier with a motorcycle at the end of its development. Everything had been tried already. Fletcher: 'We wanted to raise the exhaust port a little for more power. The Japanese engineers said they'd done it, and the piston rings would break. We were down on power so we tried it anyway. Within five laps, the rings broke.'

Yamaha made good their promise at the next round, the French GP at Paul Ricard, with an OW54 for Barry. But there was a significant difference from Roberts's bike: Kenny was able to use the latest 16-inch front tyres, made by Dunlop; Sheene couldn't get them for love or money. Burned bridges again. As it turned out, both Yamaha riders had tyre trouble in the race after tussling for the lead, dropping behind a Suzuki rostrum clean sweep: Lucchinelli, Mamola and Crosby. Barry did beat Kenny, but Mamola and Roberts were ahead on points. In Rijeka, Mamola added another win, with Roberts third and Sheene fifth.

Kanemoto remembers Assen as one of the worst races of a long career. An error setting the carburettors meant the bike wouldn't start. Barry pushed and pushed. Paused as he got to the first curve after the pits, pushed again. The bike started, idled briefly, then died. It was even worse because Roberts had a charade of his own: a brake pad had been reversed, and seized to the disc on the start-line. Unable to start, Kenny tossed his gloves down angrily and stomped away. Lucchinelli took an important Suzuki win. Since this was all in the presence of Yamaha's top brass, who'd been hoping for a demonstration of superiority, it was doubly mortifying. Kanemoto: 'I felt so bad I decided I would quit. I said to Barry: "Just keep the money. I'm going home." I felt I'd made such a stupid mistake that I didn't deserve to stay. Barry managed to persuade me to stay on, at least until he could find somebody else to take over.' Kanemoto credits a Yamaha engineer with finally changing his mind. Abe-san might have regretted this; Kanemoto's seven championships were all won on Hondas.

In Italy, where Roberts was sidelined with food poisoning, some friendly start-line tyre advice to good friend Lucchinelli ultimately helped the Italian to a third race win in succession, with benefactor Sheene second. The calls of friendship were stronger than

ABOVE *He pushed, and pushed, and pushed … but the Yamaha wouldn't start at Assen in 1981. In the background, Kenny Roberts has failed to leave the line.*

OPPOSITE *On equal bikes at last and for once, Sheene hounds Roberts at the French GP of 1981.*

those of inter-factory rivalry, he later explained. This was only one race, but it was another step towards the Suzuki rider winning the World Championship by the end of the year.

Anyway, the British GP was coming up. Silverstone might favour Sheene with good luck for a change. Yamaha provided some more chassis to choose from; he had already had the standard version braced up back in Britain. He could choose from four different versions for the race. He thought he had set fastest practice time, 'the egg-timers' thought otherwise, putting Crosby's Suzuki on pole, much to Barry's disdain.

It would have been a fascinating race: Roberts, Sheene and Lucchinelli formed up close behind early leader Crosby. Then the New Zealander lost it – too much throttle too soon at the fast Stowe corner. Roberts made it past unscathed; Sheene had to brake hard to miss the rider, and also fell. Lucchinelli promptly ran over him. Mercifully nobody was hurt. Sheene, no fan of the man on 'his' Suzuki, was livid, and said so in his *Motor Cycle News* column. 'The pace was not too hot, and I was just thinking of making an early challenge for the lead. Then Crosby made a silly mistake and got the corner all wrong. Try and keep it on the rails next time, Croz, especially if you are lucky enough to be just in front of me.'

Crosby, interviewed, hit back: Sheene had over-reacted on the front brake. Sheene replied. 'If he thinks I over-reacted, I think he's under-brained.' The argument continued when they met in the airport on the way to the Finnish GP the following weekend.

A non-finish there preceded the trip to Sweden where, after two years at Karlskoga, the race returned to Anderstorp, with its airstrip main straight. Sheene had won at both circuits, for the last five years straight. He'd first won in Sweden in 1971, on his 125. Now he won again, after stalking Boet van Dulmen through a wet race. This was his 19th win in the 500cc class, and he took it to prove that Barry Sheene was back.

Nobody could know it would turn out to be his last.

Especially not in Britain where, in spite of his usual downbeat Anglo-American performance, winning just once, he had shown himself still the dominant figure. He won the televised Donington Park *World of Sport* races at the beginning, middle and end of the year, as well as one round of the one-off Winter World Cup series. Other national wins came at Scarborough, and again he was second (to Crosby) at Mallory Park's Race of the Year.

Before smoked visors, you could see when a rider meant business. Sheene thought he was fastest in practice for the 1981 British GP, the 'egg-timers' thought otherwise.

OPPOSITE *Friendly pre-race banter between Roberts and Sheene? Or barbed comments designed to unsettle his rival. You be the judge.*

RIGHT *Barry hunts down Boet van Dulmen at Anderstorp in 1981, for his final Grand Prix victory.*

BELOW *Last taste of the winner's champagne in Sweden, with Boet van Dulmen.*

Kenny Roberts, quite simply, had invaded Sheene's territory. For the past three years he had taken control of the World Championship. Sheene was his natural rival, even if not always the closest on points. For five years, the contrast between the two men, with two very different riding styles and personalities, defined racing.

Although they were now (at least notionally) on the same team, they continued to spar in the press. Each would admit later that there was a great deal of chest-beating and trumpet-blowing involved. A bit of controversy is good for business. The nature of the bluster remains revealing, about one aspect of a sport where self-belief (call it ego, if you will) is paramount to success. Because a lot of it, especially from Sheene's side, was devoted to belittling his rival, most specifically his ability to understand motorcycles, in a way that stretched plausibility to breaking point.

Barry spoke very highly of his own technical sympathy and understanding, and few would contradict him. Here's one quote, from the mid-Eighties. 'I'm much better at setting up bikes than I am at riding them. Most of my success has been because I've got the bike right.' The statement carries a not altogether comfortable corollary; that Roberts may not know how

to get his bike right, but his riding ability made up the difference. But this is too simple by half …

Kenny's thoughtful approach to racing and his understanding of his machine was as widely respected as his hard-as-nails riding. Yet here was Sheene saying things like: 'Kenny Roberts can't develop a motorcycle. He'd have trouble developing a cold!' This was so heretical, so very Sheene, that it caught the imagination. At the time, I asked Roberts for his opinion. 'If I'm so bad, and I'm beating him, then what is he doing?'

Sheene had first articulated this opinion in 1981, when he got hold of the same square four as Roberts. In 1982, he would expand on the theme, telling me at the end of that year: 'It really opened my eyes when I rode with Kenny, because he knows nothing about setting a bike up. The thing doesn't handle. He starts with it at the beginning of the year and it doesn't handle, and he ends up at the end of the year, and it still doesn't handle. I don't think it's any fun at all riding a bike that tank-slaps all the way down the straight, and when you stick the power on in the corners, its head angle is so steep that when it steps out it's just irretrievable. It flicks you over the high side.'

There were technical reasons for the differences –

one key factor being a new generation of wide triangular rear tyres from Dunlop available to Roberts but not Sheene. More trenchant was the matter of riding styles. Dirt track schooled, Roberts liked a very quick-steering bike, and to be able to let the rear wheel spin and slide. He chose very different steering geometry: a steeper angle to the pivot and the front forks, making a twitchy and unstable motorcycle with very quick responses. Sheene's smoother style favoured less radical settings. When he rode the first of the Mk2 square-four Yamahas pre-season in 1982, he insisted Yamaha revise the chassis geometry before the first GP in Argentina. Team-mates Crosby (over from Suzuki) and Fontan both preferred Barry's way.

In the mid-Eighties, I canvassed the opinions of experts, and got a mass of contradictory views. Mechanic Ken Fletcher said: 'Barry can tell if a wheel is so much as a millimetre out of line'; while Don Mackay said: 'I've sometimes told Barry I've found and fixed a loose bolt or something on a bike when there hadn't been one. He'd then think the bike felt better, and go faster.' Parrish found Barry's settings just didn't work for him; Crosby and Fontan found otherwise. And so on, from other riders, engineers and observers.

LEFT *Victory lap in Britain in 1982, with Steve Parrish alongside.*

LEFT *France 1981, and Sheene would beat Roberts to be first Yamaha home.*

It does come down to something more than tub-thumping. Motorcycle racing is the most personal of motorsports for engineering as well as egotistical reasons. A racing motorcycle is a very personal object. Bear in mind that by moving around on the motorcycle, the rider adjusts the entire centre of gravity, changing the whole balance of what is already a very complex technical equation. It follows that each rider's physiology, and the way he moves, affects the way the machine responds to him. When you are operating at the limits of brake, tyre and engine performance, pushing the envelope of the physics, these small matters can be very important indeed.

If Barry didn't like the way Kenny had the engineers build and set up a motorcycle, and he certainly didn't, this wasn't to say that the bikes were wrong. Just wrong for Barry. Racing at the edge is very much a matter of feel, and if the bike doesn't give it to you, then you cannot use your full riding ability. Steve Harris, who had built Sheene's Yamaha chassis the year before, had found the same thing, when he offered replicas for sale. 'The bike, to Barry's specifications, was rather nervous and twitchy.' They built ten, but only South African Jon Ekerold, a past World Champion, was able to come to terms with it, and one nameless rider even sent his back.

Harris believed this showed Sheene to be a better rider, because he was able to exploit an unstable motorcycle. Was the same thing true of Roberts and Sheene?

Yamaha's task-force for 1982 comprised Roberts in the factory team in factory colours, then Sheene, Crosby and Fontan in independent teams. At the start of the year all had the new OW60 square four, the cylinders now canted forward to shorten the engine casings. It was a sign of the times, of a new commercial era Sheene had helped to usher in, that all independent teams wore cigarette livery: Crosby in Marlboro colours, Fontan in French Gauloises blue, Sheene now in John Player Special – red, white, black and gold.

There was the usual large number of Suzukis on the grid, with Mamola and Uncini on factory machines, in separate teams. Significantly, Honda had returned, soon after the embarrassing failure of their four-stroke NR500, with a two-stroke of their own, a nimble V3, ridden by the equally nimble American newcomer Spencer, already at just 19 well-nicknamed Fast Freddie.

Roberts only rode the OW60 once, because Yamaha had something special ready for him alone. That was in the season-opening Argentine GP, where he and Sheene

eventually dropped off Spencer to give a brilliant display of closely matched racing. Roberts's win was again helped when Sheene again got the worse of a back-marker on the final lap (van Dulmen, this time).

Sheene won five out of six Transatlantic Match races against a depleted American team, without Roberts or Mamola, and Spencer out after one race. Then GP racing began again … along with a big surprise. In fact, there had been plenty of rumours, but it was only a week before the race that Yamaha stopped denying everything, and released a photograph of Roberts's new secret weapon. This was the first of a long-lived generation of V4 500cc racers. Just out, and with plenty of teething troubles ahead, it offered packaging and other advantages that gave more potential than the square four. This was proven by its future success, winning six rider's titles; and the fact that V4s of one kind or another became the *sine qua non* of the 500 class, by the time it was terminated in favour of MotoGP in 2001. Of course Barry wanted one.

Sheene was second to Uncini in Austria; Roberts rode the bucking new bike to third. The next round, at Nogaro in France, was a non-event, Sheene at the fore of a faction of top riders who declined even to practise at a facility that was primitive in every aspect, including safety.

In Spain, Barry told reporters: 'I can't wait to get my hands on a V4. I'll get it handling right soon enough.' Roberts won the race, however, after a courageous battle with Barry, bouncing the unwieldy new bike off the kerbs.

Instead, it was Crosby who was first given a taste of the machine, to Barry's utter disgust, at the Italian GP. He went flying to Mitsui's Jackson. 'Look: we've been through the bad years, we've kept our mouths shut, we've gone forward as if it was good when it was lousy – and now, this is the time we make it work. And look what's happened!' It might have been politics, Crosby's team boss Agostini having a lot more clout with Yamaha than Jackson. Or it may have been, as Yamaha's Butler explained: 'The engineers felt that if Crosby got to test the bike, it would be easier for them to take it away again. There was never any question of him actually racing the V4.' Crosby pronounced it 'a camel', and preferred his square four anyway; Roberts had been mumbling that maybe he would as well.

Sheene didn't finish in Italy; Uncini won. At the next round at Assen, Barry gave a demonstration of brilliance in a race interrupted by rain. The race was his … until he hit a wet patch on the last lap. He fought the slide successfully, but in the process broke one of the fairing mounts, which then interfered with the steering. He was obliged to cruise home third, as Uncini and Roberts both rode on by.

In Belgium, Spencer won Honda's first GP for 15 years; Sheene led for a spell, and was second, ahead of Uncini and Roberts. He was closing on points, ten behind Roberts, who was in turn five adrift of Uncini. A race win would really put him back in with a chance.

He led again at Rijeka, ended up third behind Uncini and Crosby. Roberts did not finish: they were now equal on points, with Uncini drawing ahead.

The next race was Barry's home GP, at Silverstone. And Yamaha had again promised special favour. He would get the V4.

The circumstances surrounding Barry's second big crash meant he was never able to talk about it – neither up to the time that an out-of-court settlement was reached with Silverstone circuit, nor afterwards. Strong rumours put the settlement figure in Sheene's favour at about £350,000, to avoid a lawsuit alleging sundry negligence at the open practice day when it happened.

Sheene received the V4 in time to take part in a special factory-teams test session laid on by the circuit

owners. As he suspected, Kenny's 22-degree steering head angle was too steep. He shipped the bike straight to chassis builders Spondon Engineering, 55 miles away in Derby, at that time one of the few specialist manufacturers in the country equipped to cut the front off the chassis, bring the steering head back by 1.5 inches as well as raking it by 2.5 degrees, then butt-weld it together again.

By Wednesday, the modified bike was back at Silverstone, and Barry was there to test it. It was an open practice day. The track had prospective competitors for the weekend's forthcoming British GP – little 125s with a top speed barely nudging 140mph, faster 250s and 350s, and the 500s, lapping at 117mph against 106, and 40mph faster down the straights. Then there were the national Formula One class riders on big 1,000cc four-strokes. One observer counted 80 bikes on the track at the same time. This kind of thing wasn't that unusual at the time, but Kenny Roberts was one participant who felt some sort of control was needed, to split the fast bikes from the slow. Like all of them, however, including Barry, he kept getting sidetracked by important racing matters before he could do anything about it.

Sheene had plenty to do. He was delighted that his radical chassis surgery seemed to have worked perfectly. He was quickly turning in good lap times. But he was starting set-up work from zero, on a bike new to him and his mechanics. Changing carburettor jets, tucked away inside the vee, was a fiddly job. Then they kept flooding.

Late in the afternoon Sheene had one final change to try. The marshal at the end of pit lane didn't want to let him out, but Sheene was persuasive. 'Just a couple of laps, mate.' The track was packed. The incident developed with inexorable clarity.

Stephanie timed Barry's first flying lap at 1:30.006, within half a second of his own lap record, and a front-row time for Saturday's race. He had started the next, and was eyeing Middelburg's Suzuki ahead as he ran onto the long Hangar Straight.

Half a lap away, Alfred Waibel was rounding Abbey Curve on his 125 MBA, flat out and tucked under the bubble, on the racing line. Perhaps 10mph faster, French rider Patrick Igoa was approaching from behind on a 250 Yamaha. He tried to go round the outside, but was not quite fast enough, and was pushed out onto the grass at the exit. He crashed and, by a quirk, instead of

sliding off at a tangent he and his bike both careered down the track. They came to rest on the racing line, but over a blind rise, out of sight of anyone picking a high-speed exit from Abbey. There were no marshals on hand to warn oncoming riders.

Further down the track, racer Jon Ekerold was watching the end of practice by the bridge. He started to run up the track, his only thought to pull the still prone French rider, 300 yards away, off the track to safety. As he ran, he watched 20 or so bikes pass by safely.

Sheene, approaching at close to lap record speed, had passed Middelburg, who tucked in behind. He peeled fast into Abbey, glancing over his shoulder at the Dutchman, then back at the rev counter. At about 160mph, that is the last he remembered.

Ekerold saw him flash past Igoa, thought: 'That was close.' Then he saw two instant explosions. The first was Igoa's fuel tank, as Sheene's Yamaha hit the fallen bike; the second was Sheene's tank, as his disintegrating motorcycle somersaulted down the track. Simultaneously, Middelburg also ran into the wreckage. Ekerold's trousers were torn by flying debris, probably the front forks, ripped off Sheene's bike. The severity was unimaginable.

Keith Huewen was close behind, just in time to see the explosions, slamming on brakes and riding blind through a pall of smoke. He emerged to a horrifying scene, 'like an air crash'. Debris and smoking wreckage was strewn across the track. He'd stopped by chance alongside Sheene, whose body was also smoking. Huewen was sure he must be dead. Trembling with shock, he returned to the pits with the dreadful news.

Franko heard immediately, and went straight to the scene. As he approached, he met a white-faced Ekerold, who told him: 'Don't go, Franko. You don't want to see.' But Frank had to go.

Kenny Roberts had arrived by then, and carefully removed Barry's helmet. Other riders were standing around, some in tears. Marie Armes, wife of an official and a nurse by profession, inserted a breathing tube down his throat, very probably saving his life. Then Franko arrived, knelt beside him, cradled his head, and spoke to him. 'Barry. Listen son. You're alright. Speak to me.' Amazingly, Barry responded, a faint groan. Frank kept talking, willing him to consciousness.

The impact had sent Barry flying into the handlebars, knees first. His left wrist had been trapped by his knee. The bones were terribly smashed at the point of impact, lower legs flopping loosely. His hand was also badly smashed. But he was breathing.

RIGHT *Like an air crash – the remains of Sheene's short-lived V4 are removed after the smash.*

OPPOSITE *One hand left to smoke with – Sheene wears therapeutic deely-boppers in hospital after the accident.*

BELOW *Probably the most famous set of X-rays in the history of sport.*

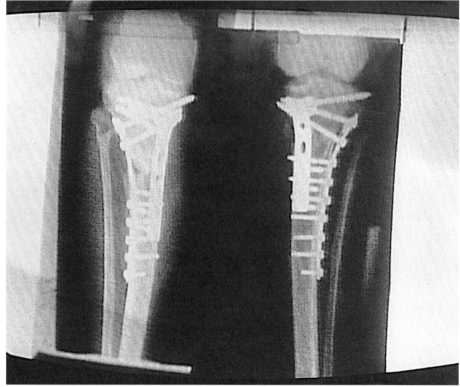

In the absence of the full medical staff, Frank took charge. Stephanie grabbed her handbag, Barry's cigarettes, and the black address book with all the doctors' names in it, coping with every pit wife's or girlfriend's horror. Barry was taken to the circuit medical centre and put on a drip. With the help of Barry's friend and fellow rider, the Venezuelan Roberto Pietri, Franko commandeered an ambulance, and was ready to jump in and drive it himself when the driver fortunately turned up. They drove to Northampton General Hospital, Barry drifting in and out of consciousness, babbling in bad Spanish to Pietri.

Northampton General was a good choice of hospital. Close to the M1, Britain's first motorway, it had much experience of high-speed accidents. Sheene's London doctor recommended one of their orthopaedic consultants, Mr Nigel Cobb, whose name was to become famous in the media frenzy that followed.

Sheene's other injuries were relatively minor; but the damage to both legs and his left hand was very serious. On each leg, the injury was confined to a small area, the top quarter of the tibia – the shinbone. The bones were shattered to a fragmented pulp. The very top of the right shin was, ironically, better protected where scar tissue from his Cadwell Park crash in 1975 had left the bone stronger. Mercifully, there was minimal skin damage, and thus no risk of bone infection … the leathers and knee-pads had saved him from that.

Cobb operated the next morning. It took seven hours to reassemble the jigsaw of bones, left leg first, a coffee break, then the right leg, then the hand. He cut and hand-shaped stainless-steel plates, located them, then assembled the shards and fragments of bone to screw them into place: first the left leg, then the right, and then the wrist. The wrist presented special problems, since it was already distorted from a previous injury. One finger was also smashed, and that was splinted to the next to heal without metalwork.

To Cobb, this was not an especially unusual or difficult operation. Merely very painstaking. Where Sheene did amaze the experienced surgeon was the speed of recovery. On his first post-operative visit, he found Sheene already moving his ankles up and down, to get his calf muscles working. 'Many patients use pain as an excuse to avoid essential exercising. Sheene didn't spend the time bemoaning his fate. He hardly wanted visitors. He just wanted to get moving, and he did the right things without being told,' Cobb remembers.

The crash happened on 28 July. On 7 August, Sheene was transferred to the private Three Shires Hospital, where he continued to amaze Cobb by being fit enough to be discharged on 20 August, just 23 days after a near-fatal crash.

Sheene didn't mean to let this slow him down. He told me in 1983: 'I never for a moment thought about retiring after the accident. I just thought about getting back. It's not as if there's some psychological thing to get over. It could have happened to anybody. It wasn't as though I messed up a corner or made a mistake. If I'd done that, I'd think I was getting a bit dodgy. The injuries were purely mechanical, physical damage, and you can fix that.'

Just part of being a motorcycle racer. His last big crash had been a huge step in his career. This one would effectively end his time as a championship contender, if not as a racer. But the injury, or more especially his conspicuous courage and good cheer in recovery, would serve him as before.

For as those X-rays were flashed on the TV screens and the newspapers, followed by pictures of Sheene on crutches, interviews and profiles, something happened to reverse the souring trend of the previous years.

The fans loved Barry Sheene once again.

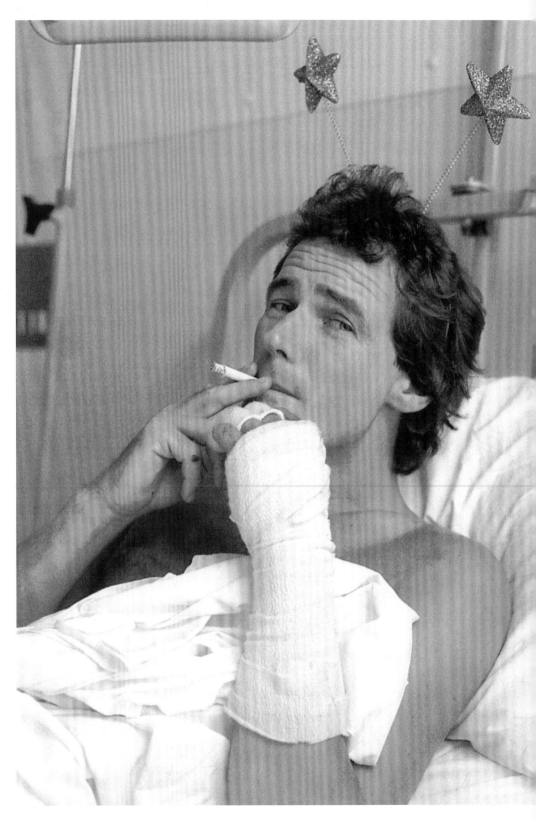

CHAPTER NINE

TIME TO RETIRE

Those X-rays were a minor icon of their time. Seen everywhere, an imprinted image. The whole world was privy to the inside of Barry Sheene's legs. How did they feel, he was asked by an ITV reporter? 'Oh, they're great,' he said. 'I wouldn't be without them.'

The jaunty responses were undimmed, the will to win still as sharp as ever. Barry's recovery was extraordinary, and much in the public eye. Courage is no less courageous for being flaunted, though it is more profitable. On 3 October, 67 days after the crash, he appeared at the big year-end meeting at Donington, where British championship races ran alongside a star-studded John Player-backed 500cc 'World Cup' (a double Mamola win), for a televised lap. He rode a Yamaha LC350 road bike, Stavros perched on the pillion just in case. He was clearly in pain, but his lopsided grin struck a chord, making fans out of the most grudging cynics.

At the time, the Seventies TV show, *The Six Million Dollar Man*, was fresh in the memory, in which a crashed NASA test pilot was scientifically rebuilt ('We have the technology') with a number of super-powers. The so-called Bionic Man. But what next for the Britain's Bionic Biker?

This issue had been open even before the crash. Mitsui's Jackson, 'very much prompted by Barry', was already negotiating for a factory Yamaha for 1984.

End of an era, and an emotional day. Sheene with Mum, Dad and Stephanie in Mayfair, for the announcement of his retirement.

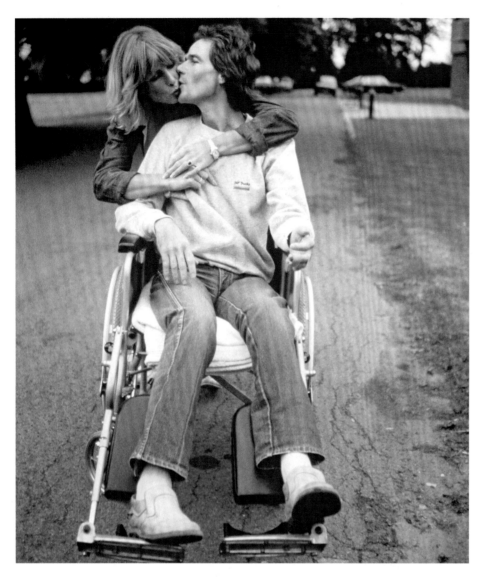

Barry's secret suitor was none other than Suzuki. Heron-Suzuki, that is, rather than the factory. A changing of the guard had seen Maurice Knight move towards retirement, and Denys Rohan appointed MD. 'When I took over, one of my objectives was to get Barry back to Suzuki. He was the man for promoting the motorcycle, not only to the enthusiast,' Rohan told me. Sheene was the only bike racer whose image would be recognised by the average man or woman, pretty much all over the world.

Rohan had been talking to Sheene in secret ever since approaching him at the Dutch TT in June, the crash coming as a major interruption. 'When he got home to Charlwood, we started talking again, and gradually found a formula for his return.' Racing, said Rohan, was only a part of it, very much at Barry's whim, and with the clear intention on Heron-Suzuki's side that Barry would get better equipment as he recovered. The major thrust of the contract was for a five-year association with Suzuki, on the promotional side.

The announcement was stage-managed with typical Sheene flair. Again it was by Frank Bough, TV presenter; but this time it was not in a hired hotel hall. It took place on national television, on the BBC's *Sports Personality of the Year*. The show had an emotional opening when special guest Sheene rode his new Suzuki onto the stage.

To the millions of viewers, simply returning to racing was an act of bravery and spirit admirable in itself. It was the same to racing insiders. And they could be forgiven for expecting that it was little more than a personal statement by Sheene, and that he would probably carry on for a year or two at reduced intensity, while the new generation of young American riders did the real racing up front. This was indeed more or less what happened. But it was not Barry's intention; he wasn't just doing this for the money. He still saw himself as a potential race winner and ultimately championship contender. Given his condition, he was prepared to start 1983 playing himself back up to speed. But he expected the level of machinery from Suzuki to improve as he regained strength.

There were two serious flaws to the plan.

Firstly, that same old difficulty, back in a different part of Hamamatsu … Japanese Suzuki staff with unhappy memories of the way Sheene had treated them and the company. They did help during 1983, but it was more token than real.

The second, insuperable, problem arose at the end of that year. Suzuki retired from racing. Their square-four RG500 was obsolete up against the V4s of Yamaha and

Mid-year, Sheene's constant demands suddenly became 'much more ferocious, really laying it on the line to Yamaha's president. He outlined what he'd done for Yamaha over the past three years, and asked why he was being treated as a second-class works rider.' He was burning bridges again. Jackson realised that Barry obviously had another alternative, and 'by September, it was all over with Yamaha'. The approaches to the factory had in any case continued to meet with indifference, especially after the crash. As Paul Butler explained: 'I suppose the Japanese could be forgiven for thinking Barry's injuries were too severe, that it would be unwise to invest the most up-to-date and highly developed equipment, which is in strictly limited supply, in Barry.'

now also Honda. In four years they would build their own V4, and rejoin battle at factory level with future champion Kevin Schwantz. For 1984, however, even if they had wanted to give Barry-san full factory bikes, they only had leftovers.

Barry claimed later that he had taken the controls of the helicopter on the first trip home from the Three Shires Hospital in August. It couldn't have been for long; but he was impatient to be up in the air again. Due for a routine medical, and in any case needing one as a matter of course after a layoff of more than three weeks, he astounded the Gatwick doctor, who told him: 'Only you could have the front to come for a pilot's medical in a wheelchair.' Sheene wheedled him into agreeing that he could be re-examined when he was on crutches.

Straight home, on the phone to Nigel Cobb, who told him that using crutches wouldn't damage his legs, though it would be excruciatingly painful. Never mind that. Sheene quickly learned how to 'quadruped' on crutches (having only had to deal with one leg at a time in the past), and presented himself for a fresh medical. He explained all this to me with a trademark one-up grin. 'Dad was with me, and after I'd got the knack of the crutches, we went straight from the hospital back to the doctor at Gatwick. I could walk on them, but I couldn't stand up or sit down. So I said to Dad, when I go to sit down, you grab me and lower me down, and you drag me up when I have to get up, right, and I'll just keep giving you a bollocking.

'So we went in, and I go to sit down, and Dad grabs the back of my trousers and lowers me gently, and picks me up again to stand up. And I'd say: "Look, Franko – will you leave me now. I'm all right. You know I've been on crutches for ages." A terrific two-man act. Dad's really great.'

Back at the manor house, Barry was putting himself through a punishing physical routine, working on the hated rowing machine upstairs, winding his handlebar-weight device in his office. I recall him greeting me, sitting, answering the inevitable question about his legs: 'They're giving me some gyp today, because I overdid it on the rowing machine yesterday.' One felt firstly that this was indubitably true, and that he would probably say the same thing the next day, with equal veracity; and secondly that he was well aware of the effect of his words.

Barry Sheene never stopped, whatever it was he was doing. And there was plenty of everything going on. Sponsorship had to be arranged, deals brokered, the future considered. Especially the future because, though he retained to the very end the fervent belief that he was as good a rider as anybody in the world, on equal equipment, even he knew it couldn't go on forever. Even if the Japanese factories did play ball.

And there was the business of being a superstar. The roistering days may have given way to red wine over dinner at home; but the fame had just been given another boost. Strike while the iron is hot!

Thence came a mercifully brief career as a star of the big screen. *Space Riders*, directed by Joe Massot, was a bike race exploitation flick, centred on Sheene as himself, returning from injury. It also starred Gavan O'Herlihy and (for the Japanese market) Toshiya Ito. The plot followed real life as Sheene had trouble getting race-winning bikes, but it deviated when he went on to win the championship anyway. Stephanie made her acting debut as Barry's girlfriend, and both carried off their roles with an amused-looking flair ... especially compared with fellow racers, including rising Briton Rob McElnea and of course Stavros, who can be seen in more than one role. The clunky plot and wooden scripting are alleviated by some quite good racing footage from 1983, although rather unexpectedly juxtaposed; the film is a 1980s period piece.

Television served Sheene rather better. He'd already shown some savvy – rejecting an invitation to appear on the very low-brow *Celebrity Squares* with comedian Les Dawson, describing the show as 'banal'. But who better than this heroic survivor to be one of three presenters of a new Saturday afternoon prime-time show, *Just Amazing!* His on-screen colleagues were entertainer and singer Kenny Lynch and comedienne Jan Ravens. Like the film, this was also much of its time ... a mélange of practical jokes, for-the-camera stunts, and some adventure footage. The first programme included a surfing rabbit, and (for Barry) a daredevil attempting to jump a gorge with a rocket-powered car. It is best remembered for a sequence of a US stuntman trying to jump over a speeding car, and not quite making it, dislocating his foot in the process. Rather lame by today's standards, and even by those of 1983. Barry's TV career in Britain never went further, but he was good at it, especially by the time series two rolled around in 1984/5, and he'd learned to relax in front of the cameras. This talent, first learned (with some difficulty, they say) when filming the Brut aftershave advertisements in the mid-1970s, would stand him in good stead in Australia in years to come.

Sheene, back once more from the dead, rode his new bike onto the stage for the BBC's 'Sports Personality of the Year' show. Interviewed by Frank Bough, it was the perfect way to announce his return to Suzuki.

ABOVE *Sunny South Africa, and rain in 1984 made for one of Barry's greatest ever races.*

RIGHT *South Africa in 1983, where Sheene made his comeback. He was tenth, and hailed as a hero again.*

Look at the records, and you will see that Barry Sheene's last two Grand Prix years included almost the worst in his career. He was 14th in 1983, although sixth in 1984, with a best finish of a single third place. As always, the results don't tell the whole story.

There were times, of course, when Barry was dispirited, but mostly he was riding as well as ever … perhaps even better, giving weight to his self-belief. I asked him after he had retired to pick out one greatest race, and it was from this period, the 1984 South African GP, 'because that was when I proved to everybody what I already knew: that I could still ride as well as ever.

'I didn't win, but I went from 45 seconds behind, and ready to retire because my bike was so sick, to third. I was only 12 seconds behind Lawson at the finish. I've never felt so good about third. I was riding a Suzuki that I'd put together myself, with one of Randy's old pre-power-valve motors in a frame made by the Harris Brothers. The thing was timed 21km/h slower than the fastest bikes on the straight, and I qualified seventh or eighth in the dry. But in the wet session I was the fastest. I've always liked racing in the wet.

'It was pouring with rain for the race, so I felt pretty good. But when the flag fell, things went bad. I pushed,

and it didn't start. I pushed again, and still it didn't start. I pushed again, and it did start, but only on one cylinder. It was missing and spluttering all through the first lap, and at the end of it, I thought that really I might as well stop. But I thought: what the hell, I've come all this way to race, I'll press on.'

With Lawson's Yamaha doggedly drawing away up front in the spray, Sheene's bike gradually chimed onto three and then four cylinders. 'By now, I was 45 seconds down, and there didn't seem too much point in carrying on, but I didn't think there was much point in stopping either.

'I couldn't see anyone ahead of me, but after a while I started passing two or three riders a lap. When I got a pit signal P9 I thought, that's OK, at least I'll get some points. Then it went P6, P5, P6 again and I thought well, maybe it's been worthwhile.

'I started the last lap six seconds behind Raymond Roche on the three-cylinder Honda. I could see him ahead, but I didn't know who it was, or what position he was in. I only knew that he was going so slowly that I thought there must be something wrong with the bike. I didn't worry too much about him. At the last corner, I had caught right up, and was on his tail and going much quicker than him.

'Then I saw the whole grandstand rise to their feet, and I realised that he was the second-placed rider. Roche obviously noticed as well. He turned round, saw me, and gassed it up. I couldn't match the Honda's acceleration, and ended up just behind. It was a pity not to get second, but I was so pleased to have caught up to almost within ten seconds of the leader that I honestly didn't mind. I knew I had proved a point ... I was the fastest rider out there, and all those knockers who had written me off had to eat their words. That was the best feeling of all.'

Sheene had everything to prove when he returned for 1983, because just being courageous wasn't enough. He wanted results. When they didn't come that year, there were plenty of critics, once people had got over their sheer admiration for the fact he was racing at all. One of the knockers was his Suzuki team-mate Keith Huewen, who had spilled the beans in an unguarded interview with *Motor Cycle News*, after twice finishing ahead of him in spite of Sheene's better machinery. Huewen called him 'chief bullshitter and superstar'; Sheene responded in his column that Keith should 'write a book on how to win friends and influence people'.

Above all else, there was the question of equipment. Barry did what he could with his Suzuki, once again

commissioning a chassis to his preference, from Harris; Heron-Suzuki did what they could, getting ex-Mamola engines, and a few other development parts from the third GP onwards. By mid-season he was running in the same HB colours as Mamola's factory bike and a host of others, but when there was some works-bike largesse mid-season, he was not included. In any case, even the factory RG was outclassed, and Fast Freddie Spencer was the leader of a new generation who would also (narrowly) oust Kenny Roberts.

Sheene had tested his Suzuki, an over-the-counter RG500 Mk8, for the first time at Donington Park in February, a little over six months after the crash. He did four laps before it started snowing. He was out again at Brands Hatch in March, the footrests lowered to accommodate his less flexible knees, and worked himself up towards a respectable speed. His race debut was just a couple of weeks hence, at the South African GP.

Sheene was the star of the show, having already flown out to do pre-race publicity work – driving round in a borrowed Rolls-Royce that he would park right outside the front door of the upmarket Sandton Holiday Inn; his insistence on wearing jeans forced them to relax their evening dress code for the duration of his stay. If it had

rained he might have had a result worthy of the fuss. As it was, he finished tenth, first privateer behind the factory bikes. It was impressive enough that he had managed the push start.

Seventh in France was better, but he was two places behind team-mate Huewen, and miserably cold and stiff in the damp weather. The reward was an ex-Mamola engine, fitted to his chassis, for a televised home race at Donington. The engine went sick while Huewen won. Then to Monza for the Italian GP, where he was ninth, and – he openly admitted – getting fed up, and riding at only eight-tenths of his ability (similar to the figure that he'd said had been enough to win him the title in 1976). At the same time, screws were loosening in his wrist, a painful problem. He was, quite literally, coming undone.

Now was the time for Suzuki to demonstrate their intent. They did so, after some fancy footwork at headquarters in Britain had delayed the shipment of certain crates back to Japan. Inside was a year-old factory chassis, made of aluminium rather than the steel tubes of the Mk8. Ken Fletcher put the bike together for the German GP at Hockenheim. Sheene was preparing for the first practice session, when the

phone rang. It was Denys Rohan. The Japanese had withdrawn permission. Earlier in the year, interviewed for a Japanese magazine, Sheene had taken the opportunity to tell me: 'It's time the Japanese were men enough to admit they were wrong at Imatra.' This clearly hadn't had the desired effect.

Thoroughly disgruntled, Sheene refused even to go to the next round in Spain. This brought about a change of mind in Japan. He would be allowed to ride the old bits-and-pieces factory machine after all. But it was made clear there would be no chance of this year's factory bike. From now on, the glory of victory was for the younger generation, and Barry was obliged to slip into the role of a mere top-ten rider.

This machine turned out to be a prize barely worth the difficulty in winning it. Barry switched back to his own bike in Austria, to 13th; used the hybrid for the same no-points position in Yugoslavia, then a retirement in Assen. A dose of flu put him out of the Belgian GP the following weekend.

Suzuki's position was getting weaker at the same time as Sheene's; the manufacturers' World Championship they had won for the past seven years was now under serious threat. They had a big HB team

backing up factory riders Mamola and Uncini, but had lost one when Loris Reggiani was injured at Le Mans, and had been without Toni Mang from the start of the year, after a skiing accident. Now Uncini was badly hurt at Assen, lucky to escape with his life. Their response was to make factory bikes available to other riders. With the British GP next on the calendar, surely Sheene would have been top of the list?

No. Of eight riders mustered under the HB banner, Sheene was left out. Van Dulmen was given Uncini's factory bike, and Swiss rider Sergio Pellandini another, and the returned Reggiani an upgrade as well. The race was split in two after a horrendous double-fatality in the early stages, when Briton Norman Brown and Swiss Peter Huber collided. At first, the organisers proposed that a points system, taking both halves into account, should determine the final results. Sheene, racing only for position, put on a good show for the crowd in race two, battling with Boet van Dulmen, making sure to lead him over the line by a tenth of a second for eighth. After the race, at the end of a shocking afternoon, the crowd invaded the track on the slowing down lap, to give Sheene a hero's welcome.

The points system, however, didn't work out. Officials decided to take aggregate times from both races into account instead. Thanks to 'the egg-timers', and a federation that was still making up rules as it went along, this reversed their positions, Sheene ninth to van Dulmen by one hundredth of a second! 'If I'd known they were going to do that, I'd have beaten him by more,' said Sheene. This was just another kick in the teeth.

Barry might have opted out of the last two rounds, but for the filming demands of *Space Riders*. Sweden brought another non-finish, but put some footage in the can; ditto at the San Marino round, a historic race where Spencer's Honda finally prevailed over Roberts's Yamaha, after a neck-and-neck battle all year long. Barry simply hadn't played a part in it, finishing 14th overall. Soon afterwards, Kenny announced his retirement from racing. It was reckoned by all to be the end of an era, one in which Sheene had played a leading role.

His gloom worsened at the year-end British races, where he twice pulled in after finding himself simply out of touch with the leaders. His column in *Motor Cycle Weekly* of 17 September led many to predict imminent retirement. He had left Donington, he said 'as depressed and miserable as I've felt for a long time.

After spending the winter fighting to get fit, I was really fired up. After taking tenth in South Africa, I thought everything was going to work out fine … but my keenness and enjoyment started to wane when I realised I was not going to get a works bike. My lowest ebb was as Silverstone, when HB Suzuki gave a works bike to Boet van Dulmen, and then to everybody except me. I knew I was banging my head against a brick wall. It's not the first time in my career I've felt like this, but there's always seemed to be a solution in the past. I'm not so sure if it's the case this time.'

If he was hinting at following Roberts into retirement, he confused everybody one week later. After racing to a pair of sevenths at Scarborough, he cheered right up, writing: 'For the first time in a few months, I really enjoyed my racing.'

Perhaps a reasonable man would have retired at the end of 1983. But a reasonable man would also probably have quit racing after the first big accident … let alone

a second. Sheene knew very well now that there wasn't the smallest hope of being involved in the championship, but he'd also said he would carry on racing until he stopped enjoying it, and obviously he still was. To the extent that at the end of 1984 the annual review, *Motocourse*, wrote that, in spite of having no ostensible need to race, Sheene 'has ridden superbly all year … and has at last begun to enjoy the position of underdog'.

Suzuki's withdrawal from racing perversely freed Sheene somewhat. He continued as part of the loose-knit Heron-Suzuki squad, operating quite independently, and now having secured important sponsorship from DAF Trucks. Years of practice at scouring for parts meant he had been able to acquire a factory XR45 engine from the previous year, and immediately commissioned another Harris chassis. His crew chief Ken Fletcher worked with London racer and tuner Jim Wells to maximise horsepower, one change being to ditch the factory exhaust power valve

OPPOSITE *Nose taped to stop his visor fogging, Sheene stands with Lawson before the 1984 South African GP. Sheene took fastest lap, and a very close third. Lawson won.*

BELOW *The last hurrah. Sheene at Mugello in his final Grand Prix.*

that Sheene had so coveted the previous year. It was almost Queen Square-style racing again.

After his epic season-opening ride in South Africa, Sheene retired from the Italian GP, was a fighting seventh in Spain, and a short-of-power tenth in Austria, lapped by winner Lawson. Tenth again in Germany, he had a fine ride in France, heading a pair of private Hondas over the line for fifth at Paul Ricard, best Suzuki finisher. Sheene's chassis now had the benefit of adjustable steering geometry, thanks to some innovative engineering by Harris, as well as adjustable rear suspension. It took him to seventh at Rijeka, top Suzuki once again.

He was doing much better than that at Assen, running with leaders Haslam, Lawson, Roche and winner Mamola – until one of the old Suzuki's over-stretched con-rods failed under the exertion. Once again, though, at a riders' track, he had shown he was the equal of anybody, and this race was another fond memory. 'I could have been in the top three, on a bike that was well outclassed.'

There were to be more fine rides in that year … to ninth in Belgium, then to fifth in Britain, after pushing hard in the early stages, trading blows up front with Mamola, who won from Lawson. This was the first time Michelin had given him access to the latest 17-inch rear tyre, which the factory teams had been using for the full season. Then he crashed at Anderstorp in Sweden, flicked over the high side after getting put off line to avoid a fallen rider. His last GP, though not even he was sure of that at the time, was at Mugello in Italy, and he retired with ignition problems.

It had been a year of valiant effort; and the reward was a somewhat better and certainly hard-earned sixth place in the championship, albeit a long way behind runaway winner Eddie Lawson. There was at least a symmetry. In 1974 he had opened his 500-class GP career on a square-four Suzuki RG500, finishing sixth overall. In 1984, he closed it on the same type of machine, in the same position.

Back then, his confidence in his own ability had been unshakeable, and he'd gone on to prove it with dominant title wins in 1976 and 1977. That opinion was unchanged at the end of his career. As he told me: 'That was why, at the end of '84, I could give up easily … because I knew I was riding as good as ever. I couldn't have stopped at the end of '83. And I could never understand James Hunt, who decided to quit, but only after finishing the season. When I decide, it'll be right then.'

Sheene played at truck racing with DAF Trucks and best-mate Stavros.

There was a final flourish in Britain to come before that. Sheene took one last win at Scarborough, where (just like old times) he had duelled with Mick Grant. There was another race of old memories at Donington Park, for ITV's *World of Sport*. A race-long duel with Ron Haslam ended in a photo-finish. They gave the race to Haslam; Sheene congratulated him happily. 'It was just like ten years ago … really good fun,' he told the TV interviewer.

And that was Barry Sheene's last motorcycle race. Or at least his last for more than 15 years, until he returned on a classic Norton in the final years of his life.

It wasn't the end of racing, however. Sheene had a deal with DAF Trucks, and later that same month took part in an inaugural truck race in one of their products at Donington. He would do several more over the coming years, in Britain and Australia, and even win a couple. But he never took it seriously, more as a bit of fun with his mate Stavros, who took it seriously enough to win five European Championships. Nor was Sheene's single season as a saloon car racer especially memorable. He raced a Toyota Supra for Hughes of Beaconsfield in the RAC British Saloon

Car Championship, forerunner of today's BTCC series, and started well in a car developed and set up by well-known driver Win Percy. Up at the front after the start of his first race, he got hit from behind 'and then T-boned at about 130mph'. The car was destroyed, and 'the next car they built wouldn't do within two-and-a-half seconds of it. So after that I lost interest.' He managed a couple of rostrum finishes all the same, and finished fifth in his class.

And then happily gave it up.

'I put everything I had, all my competitive spirit, into bike racing,' he said. 'After that, I couldn't take anything else seriously enough.'

Barry announced his retirement at a Mayfair hotel, in a press conference that made the main evening news bulletins. It was not accomplished without a final practical joke on *Motor Cycle Weekly*, which had frequently displeased him, especially in the last two years. Timing the conference for the day after they'd gone to press, he 'revealed to them exclusively' that he was planning to race on for another year. Banner headlines proclaimed SHEENE TO HONDA. To the rival publication, *Motor Cycle News*, which carried his column, he told the truth.

Barry did a season in British Saloons in a Toyota – but found his competitive edge had been all used up in motorcycle racing.

FAMILY GUY

Sheene's departure from Suzuki at the end of 1979 had been headlong and ill-considered. He'd assumed that certain alternatives would naturally fall into place. They had not, and ultimately his top-flight racing career came to a premature end. He never made the same mistake again. From now on he made sure of things in advance. So it was that, after he quit racing, he moved seamlessly into a highly active retirement. Then, when he moved to Australia, it was another well-cushioned transition. If he was itching with frustration and missing his old life, this didn't show, because he was headlong into the new one.

Who knows what Barry might have achieved had he stayed in Britain. *Just Amazing* hadn't gone into a third series, but there would surely have been other TV opportunities for so practised and popular a personality. (Just imagine Barry, for instance, on *Celebrity Big Brother*... who would bet against him winning?) Barry was also now developing interests in property and other business in the UK that he would maintain to the end of his life, flying back to Britain regularly to meet with his partners. But to tell the truth, Barry's 'Real Life – Part 2' never properly got going in Britain before Australia took him away.

Blame George Harrison. Blame the British weather. Blame Barry's legs. It was a combination of these things that dictated that Barry would move to

Barry at home in 1991: Sidonie and Freddie use Dad's title-winning Suzuki as a climbing frame.

Queensland's kinder climate, and find a new flowering of national fame that would rival anything in Britain.

It began when George invited Barry to the first F1 Australian Grand Prix, at a new street circuit in parkland at Adelaide, on 3 November 1985. The GP was won by Keke Rosberg, but for the pair of English celebrities, glad-handing in the paddock and hob-nobbing with Barry's driver pal Gerhard Berger, the race was just the start.

Harrison owned a palatial Mediterranean-style villa (coyly named 'Let's Be Avenue') on 2.4 hectares on Hamilton Island, a resort that developer Keith Williams had created on one of the Whitsunday Islands, off the coast of Queensland. Sheene had the time of his life – and Williams, a motorcycle enthusiast with a vast private collection, was glad to welcome him. It was a captivating lifestyle and, best of all, with the winter approaching in Britain, a captivating climate. Every year the winters would get harder for Sheene: all the metalwork was still in his legs and his wrist, and the cold and damp meant the aches kept getting worse.

Sheene didn't take much persuading that the warmth of an Australian summer would be a boon to his health, both in the short-term and the long. He decided pretty much there and then to buy a place where he could

spend three months a year. And not long after that, when he returned for another look around, this time with Stephanie, they decided to move to Australia for good.

There were considerations other than Barry's knees, important though these were. Sidonie was now rising three, and winter is school time in Britain – just when Barry wanted to be out of the country. It was an easy conclusion. Barry found a property a long way south of Hamilton Island, south of Brisbane, though still just in Queensland. With typical flair, it was a superb buy: a waterfront stretch upstream on the Nerang River at Carrara, a few kilometres inland from the Gold Coast and the famous Surfers Paradise beaches. There he built a fine large house, in the Spanish mode. There was room aplenty for his soon-to-grow family, as well as cottages in the grounds for Franko and Iris and for Stephanie's parents. And a workshop equipped with all the tools and equipment from Charlwood, with space for his collection of eight of his racing motorcycles, including that first 125 Suzuki. As Barry finished restoring each one, it would be moved into the spacious hallway of the main house.

The upheaval was complete, but while Franko would go anywhere Barry went, especially if there was a workshop attached, it was especially hard for Iris. Maggie

ABOVE *The Manor House Mk2. Sheene built a fine riverside residence, in the Spanish style, at Carrara.*

OPPOSITE *The Gold Coast's sunny climate suited Barry's lifestyle, his growing family, and his legs.*

recalls: 'He wasn't my favourite person for a while, taking my Mum and Dad away, but we got over this. It really tore my Mum in two. Because she'd got her first two grandchildren here, and was now going off to the other side of the world with Stephanie, and obviously Sidonie.' Whether it was the stress or not, Iris lived only three years after arriving in Australia. She fell ill with a brain tumour, and succumbed soon afterwards. For a family that had always been close-knit, even if now far-flung, it was a heavy blow.

Four years after Sidonie, Freddie was born. Barry, still back and forth to Britain on business, had developed similar interests in Australia, buying and letting commercial property, as well as leasing helicopters. It was an idyllic lifestyle for a young family – on the river banks in the Queensland sunshine, Sheene was able to indulge his passion for water-skiing and jet-skiing as much as he wanted, and with his Hughes 500E/AS3500 helicopter parked in the back yard.

Barry was to become revered by the public, and influential in Australian racing. He took the role of talent spotter, and would help promising riders onto the world stage. None more famously than Mick Doohan. A word in the right ear went a long way when it came from

Barry Sheene, and he could see just how fearsomely competitive this young Queenslander might become. Thanks to Barry, Mick was at an advanced stage of negotiation with Suzuki, to sign for the factory Grand Prix team. According to team manager Garry Taylor: 'We had agreed the money, and to keep talking.' Then a much more attractive offer came from Honda. How to withdraw from Suzuki? Taylor: 'I got a phone call, not from Mick but from Barry. He told me a story about how Doohan was very superstitious. He'd had a vision during the night about how it would be really bad luck to ride for Suzuki.' It was obviously rubbish, but, as Taylor says: 'You can't force a rider to ride for you if he doesn't want to. Anything with Barry Sheene involved often had a way of getting complicated.'

Sheene helped several other Australian riders, including ex-speedway rider Garry McCoy, who went on to win three 500-class GPs; and more recently Chris Vermeulen, now with the Suzuki MotoGP team, originally moving to Europe after Sheene contacted old rival, and now UK team manager, Mick Grant.

Sheene's shenanigans, as ever, both endeared and sometimes appalled. He loved telling stories about his scrapes, his jokes, his conquests. How when young he'd

OPPOSITE *Ex-racer at work – Sheene in his Australian home office.*

RIGHT *For Franko, home was wherever Barry went, as long as there was a workshop attached.*

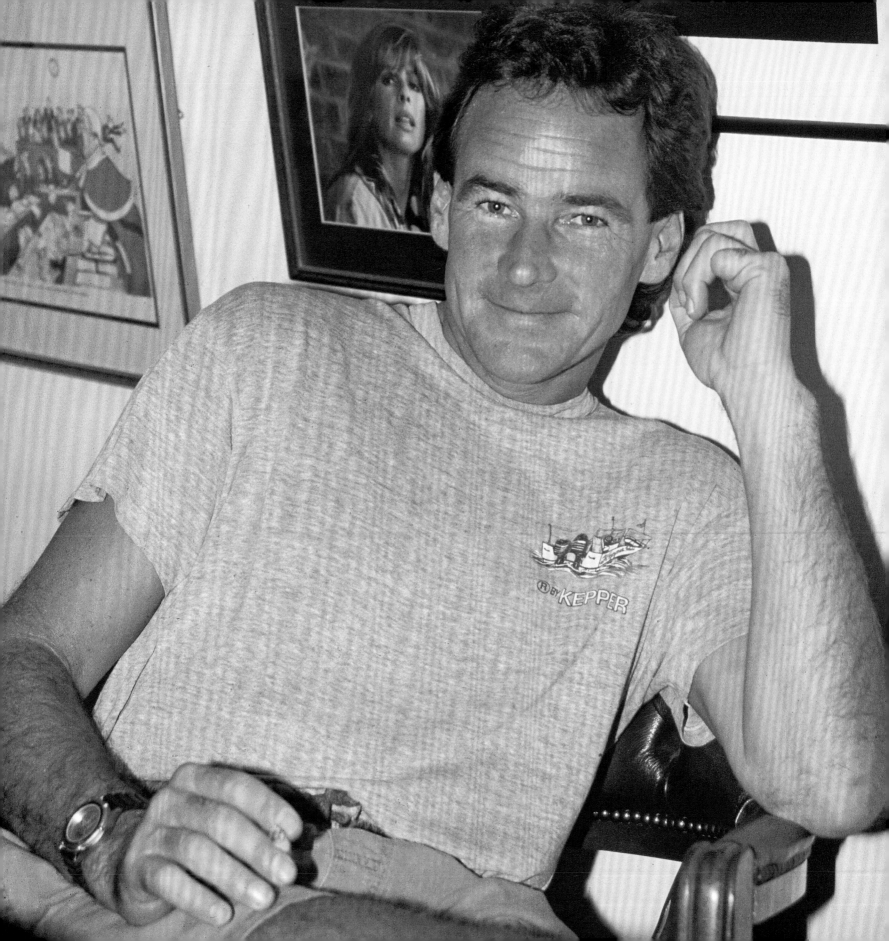

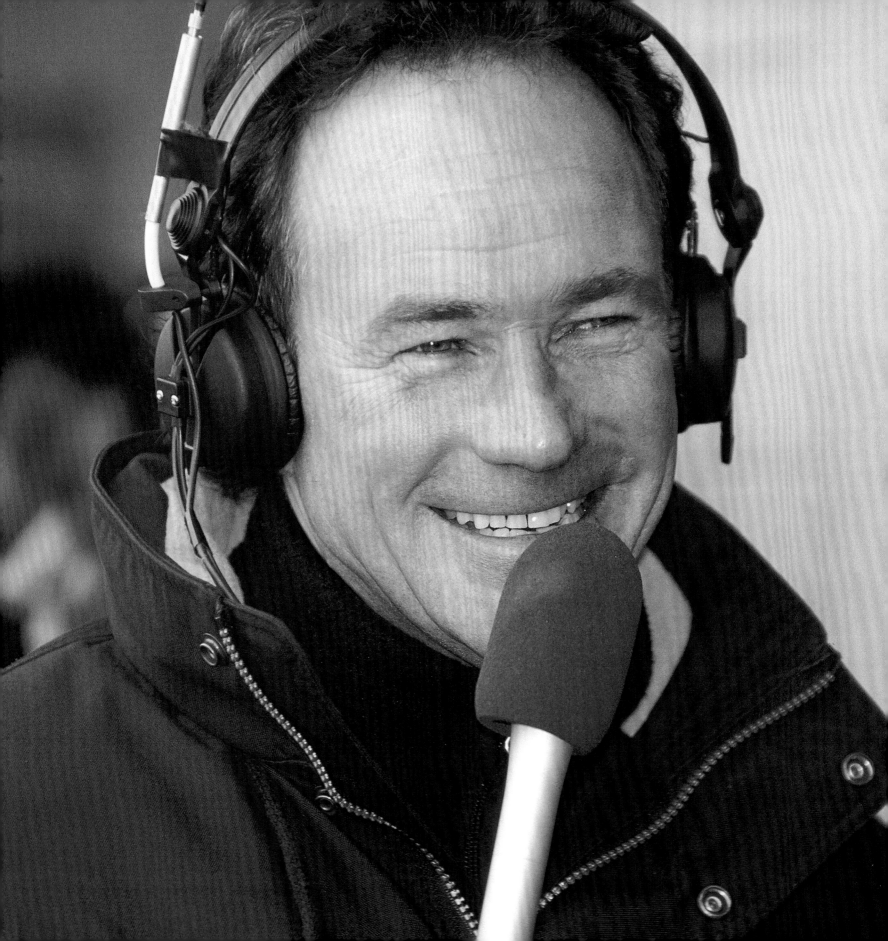

rented a Transit van, swopped its engine for the worn-out one from his own van, then handed it back. How after losing his finger in 1980 he'd bought a joke-shop finger, and used to slip this onto guests' dinner plates under the Yorkshire pudding. How he used to land his helicopter in a park across the river from Harris Performance Products, when going to pick up parts or check on a chassis, and would ask the stunned schoolkids playing there to 'keep an eye on it for me'. How as a kid he had shaved the family cat. About foreign currency coups, and other financial scores he'd made. And an inexhaustible fund of quite unprintable sagas: sex in hospital wards, in cars and cabs, on the back stairs at Earls Court exhibition centre. This was all part of the image he'd built for himself: the lovable larking about, the canny Cockney on the loose. He fostered it with enthusiasm.

Perhaps it was predictable that one day – actually in the week before the season-opening F1 car GP at Melbourne in March 1996 – this would go out of control. And when the story broke, fully two months later, it was headline news in Australia, and all over the world. Sheene and Berger were the stars of a sex scandal. Old pal Gerhard was visiting Sheene before the GP. A 19-year-old girl, named as Melanie Hilzinger, had reported to police that she had been sexually assaulted (although not actually raped) in the rest-rooms of a shopping centre on the Gold Coast. Both men had promptly been questioned by police, and a report had been sent to the Queensland Director of Prosecutions, to decide if there was a case to answer. No decision had been reached by the time the story broke in mid-May. Then things moved fast; the matter was settled out of court within two weeks, after the girl withdrew the allegations. Rumours continue to circulate: that F1's ringmaster Bernie Ecclestone had stepped in firmly to stop the stories, and that the girl had been paid a significant sum to secure her cooperation. Or was it, as the Sheene/Berger camp alleged, just another case of a gold-digger targeting two multi-millionaires for a fast buck?

Sheene's punishment was not over. Stephanie left. Well – not exactly. But she did buy her own house, not far from the family home. It was her house, and though she might sometimes sleep at the family house, Barry never slept at hers. There followed a spell of penance but Sheene, always strongly family orientated, was determined not to let his own family break apart, and in any case they were made for one another, surely. At the time he told me how, in spite of the living arrangements, they were still together. As we have seen, when Barry was determined something would happen, he moved heaven and earth. The split was partial and temporary, and by the time Barry was diagnosed with cancer Stephanie had left her new house, never to return.

As it happened, the timing of the family move to Queensland was impeccable. Circumstances meant that Australia was as ready for Barry as he was ready to exploit it. Always a commercial animal with an unerring instinct for upcoming opportunity, he found himself in the right place at the right time, and immediately started to make the most of this.

The first level of public recognition came through motorcycle racing, which was riding the crest of a wave. Barry started out as a guest TV commentator, but rapidly became a hugely popular fixture. The second step came via a spin-off advertising campaign for Shell. That, like Brut and Texaco in the past, projected Barry right into prime-time mainstream Australian consciousness.

Since Barry's retirement, the 500cc World Championship had been dominated by Americans – with Freddie Spencer and Eddie Lawson sharing honours year by year for Honda and Yamaha respectively. As we know, American riders had two advantages. They started young, and they learned on loose surfaces. Exactly the same conditions prevailed in Australia, where lively and highly competitive domestic racing was about to throw up a slew of talent, including GP winner Kevin Magee and the ultimately dominant Mick Doohan. The first Aussie star had already arrived, in the feisty form of Wayne 'Digger' Gardner. By 1986, up via the British championships to a factory Honda, he was winning GPs, and second overall to Lawson. Thanks to Wayne, Australia was reawakening to motorcycle Grand Prix racing in the biggest possible way. Barry was in on the ground floor.

His first commentating job came even before he had moved, during 1986, with the relatively small, Sydney-based public broadcasting channel SBS, which then held the motorcycle Grand Prix rights. The programme was rapidly gaining popularity. Presenter Will Hagon originally invited Sheene, at that stage to and fro from Australia, if he would make a guest appearance. Back came the demand: two first-class air tickets, a week at the Regent, and so on. 'I told his agent, no, this is public broadcasting. If when he is next in Australia he would like a taxi docket to come round, we'd love to have him.' Barry, quick to grasp the opportunity, was an immediate success, with the viewers and with the station

The wicked grin usually accompanied a wicked comment: Sheene – here at the 2000 Australian GP – carved himself a niche in Australia as a motorsport commentator.

management. When he did move to Australia, he was taken on to the GP commentary team full time.

He was an excellent commentator: though not always right, and not always thorough. There was a blue, for instance, with Mick Doohan's people a little further down the line, because sound-bite-conscious Barry was a little too free on air in describing chats and phone calls with Mick that hadn't actually happened. But to the viewers the Sheene persona had a strong and instant appeal. Never shy with his opinions – usually scathing, frequently very funny – he was a hit. As Hagon observed, he had grudges galore. 'He was narked at Kenny (Roberts), narked at Dunlop – because one had thrown him off. Then he was narked with Honda, because he'd never got a ride with them, narked with Michelin because they were French.' And so on, with, of course, Suzuki and Yamaha thrown in for good measure. 'There was always a good reason for hating somebody.'

But Hagon recognised something else behind the gibes and between the lines of the partisan patter and tendentious tittle-tattle. 'I think the way he got through to Aussies was that they saw an honesty in him. As with a lot of those people who appear to be honest, a lot of the time they are grinding a particular axe. But a lot of the time too they're being up front, and just saying what they think … this bloke can't ride, or he shouldn't have that bike … the punters loved that.'

With the growing audience figures, it was only a matter of time before one of the commercial networks would snap up bike GP racing, and Kerry Packer's Channel Nine did so. It was a tribute to Sheene's popularity, and his political skills, that he managed to move along with it. At Nine he teamed up for the first time with Darrell Eastlake, a long-standing channel sportscaster with a booming voice and a penchant for ramping up the excitement. Eastlake was no bike expert, and when there was at first a groundswell against his involvement in the GP series, Sheene was quick to support him. 'If he goes, I go too,' he insisted. It was a smart move; Barry had a new ally as well as a firm friend.

The Darrell and Bazza show was the trademark of motorcycle GP racing in Australia, as Gardner came and went; then Americans Wayne Rainey and Kevin Schwantz, before the next Australian succeeded to the throne. Mick Doohan was king of the 500-class five times, from 1994 to 1998, in an unbroken reign of dominance that kept the sport at the forefront of attention in Australia.

At the end of 1996, in the middle of this spell, there was another change of broadcaster, when Ten Network took over motorcycle racing. Once again Sheene made the transition with the sport, not only covering the GPs but soon the whole panoply of motorsport, including World Superbikes, Formula One, and the popular Australian V8 Touring Car series. On top of the commentating, he was also co-presenter of their weekly motoring show, *RPM*. Sheene had managed to carve himself a niche whereby he was not only bigger than the national television rivals bickering over bike racing, but ultimately much bigger than bike racing as well.

He'd had a bit of help in this … from, in his inimitable way, one of the biggest sponsors around: Shell Australia. It had all happened through contacts in Britain, and was a major coup. Sheene and Australian touring car legend Dick Johnson were the highlight of a series of prime-time adverts for Shell Helix oil. Barry was cast as a motor-mouth Pommy larrikin who just didn't stop talking, bugging the gruff Johnson. In the first ad, Johnson, anxious to shut him up, suggests Sheene might buy a pair of socks at the Shell shop. Sheene's reply: 'What would I want a sock for?' became an instantly recognised catchphrase across the whole of Australia. The stories developed, including one where the pair got lost in the outback because Barry had the map upside-down.

ABOVE *Hard talk, man to man, with four-times World Superbike Champion Carl Fogarty. Britain's previous 500cc World Champion didn't take kindly to his successor.*

OPPOSITE *With Mick Doohan in Australia in 1998. Sheene used subterfuge to steer him away from Suzuki to Honda, and five World Championships.*

LEFT *With a young Valentino Rossi in 1997. Sheene was a hero to the Italian superstar. After winning the Australian GP in 2003, Rossi carried a Number 7 flag round the track in tribute.*

OPPOSITE *Greats on the grid at Goodwood in 1999 – from left, F1 star Gerhard Berger on a BMW, World Champions Damon Hill and Barry Sheene on Nortons, and John Surtees on his title-winning MV Agusta.*

LEFT *Sheene tries his Goodwood Norton for size. It would be his first public ride on a racing bike since 1984.*

LEFT *Hands on and tinkering, Sheene felt right back at home.*

Sheene did the occasional truck race in Australia, just for fun, but turned his back on any other opportunities. Although it might have been the other way around, when he was invited to drive one of the Pete Brock Ford V8s from the fearsome Australian Touring Car Championship, at Winton. He thought this was just for fun, but when he arrived it turned out to be a full-on test for the famous Bathurst race. Sheene didn't want to do that race, but they let him have a go in the car anyway. On his last lap, caught out by the surge of the turbocharger, he half-spun, then speared across the track into the pit-lane entry wall. He cracked a rib and an ankle bone, and destroyed the Ford, earmarked for driver Brad Jones.

From now on, Sheene was firmly on the Australian celebrity circuit, an adopted national icon.

What could be missing from Barry's perfect life in Australia? It turned out – apparently to his own surprise, if nobody else's – to be what had defined him all along. Motorcycle racing.

Having turned his back on the sport, it crept back into his life little by little. He was very much hands-on – more so than for many years. There were those eight

classic racing motorcycles and their riders ever seen. Among past World Champions were MV riders John Surtees, Giacomo Agostini and Phil Read, as well as Jim Redman, Kork Ballington, Carlo Ubbiali and Luigi Taveri. Almost 50,000 fans packed the circuit, known as 'the cathedral of motorcycle racing', to watch their past heroes. Especially Barry Sheene, reunited with the RG500 XR14 on which he had won his first 500-class GP at the same circuit in 1975.

Although he said at the time that this parade had just been a bit of fun, it clearly tickled Barry's fancy. Many of his contemporaries were already, or would soon be, re-exercising themselves in the classic class, including Phil Read, Chas Mortimer and Paul Smart. On relatively slow bikes, on narrow tyres, and for lower stakes, it was only a little less competitive than what they always used to do, and barely less dangerous. But the quaintness of the booming exhausts of the single-cylinder Nortons and Matchlesses, of the delicately laced spoked wheels and trim seat humps, somehow anaesthetised the effect.

The next chance arose with the first Revival at the Goodwood circuit reconstituted by Lord March, whose grandfather had founded the Sussex track. Lord March was another in Sheene's extensive network, and Barry was invited to ride a Manx Norton this time, and to race it, rather than just parade. He had to renew his lapsed racing licence to take part. He also didn't want to turn up unprepared. In Australia, he was already in contact with ex-Speedway rider Mike Farrell, who had done some specialised engineering for the rebuild of Barry's 125 Suzuki racer. Farrell arranged a test at the privately owned Darlington Park, near Brisbane, and – when the borrowed Manx broke down – lent Sheene his own G50 Matchless. He needn't have worried about his speed, his lines, or his prospects.

At Goodwood, Sheene promised he was just there to have fun – 'I won't be under the red mist.' And he was smooth and controlled, but fast enough to make second and third places in the pair of Lennox Cup races, among a number of seasoned classic racing specialists.

It was still a demo race, however; as was another outing a year later, also at Goodwood. This time Barry took a couple of wins on the Norton. His first real race since 1984 came after that, back in Australia. Farrell invited him to ride the Matchless in the Historic National Title races at the Queensland Raceway.

By now the bug had bitten. Barry bought a Manx of his own – the Nortons being remanufactured to

ex-race bikes he had accumulated. He'd lent them to the Keith Williams collection on Hamilton Island, but then brought them all home, complaining that they were being allowed to deteriorate in the harsh climate. One by one, he was rebuilding them, starting with the little 125 Suzuki.

His first actual track outing was as a star of a major classic event at Assen, in Holland, in 1998. His second-last major public appearance, only months before he died, was going hell-for-leather on a Manx Norton, and sharing race wins with none other than Wayne Gardner. By then, the bug had clearly got him again.

Barry told a TV interviewer in the early 1990s that to go bike racing again, 'I'd have to have a frontal lobotomy'. And his first outing wasn't a race, but a parade. A massive one, over three days in May – the Assen Centennial Classic. Organised by Dutchman Ferry Brouwer, Arai helmet importer and a long-time racing man, it assembled the biggest collection of

original pattern, which was prepared in Britain by specialist Fred Walmsley. He flew the bike out to Australia to take a couple of wins and the classic title at Phillip Island, and over the coming years raced that Norton and the Matchless several times in Australia and Britain.

It was in Australia that he had yet another crash at more than 100mph, when his Norton seized at Phillip Island, throwing him over the high side. All the internal metalwork held up and, though he was detained in hospital for some hours with concussion, he was not seriously hurt.

His British races were confined to Goodwood, gaining a couple more wins in 2001, and the classic race at the British GP at Donington Park. Here, up against the most committed classic racers in the world, Barry was in his element. He gained a second in 2000,

a first place in 2001, and won both races in 2002. 'I'm enjoying this racing as much as I ever did when I was going for the title,' he bubbled at the time. But now there was a shadow hanging over him. The symptoms of the disease that would kill him were making themselves felt. He would fly home from that race for medical consultations. Within a week, he would know the truth.

'I'm not going to let that stop me enjoying myself,' he declared, and prepared for one last outing at Goodwood in September. The two races turned out to be thrilling battles against Wayne Gardner, riding a G50 Matchless. Gardner won the first by inches, Sheene the second by a fractionally greater distance, taking his third Lennox Cup on aggregate time. He could hardly have wanted a better way to say goodbye to motorcycle racing.

ABOVE *Barry raced at Goodwood in 2002, after he had embarked on treatment for cancer. He was a crowd favourite.*

OPPOSITE *Last action for a racing hero: Sheene's final ride at Goodwood.*

Barry Sheene MBE

September 11, 1950 – March 10, 2003

...SHEENE died on March 10, beaten cancer he'd refused to refer to as other than 'a right pain in the arse'. ...ree weeks before, too ill to complete ...gular column for Bike, he'd been ...g ahead to when he'd next be able to ...knocked back but typically refusing ...mit defeat. It was an attitude core to ...ne's thinking and one that took him ...asthmatic Cockney youngster to ...national sporting celebrity, at a time ...en the term was pretty much unknown ...motorcycle racing.

...Sheene was born on September 11, ...50 in Holborn, London. His father, ...ank, worked as a maintenance man at ...e local Royal College of Surgeons, but ...ent most of his spare time messing about ...ith bikes, later forging close associations ...ith the Spanish Bultaco factory and ...arning himself the still-present 'Franco' ...nickname. By the mid-Sixties, Frank was ...prepping engines for the likes of Phil Read ...and Bill Ivy and his expertise as an engine ...builder and tuner, passed on to his son, ...played a large part in Sheene's success.

...Riding from five years old, on a 50cc ...Ducati spared from the scrap by Frank, ...Sheene thrived around bikes. He spent ...weekends with his dad in race paddocks

to run-in Frank's new 125 and 250 Bultacos at Brands. He rode so well that he entered them for two races the following week, crashing in the first when the 125 seized.

Despite smacking his head and losing skin off his hands, he showed signs of the resilience for which he would become famous, taking the 250 out later that day and coming third. Eight years later he'd be 500cc World Champion, riding with a style that combined the best of the smooth old-school and shoulder-in, knee-down modernism. It was a beautiful style that enabled him to get on a classic in recent years and start winning all over again.

By the time you read this, a month after his death, Sheene's racing exploits will have been gone over time and again in countless articles. For the record – and what a great record it is – we list the man's career highlights in the feature starting on page 126. But there was so much more to the man than Sheene the racer.

Other British racers have been more successful than Barry Sheene. Mike Hailwood, John Surtees and Geoff Duke all won more 500cc titles, but none had the same impact outside the sport. It's true that the gruesome tabloid column inches dedicated to his two big crashes (Daytona ...ctice in 1975 and British GP practice at

The One And Only

racing was cool ...Sheene in the p... a champagne ... Stephanie Mc... epitomised ev... Makers of aft... thousands to ... or bike. TV ... mums love... of mischief... mind that ... as a motor...

But yo... famous w... and Shee... office w... things ... column ... and al... final ... judge... chan... sofa ... and ...

th... m... fil... f...

Barry Sheene is gone but not forgotten

BY MICHAEL SCOTT
PHOTOS BY GOLD & GOOSE
FROM THE C...

national ...

L'ult... ba...

...di Stefano S...

Donald sur l'intégral, le numéro 7, et un charisme à tout casser. C'est sous cette image que Sheene fit souffler un vent nouveau sur le Continental Circus.

C'est au guidon de la Suzuki Heron qu'il a connu ses plus belles heures de gloire, dont deux titres mondiaux 500 en 76 et 77.

Amoureux de la vie et pil... de génie, Barry Sheene ... a abandonnés dimanche... Ses copains et ses fans... du Continental Circus se souviennent...

Par Jacques Bussillet et Bruno Gillot...

Barry Sheene, 1950-2003

Obituary

Barry Sheene 1950-20...

MOTORCYCLING and motorcycle racing can be neatly divided into two eras – before Sheene and after Sheene. Such was his impact on biking when he exploded onto the scene in the early Seventies that he remains the only mainstream name the sport has ever produced. He was also the last Brit to win a 500cc Grand Prix (way back in 1981) and the last to win a 500cc world title which he did for the second time in 1977 after winning in '76 too.

No-one did more for motorcycling ...

friends, who had dinner with Cary Grant, who judged Miss World competitions and who considered himself an equal of George Best when it came to dating leggy blonde models. Here was a superstar.

But it wasn't all glitz and glamour and Sheene proved he was no celebrity prima donna by overcoming horrendous injuries with a determination rarely seen outside of Hollywood movies: it won him the hearts of mil...

As a mult... worldwide celebr... have raced again... the opening Grand... production RG500... the house down wi... place. No punishm... itself could stop Ba... wheels off a racing... he was born to do.

His ready wi...

CHAPTER ELEVEN

THE BIG C

Cancer, according to Barry Sheene, is 'a horrible cretin of a disease – and I am not going to make any room in my life for it.'

This was an opinion he repeated frequently over the last eight months of his life, with a confidence that hardly flagged right to the very end. He really did believe he could beat it, his own way, without giving in to the disease, or to the medical establishment and the expensive, painful and risky treatment the doctors offered. His opinion of that never altered. Cancer was, he said in a September 2002 interview in London's *Evening Standard*, 'a trillion-dollar business in the USA. More people make a living off cancer there than die of it.' And, in terms of treatment, 'if they can't make a buck out of it, they're not interested.'

He rejected surgery and chemotherapy, saying: 'I believe we were given a whole body, and that's the way we should stay.' Instead, he took the cancer on in characteristically individual style, fighting it on his own terms, in his own way, espousing alternative medicine and his faith in God. 'I've always believed in God. He's always looked after me in the past, and I am sure He will look after me this time. If it doesn't work out that way, then that's the way it's meant to be,' he told the paper.

The first symptoms became apparent early in 2002. His sister, Maggie, recalls: 'I was over there, for my usual

Charismatic in life, and in death it was the same. A selection of tributes comes from (clockwise, from top left) Bike Magazine (UK), Cycle News (USA), Motosprint (Italy), Cycle Sounds (Japan), Two Wheels Only (UK) and Motojournal (France).

three months or so. And round about January or February, he kept complaining that when he ate anything, it felt like it was getting stuck. He'd need a drink to wash it down. That was the first symptom, but you don't think anything of it. I can remember him at lunch several times, getting cold water from the fridge.'

Maggie and Barry flew back to Britain together in April: Barry had a job promoting (of all things) the North-West 200 road race in Northern Ireland, demonstrating some flexibility of principles perhaps. The fast and notoriously dangerous public-roads circuit near Coleraine was shorter but otherwise little different from the Isle of Man. This was the race that had claimed the lives of (among many others) his Suzuki team-mates John Williams, John Newbold and Tom Herron. Early in May, he, Maggie and Stavros took a helicopter from Biggin Hill, in Kent, over the Isle of Man and across the Irish Sea. It was a good laugh, but would turn out to be the last such outing for the trio. He looked, thought Maggie at the time, a bit pale. The disease was stealthily progressing.

Barry, in the meantime, had been lusting after a particular helicopter, a 7/8-seater Agusta A109C. He'd been phoning back and forth, and had finally tracked

one down. He had to flip back to Australia for a Channel Ten TV commitment, then came straight back to pick up Maggie for a last trip that she treasures in her memory.

'We flew, Easyjet, to Zurich. The weather turned horrendous, and we had to wait a while in the little airport before we could take off. Then eventually a window came, we took off, and flew out. Once we got over Basle, it started to clear, and we had this amazing flight home. We had another pilot with us. We stopped at Reims in France to refuel, and then dropped him off somewhere, and then we flew on our own, over London, and we landed back in Biggin Hill with this beautiful helicopter. I am so happy we did that together.'

The machine was stripped to be delivered to Australia; Barry returned also, then was back in Britain a few weeks later, for his double victory in the classic race at the British GP. Nephew Scott Smart had also noticed the deterioration now. 'He actually rang me up,' remembers Maggie, 'and said "is Barry all right, Mum? I don't think he looks very well."'

He had still not sought treatment, confirms Maggie, but on his return home Stephanie insisted. A doctor friend commissioned an endoscopy – where a fibre-optic instrument is fed down the throat for on-the-spot visual

BARRY SHE

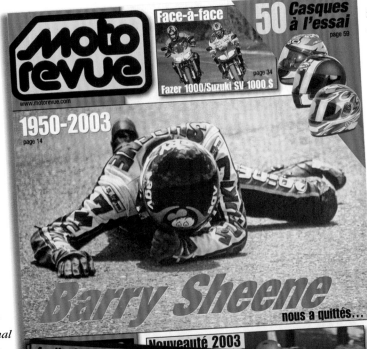

Powerful images from international magazine covers and stories bade sad farewell to a departed hero.

investigation. This requires an anaesthetic, so Stephanie dropped him off for the tests.

When he came round from the anaesthetic, as he told Sue Mott of the *Daily Telegraph*, he got dressed and went into the doctor's office. "'Bloody hell, Baz, it's cancer," he said. 'Best way to tell me. Straight out with it.' It was almost the same day that his new helicopter arrived.

The cancer was right at the bottom of the oesophagus, the alimentary canal, and the cause was indeterminable. Barry had always been a heavy smoker – 40 or more a day, usually Gitanes with the filter snapped off – but had in fact given up five years before, a matter for which Gary Nixon claimed the credit, and about which Barry proudly bragged to me at Donington Park soon afterwards. He himself didn't blame smoking, but 'all the poisons and things we eat'. As he told the *Standard*: 'Hormones are pumped into the meat, and there are pesticides on most fruit and vegetables.' But the reason was rather academic anyway.

The cancer was, thought the doctor, operable. It would be major surgery, excising the top of the stomach and the bottom of the oesophagus, lifting the stomach to reattach it higher up the alimentary canal. The surgery alone was bad enough – the equivalent, said Sheene, of a heart-lung transplant. One effect is to remove the flap valve that prevents food being regurgitated, so that the patient can never again lie down to sleep, having to stay in a more-or-less upright position. As Sheene told the *Telegraph*: 'I refused the operation. I don't want to be opened up … so that forevermore if I bent over to tie my shoelaces, everything I'd just eaten would end up all over the floor. That's not quality of life. I don't want my children to see me in that state.' And not just his children, either. As Paul Smart said: 'He was always very conscious of his appearance, his fitness, his hair and things like that. He was Barry Sheene.'

He was equally vehement about the reason for refusing the associated chemotherapy. 'Anybody I've ever known who has had it has been, basically, completely destroyed. I can't let someone put an IV drip in my arm and inject me with poison. I've seen friends of mine after chemo. They look like dead people who can still talk.' Instead, Sheene put himself energetically into seeking alternatives, for which he had an evangelical enthusiasm. 'When I do get better I'm going to spend my money going round the world telling people there is an alternative way to recover. You don't have to be cut open or poisoned to survive.' His belief in his recovery, at least outwardly, was total, and affected all those close to him. 'He was convinced,' says Maggie, 'he was so convinced he would beat it. And we all thought so too. You think, he's beaten everything else.'

Sheene told his family, taking his children out of their Geelong boarding school to break the news to them face to face. He promised them he would recover, saying later: 'I can't let them down.' In spite of his bravery, it was a devastating time for all. 'Everyone thinks that cancer is a death sentence,' he said. He took three telephone calls in the space of a week before he was able to tell Maggie and Paul.

Almost a month after the diagnosis, he made the illness public with a brief and characteristically defiant press statement on 22 August. 'This is a total pain in the arse, but I'm going to deal with it,' he said. The statement continued: 'Although tired, Barry is in reasonable spirits and just yesterday picked up a new helicopter from Melbourne.' He was staying at his home on Australia's Gold Coast, and 'politely requests that no-one contacts him at this time'.

By then, after a spell of intensive research, he was already deeply invoved in finding his own solution. 'I read everything I could lay my hands on, and found out that a massive number of people have been cured by alternative treatments.'

His first port of call was a diet devised by Austrian naturopath Rudolf Breuss, who based his treatment on the belief that cancerous cells need protein to survive, and that starving them of protein will kill them off. As well as diet, the treatments include herbal extracts. And there was B17, made from apricot seeds, which is claimed to mix with a glucose given out by the cancer cells to produce a natural cyanide that kills them. Breuss claimed a 96 percent success rate for his diet, a 42-day course, although medical experts remain dubious. Barry believed in it anyway, and for three weeks submitted to a diet of liquidised organic vegetables – primarily beetroot, carrot, celery, radish and Chinese cabbage – before moving onto the second phase, still eating only vegetables.

Whatever effect this had on the cancer, it was certainly debilitating for the patient, and Maggie was one of many to wonder whether it might even have hastened the end. Sheene never did have much in the way of surplus flesh, and without fat he instead suffered muscle waste, his weight dropping from 154lb to 133, his thin frame getting thinner still. He regained a little weight when he went back onto solids.

It was in this condition that he returned to Britain in September to race (and win) at Goodwood. For the old

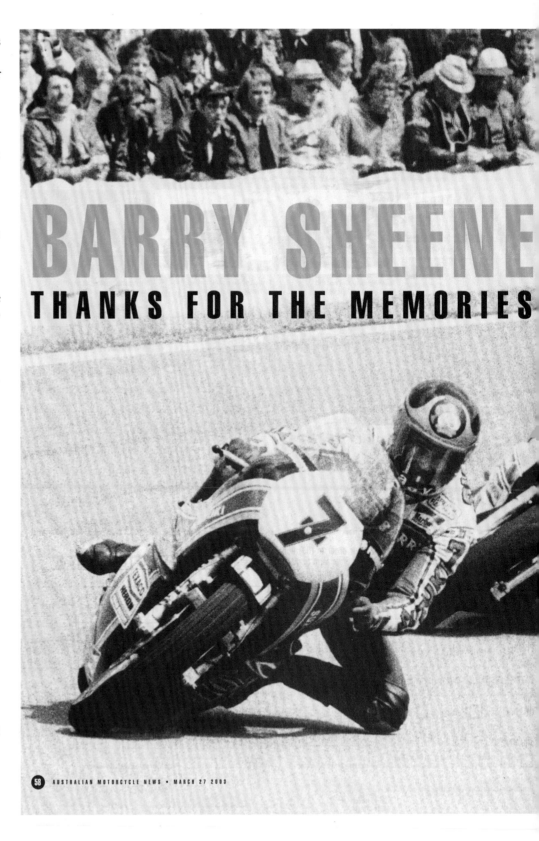

BARRY SHEENE
THANKS FOR THE MEMORIES

58 AUSTRALIAN MOTORCYCLE NEWS • MARCH 27 2003

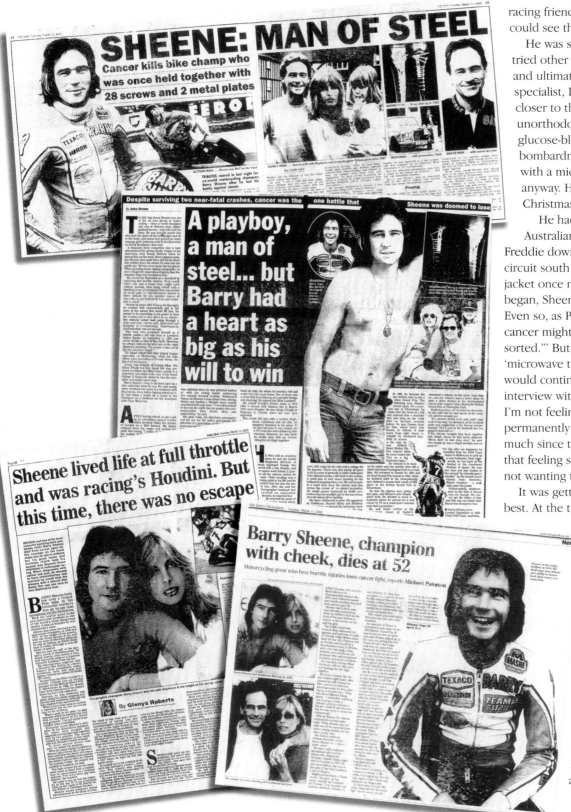

racing friends he met there, it was a sad occasion. 'You could see the shine had gone off him,' said Mick Grant.

He was still determined to beat the cancer, and now tried other therapies, including a visit to a clinic in Mexico, and ultimately a course of treatment by a British cancer specialist, Dr John Holt, in Perth, Australia. This was closer to the original medical recommendations, but still unorthodox – entailing thrice weekly injections of a glucose-blocking cytotoxic agent, combined with bombardment by UHF waves that have much in common with a microwave oven. That's how it felt to Barry anyway. He took a break in this treatment to spend Christmas at home with his family.

He had made one last public appearance, at the 2002 Australian GP on 20 October, when he flew his son Freddie down from the Gold Coast to the Phillip Island circuit south of Melbourne, and donned his Channel Ten jacket once more for 'light duties'. But as the New Year began, Sheene, quite simply, was getting sicker and sicker. Even so, as Paul Smart recalled, he didn't accept that the cancer might beat him. 'He still kept saying: "We'll get it sorted."' But early in February 2003, he announced that the 'microwave treatment' had not been successful, but that he would continue his quest for other solutions. In an interview with *Motor Cycle News*, he said: 'I have to admit I'm not feeling particularly great at the moment. I just permanently feel sick. I've been feeling like this pretty much since the beginning of November, and I can tell you that feeling sick 24 hours a day is not pleasant. It isn't nice not wanting to eat anything at all.'

It was getting harder to remain positive, but he tried his best. At the time he had a column for Britain's *Bike* magazine, and after his death deputy editor Mick Phillips wrote how, for his final column, Sheene had dictated: 'It's a situation I can't sort out. And that's something I'm not used to. That's the most frustrating thing, that there's nothing you can do about it.' When Phillips read that back to him, he asked for it to be struck out.

Sheene had withdrawn from public appearances, and was selective in who he would allow to visit, turning away some old friends. Always very aware of his image, he didn't want to be seen like this. One welcome visitor, of course, was Steve Parrish, who was shocked at how tired and weak he was – although he was still the same old Barry. '

When I left, he said to me: "Stavros, at least we won't die wondering."'

Paul and Maggie Smart were there to the end. Their son Scott had to fly back to Britain shortly before Barry died – his own racing season was about to begin. But before that he and Barry had been able to heal some differences and become closer. Scott, briefly a GP rider and still a highly regarded British Superbike racer, had followed a difficult career with plenty of talent but little in the way of luck, and no help whatsoever from his illustrious uncle, who could certainly have eased the way. The reasons must be guessed at, but one might be that Barry was anxious to protect his own image, and he didn't want to be outshone by any other British rider, especially one from his own family. The same restrictions, clearly, didn't apply to Australian riders that he willingly helped.

The last weeks were very difficult, as Maggie confirmed. Sheene had difficulty in swallowing food, and in keeping it down. He was making frequent visits to hospital for treatment; Stephanie cared for him with, according to Maggie, the patience of a saint, but the deterioration was becoming more rapid. On Friday, 7 March 2003, he was admitted to hospital, and three

RIGHT *Spontaneous gesture – at the Catalunya GP circuit in Spain, an anonymous bouquet was laid at the feet of a statue of Snr Francesco Bulto, whose motorcycles were so important to Barry in the early days.*

BELOW *Cartoonist Sprocket (John Mockett) deftly portrayed the emotion of Sheene's passing.*

OPPOSITE *Farewell. A classic photograph from 1976.*

days later, at 2pm, he finally lost the last and toughest battle of his life.

The funeral was private. Franko, by now suffering from Alzheimer's and in a local care home where he still lives today, did not attend. Mercifully, he did not seem to understand what had happened.

The tributes came from far and wide – by e-mail, by post, and in the press, from rivals, friends, and from tens of thousands of fans. All reflected the same bewilderment, that a man who had survived so much and, as a result, been a beacon of hope to so many, could be struck down so cruelly, and so prematurely. He died almost exactly six months before his 53rd birthday. The memorial meetings, the annual charity ride to the Australian GP and similar events in Britain continue to this day.

Sheene, in his remarkable life, had done more than anybody to promote not only himself, but at the same time motorcycling and racing. Much more importantly, he had been an example of sportsmanship, courage, individuality, humour and humanity. In death, his popularity remained. He had been bigger than his sport, and in the end he was bigger than his own mortality too.

Rest in peace.

APPENDIX

The following listing contains all Barry Sheene's Grand Prix results and the notable home and international meetings.

Key: DNS – Did Not Start, DNF – Did Not Finish,
GP – Grand Prix, TT – Tourist Trophy,
Prod – Production Motorcycle

1968

First race, March	125cc	DNF (Bultaco)
Brands Hatch	250cc	3rd
First wins, April	125cc	1st
Brands Hatch	350cc	1st

1969

Notable National Meetings

Hutchinson 100, Brands Hatch	250cc	4th (Bultaco)
Race of Aces, Snetterton	350cc	2nd (Cliff Carr 1st)
	125cc	2nd (Chas Mortimer 1st)

National Championships

ACU, British Championships	125cc	1st Chas Mortimer (64pts)
		2nd Barry Sheene (48pts)

1970

Notable National Meetings

Hutchinson 100, Brands Hatch	250cc	4th (Bultaco)
Race of Aces, Snetterton	500cc	DNF (Suzuki 500)

National Championships

ACU, British Championships	125cc	1st Barry Sheene
		2nd Chas Mortimer
		3rd Cliff Carr

World Championship Meetings

Spanish GP, Montjuich Park, September	125cc	1st Angel Nieto (Derbi)
		2nd Barry Sheene (Suzuki)
		3rd Bo Jansson (Maico)

1971

Notable National Meetings

Mallory Park, March	125cc	1st (Suzuki)
	250cc	1st (Yamaha)
	350cc	1st (Yamsel)

Mallory Park, Post-TT, June	500cc	1st Giacomo Agostini (MV Agusta)
		2nd Barry Sheene (Suzuki)
British 'Grand Prix' Silverstone August	125cc	1st (Suzuki)
	250cc	1st (Yamaha)
	500cc	1st Giacomo Agostini (MV Agusta)
		2nd Barry Sheene (Suzuki)

National Championships

ACU, British Championships	125cc	1st Barry Sheene
	250cc	1st Steve Machin
		2nd Barry Sheene

World Championship Meetings
50cc Kreidler Van Veen
125cc Suzuki
250cc Derbi and Yamaha
350cc Yamaha

Austrian GP, Salzburgring	125cc	3rd
German GP, Hockenheim	all	DNF
Isle of Man TT	125cc	DNF
	250cc Prod	DNF
Dutch TT, Assen	125cc	2nd
Belgian GP, Spa-Francorchamps	125cc	1st
East German GP, Sachsenring	125cc	2nd
	250cc	6th (Yamaha)
Czechoslovakian GP, Brno	50cc	1st
	125cc	3rd
Swedish GP, Anderstorp	50cc	4th
	125cc	3rd
Finnish GP, Imatra	125cc	1st

(injured at international, Hengelo, Holland)

Italian GP, Monza	125cc	3rd

(injured again at Mallory Park Race of the Year)

Spanish GP, Jamara	50cc	2nd
	125cc	3rd

Final Positions – 125cc World Championship

1st	Angel Nieto (87pts)
2nd	Barry Sheene (79pts)

1972

Notable National Meetings

Race of Aces, Snetterton, August	250cc	1st (Yamaha)
	350cc	1st (Yamaha)
	500cc	1st Giacomo Agostini (MV Agusta)
		2nd Barry Sheene (Yamaha 356)

National Championships and Awards

Shellsport 500 Championship	1st Pat Mahoney
	2nd Barry Sheene

King of Brands

World Championship Meetings
250cc and 350cc Yamaha

German GP, Nürburgring	250cc	DNF
	350cc	DNF
French GP, Clermont-Ferrand	250cc	DNS
	350cc	DNS
Austrian GP, Salzburgring	250cc	4th
Italian GP, Imola (injured in practice)	250cc	DNS
	350cc	DNS
Swedish GP, Anderstorp	250cc	DNF
	350cc	DNF
Spanish GP, Montjuich Park	250cc	3rd

250cc World Champion – Jarno Saarinen (Yamaha)
350cc World Champion – Giacomo Agostini (MV Agusta)

1973

National Championships and Awards

Shellsport 500 Champion

MCN Superbike Champion

MCN Man of the Year

King of Brands

FIM Formula 750 European Championship Meetings
Seeley-Suzuki three-cylinder 750

France, Rouen	F750	DNF
Italy, Imola 200	F750	DNF
France, Clermont-Ferrand	F750	1st
Sweden, Anderstorp	F750	3rd

Finland, Hameenlinna	F750	2nd
Great Britain, Silverstone	F750	Disqualified
Germany, Hockenheim	F750	4th
Spain, Montjuich Park	F750	2nd

Final Positions – F750 Championship

1st	Barry Sheene	61pts
2nd	Jack Findlay	51pts
3rd	John Dodds	47pts
4th	Stan Woods	46pts

World Championship Meetings
Suzuki twin-cylinder 500

Finnish GP, Imatra (500cc debut)	500cc	DNF

1974

Notable Home Internationals

British 'Grand Prix', Silverstone	1st (first Suzuki RG500 race win)
Race of the Year, Mallory Park	1st

National Championships and Awards

Shellsport 500 Champion

MCN Superbike Champion

MCN Man of the Year	1st – Phil Read
	2nd – Barry Sheene

FIM F750 European Championship Meetings

USA, Daytona 200 (non-championship)	F750	DNF
Italy, Imola 200	F750	5th
Great Britain, Silverstone	F750	1st

World Championship Meetings
Suzuki RG500

French GP, Clermont-Ferrand	500cc	2nd
German GP, Nürburgring	500cc	DNS
Austrian GP, Salzburgring	500cc	3rd
Italian GP, Imola	500cc	DNF
Dutch TT, Assen	500cc	DNF
Belgian GP, Spa-Francorchamps	500cc	DNF
Swedish GP, Anderstorp	500cc	DNF
Czechoslovakian GP, Brno	500cc	4th

Final Positions – 500cc World Championship

1st	Phil Read (MV Agusta)	
2nd	Barry Sheene (Suzuki)	

1975

Notable Home Internationals

Race of the Year, Mallory Park	750cc	1st

National Championships and Awards

MCN Superbike Championship   3rd

MCN Man of the Year

International 750 Races
Suzuki three-cylinder 750

USA, Daytona 200	750cc	DNS (injured in pre-practice)
France, Magny-Cours	F750	1st
Sweden, Anderstorp	F750	1st
Great Britain, Silverstone	F750	1st

Final Positions – F750 Championship

1st	Jack Findlay	
2nd	Barry Sheene	

World Championship Meetings
Suzuki RG500

Austrian GP, Salzburgring	500cc	DNS
German GP, Hockenheim	500cc	DNF
Dutch TT, Assen	500cc	1st
Belgian GP, Spa-Francorchamps	500cc	DNF
Swedish GP, Anderstorp	500cc	1st
Finnish GP, Imatra	500cc	DNF
Czechoslovakian GP, Brno	500cc	DNF

Final Positions – 500cc World Championship

1st	Giacomo Agostini (Yamaha)	
6th	Barry Sheene (Suzuki)	

1976

Notable Home Internationals

Transatlantic Trophy Races	1 x 1st, 1 x 2nd, 3 x 3rd, 1 x 13th	
Race of the Year, Mallory Park	1st – Stevie Baker (Yamaha) 2nd – Barry Sheene (Suzuki)	

National Championships and Awards

Shellsport 500 Champion

MCN Superbike Champion

MCN Man of the Year

International Meetings

USA, Daytona 200	750cc	34th

Venezuela, San Carlos	F750	DNF
Italy, Imola 200	F750	3rd
Belgium, Nivelles	F750	DNF
France, Nogaro	F750	DNF
Belgium, Chimay International	500cc	1st
Great Britain, Silverstone	F750	DNF

World Championship Meetings
Suzuki RG500

French GP, Le Mans	500cc	1st
Austrian GP, Salzburgring	500cc	1st
Italian GP, Mugello	500cc	1st
Isle of Man TT	500cc	DNS
Dutch TT, Assen	500cc	1st
Belgian GP, Spa-Francorchamps	500cc	2nd
Swedish GP, Anderstorp	500cc	1st
Finnish GP, Imatra	500cc	DNS
Czechoslovakian GP, Brno	500cc	DNS
German GP, Nürburgring	500cc	DNS

Final Positions – 500cc World Championship

1st	Barry Sheene (72pts)	
2nd	Tepi Lansivuori (48pts)	
3rd	Pat Hennen (46pts)	
4th	Marco Lucchinelli (40pts)	

1977

Notable Home Internationals

Transatlantic Trophy Races	1 x 1st, 2 x 2nd, 1 x 3rd, 1 x 4th, 1 x 11th
Race of Aces, Snetterton	1st – Pat Hennen (Suzuki) 4th – Barry Sheene (Suzuki)
Race of the Year, Mallory Park	DNS
Gauloises Power Bike, Brands Hatch (long circuit)	5th

National Championships and Awards

Shellsport 500 Champion

MCN Superbike Champion

MCN Man of the Year

International Meetings

USA, Daytona 200	750cc	DNS

USA, Long Beach	750cc	1st – Skip Aksland (Yamaha) 2nd – Gene Romero (Yamaha) 3rd – Barry Sheene (Suzuki)
Belgium, Chimay, GP des Frontières	750cc 500cc	1st 2nd

World Championship Meetings
Suzuki RG500

Venezuelan GP, San Carlos	500cc	1st
Austrian GP, Salzburgring	500cc	DNS
German GP, Hockenheim	500cc	1st
Italian GP, Imola	500cc	1st
French GP, Paul Ricard	500cc	1st
Dutch TT, Assen	500cc	2nd
Belgian GP, Spa-Francorchamps	500cc	1st
Swedish GP, Anderstorp	500cc	1st
Finnish GP, Imatra	500cc	6th
Czechoslovakian GP, Brno	500cc	DNS
British GP, Silverstone	500cc	DNF

Final Positions – 500cc World Championship

1st	Barry Sheene (107pts)
2nd	Steve Baker (Yamaha) (80pts)
3rd	Pat Hennen (Suzuki) (67pts)
4th	Johnny Cecotto (Yamaha) (50pts)

1978

Notable Home Internationals

Transatlantic Trophy Races	1 x 1st, 1 x 2nd, 2 x 3rd, 2 x DNF
Snetterton, Races of Aces	1st
Mallory Park, Race of the Year	1st
Brands Hatch, Gauloises Power Bike	1st

National Championships and Awards

Shellsport 500 Champion

MCN Superbike Champion

MCN Man of the Year	1st – Mike Hailwood 2nd – Barry Sheene

Notable International Meetings

Belgium, Chimay, GP des Frontières	750cc 500cc	1st 1st
Italy, Imola, AGV Cup		Highest individual scorer in a series of team races

World Championship Meetings
Suzuki RG500

	Sheene	Roberts*
Venezuelan GP, San Carlos	1st	DNF
Spanish GP, Jarama	5th	2nd
Austrian GP, Salzburgring	3rd	1st
French GP, Nogaro	3rd	1st
Italian GP, Mugello	5th	1st
Dutch TT, Assen	3rd	2nd
Swedish GP, Anderstorp	1st	DNF
Finnish GP, Imatra	DNF	DNF
British GP, Silverstone	3rd	1st
German GP, Nürburgring	4th	3rd

* Kenny Roberts's places are included to
  illustrate the battle between the two men.

Final Positions – 500cc World Championship

1st	Kenny Roberts (Yamaha) (110pts)
2nd	Barry Sheene (Suzuki) (100pts)
3rd	Johnny Cecotto (Yamaha) (66pts)
4th	Wil Hartog (Suzuki) (65pts)

1979

Notable Home Internationals

Transatlantic Trophy Races	3 x 1st, 1 x 2nd, 2 x DNF
'World of Sport' Superbike, Donington Park	1st
AGV Nations Cup, Donington Park	4 x 1st
Race of the Year, Mallory Park	2nd

National Championships and Awards

MCN Man of the Year

World Championship Meetings
Suzuki RG500

Venezuelan GP, San Carlos	500cc	1st
Austrian GP, Salzburgring	500cc	12th
German GP, Hockenheim	500cc	DNF
Italian GP, Imola	500cc	4th
Spanish GP, Jarama	500cc	DNF

Yugoslav GP, Rijeka	500cc	DNF
Dutch TT, Assen	500cc	2nd
Belgian GP, Spa-Francorchamps	500cc	DNS
Swedish GP, Karlskoga	500cc	1st
Finnish GP, Imatra	500cc	3rd
British GP, Silverstone	500cc	2nd
French GP, Le Mans	500cc	1st

Final Positions – 500cc World Championship

1st	Kenny Roberts (Yamaha) (113pts)
2nd	Virginio Ferrari (Suzuki) (89pts)
3rd	Barry Sheene (Suzuki) (87pts)
4th	Wil Hartog (Suzuki) (66pts)

1980

Notable Home Internationals

Transatlantic Trophy Races	1 x 4th, 1 x 5th, 1 x 8th, 1 x 16th, 2 x DNF
World of Sport Superbike, Donington Park, April	DNF
World of Sport Superbike, Donington Park, June	DNF
World of Sport Superbike, Donington Park, August	1st
Gauloises Power Bike, Brands Hatch	DNF
Race of the Year, Mallory Park	2nd

National Championships and Awards

MCN Man of the Year	2nd

World Championship Meetings
Yamaha TZ500

Italian GP, Misano	500cc	7th
Spanish GP, Jarama	500cc	5th
French GP, Paul Ricard	500cc	DNF (injured in race crash)
Dutch TT, Assen	500cc	DNF
Belgian GP, Zolder	500cc	DNS
British GP, Silverstone	500cc	DNF

Final Positions – 500cc World Championship

1st	Kenny Roberts
14th	Barry Sheene

1981

Notable Home Internationals

World of Sport Superbike, Donington Park, April	1st
John Player Gold Cup	3rd
Transatlantic Trophy Races	1 x 1st, 1 x 3rd, 1 x 6th, 1 x 7th, 2 x DNF
'World of Sport' Superbike, Donington Park, June	1st
'World of Sport' Superbike, Donington Park, August	1st
Winter World Cup, Donington Park	1st
Race of the Year, Mallory Park	2nd

National Awards

MCN Man of the Year	2nd

World Championship Meetings
Yamaha YZR500 and OW54

Austrian GP, Salzburgring	500cc	4th
German GP, Hockenheim	500cc	6th
Italian GP, Monza	500cc	3rd
French GP, Paul Ricard	500cc	4th
Yugoslav GP, Rijeka	500cc	5th
Dutch TT, Assen	500cc	DNF
Belgian GP, Spa-Francorchamps	500cc	4th
San Marino GP, Imola	500cc	2nd
British GP, Silverstone	500cc	DNF
Finnish GP, Imatra	500cc	DNF
Swedish GP, Anderstorp	500cc	1st

Final Positions – 500cc World Championship

1st	Marco Lucchinelli
5th	Barry Sheene

1982

Notable Home Internationals

Transatlantic Trophy Races	5 x 1st, 1 x 2nd
'World of Sport' Superbike, Donington Park, April	DNF
John Player Gold Cup	2 x 2nd
'World of Sport' Superbike, Donington Park, June	DNF
John Player International	3rd and 6th

World Championship Meetings
Yamaha OW60 and OW61

Argentine GP, Autodromo de la Cuidad	500cc	2nd
Austrian GP, Salzburgring	500cc	2nd
French GP, Nogaro	500cc	DNS
Spanish GP, Jarama	500cc	2nd
Italian GP, Misano	500cc	DNF
Dutch TT, Assen	500cc	3rd
Belgian GP, Spa	500cc	2nd
Yugoslav GP, Rijeka	500cc	3rd
British GP, Silverstone	500cc	DNS (injured in practice crash)

Final Positions – 500cc World Championship

1st	Franco Uncini
5th	Barry Sheene

1983

Notable Home Internationals

Transatlantic Trophy Races	1 x 4th, 1 x 5th, 1 x 6th, 1 x 7th, 2 x 8th

National Championships and Awards

Shell Oils 500 Championship	7th	
MCN Masters Championship	12th	(only two rounds entered)

World Championship Meetings
Suzuki RG500

South African GP, Kyalami	500cc	10th
French GP, Le Mans	500cc	7th
San Marino GP, Monza	500cc	9th
German GP, Hockenheim	500cc	DNF
Spanish GP, Jarama	500cc	DNS
Austrian GP, Salzburgring	500cc	13th
Yugoslav GP, Rijeka	500cc	13th
Dutch TT, Assen	500cc	DNF
Belgian GP, Spa-Francorchamps	500cc	DNS
British GP, Silverstone	500cc	9th
Swedish GP, Anderstorp	500cc	DNF
Italian GP, Imola	500cc	DNF

Final Positions – 500cc World Championship

1st	Freddie Spencer
14th	Barry Sheene

1984

Notable Home Internationals

Transatlantic Trophy Races	2 x 9th, 1 x 10th, 2 x 11th, 1 x DNF
'World of Sport' Superbike Challenge	6th
Motor Cycle News Masters	12th=

World Championship Meetings
Suzuki RG500

South African GP, Kyalami	500cc	3rd
Italian GP, Misano	500cc	DNF
Spanish GP, Jarama	500cc	7th
Austrian GP, Salzburgring	500cc	10th
German GP, Nürburgring	500cc	10th
French GP, Paul Ricard	500cc	5th
Yugoslav GP, Rijeka	500cc	7th
Dutch TT, Assen	500cc	DNF
Belgian GP, Spa-Francorchamps	500cc	9th
British GP, Silverstone	500cc	5th
Swedish GP, Anderstorp	500cc	DNF
San Marino GP, Imola	500cc	DNF

Final Positions – 500cc World Championship

1st	Eddie Lawson
6th	Barry Sheene

Classic Bike Racing

Goodwood, 1998	500cc	2nd, 3rd
Goodwood, 1999	500cc	1st, 1st
Phillip Island, 2000	500cc	1st, 1st, DNF
Donington Park, 2000	500cc	DNF, 2nd
Goodwood, 2000	500cc	DNF, 2nd
Phillip Island, 2001	500cc	3rd, 3rd, DNF
Eastern Creek, 2001	500cc	3rd, 3rd
Donington Park, 2001	500cc	4th, 1st
Goodwood, 2001	500cc	1st, 1st
Phillip Island, 2002	500cc	2nd, 2nd, 2nd
Eastern Creek, 2002	500cc	5th, 4th, 6th, 2nd
Donington Park, 2002	500cc	1st, 1st
Goodwood, 2002	500cc	2nd, 1st

INDEX

ACU 131
Adelaide 195
Agg, Peter 53, 89
Agostini, Giacomo 45-46, 49, 59-60, 74, 78-79, 82, 85, 93, 97, 101-102, 106, 109, 159, 169, 204
Agusta A109C helicopter 210
Agusta, Count 78
AGV Nations Cup 141
AJS 7R 26
Akai hi-fi 150
Alderbrook 111
Alexander Butterfield & Ayres 26
AMA Grand National Championship 60, 79, 133
Anderstorp 40, 43, 79, 85, 94, 163-164, 190
Andrews, Eamonn 108
Annabel's, Mayfair 114, 117
Anne, Princess 114
Araoke, Ken 59, 79
Argentine GP 1982 166, 168
Armes, Marie 172
Arrows F1 team 124
Assen 44, 78-79, 85, 94, 102, 134-135, 141, 155, 161, 169, 186, 188, 190, 204
    Centennial Classic race 204
Aurora F1 series 124
Austin Ten 25
Australian F1 GP 195, 199
Australian GP 216; 2002 8, 214
Australian V8 Touring Car series 201, 203
Austrian GP 1974 78; 1975 82, 85, 117; 1976 93; 1977 99, 102, 150; 1979 139, 141; 1980 153; 1981 159; 1982 168; 1983 186; 1984 190

Bailey, David 71, 117
Baker, Steve 96-97, 99, 101, 103, 105, 134
Bali Hai, Streatham 26, 114
Ballington, Kork 168, 204
Barcelona 24-hour event 21
Barry Sheene Fan Club 49
Bartlett, Chris 156
Bartusch, Gunther 38
BBC 96
    Great Sporting Moments 142
    Sports Personality of the Year show 178, 181
Belgian GP 1971 43; 1974 79; 1975 73, 83; 1979 142; 1980 153; 1982 169; 1983 186; 1984 190

Bender, Gert 44
Berger, Gerhard 195, 199, 203
Biaggi, Max 159
Bike magazine 214
Blue, Adrianne 113
BMW 900cc 63
Boddice family 25
Bonera, Gianfranco 73, 78, 82
Bough, Frank 150, 178, 181
Bourne & Hollingsworth 30
Brands Hatch 19, 25-26, 28, 30, 37, 40, 49, 59-60, 111, 124, 127, 130, 139, 185
    Hutchinson 100 race 32, 40, 46
    King of Brands 48-49, 55, 60, 63
    Race of the South 117
Braun, Dieter 38, 44, 99
Brearley, Mike 127
British GP 1977 105; 1978 136, 139; 1979 142, 152; 1980 153, 155; 1981 163; 1982 169; 1983 188; 1984 190, 2001 207; 2002 210
British Superbikes 215
Brno 35, 40, 44-45, 79, 85, 105, 152
Brock, Pete 203
Brooklands 18
Brouwer, Ferry 204
Brown, Gerald 32
Brown, Norman 188
Breuss, Rudolf 213
BSA 40, 44
    Bantam 26
Buckingham Palace 106, 127
Bultaco 19, 21-23, 26, 32, 67
    Sherpa 25, 35, 37
    125cc 21-22, 25-26, 31-32, 35
    250cc 21-22, 26, 31-32
    350cc 26, 31-32
    360cc 74
Bulto, Don Paco 38
Bulto, Francesco 21, 109
Butler, Paul 150, 169, 178
Buxton, Dave 26, 28, 30
Byrne, Ian 23, 25-26

Cadalora, Luca 159
Cadwell Park 30, 60, 67, 80, 85, 155-156, 175
Café des Artistes, Earls Court 26
Carney, Martin 26
Carr, Cliff 32, 53, 59, 74-75
Carrara, Queensland home 195, 199

Carruthers, Kel 133
Castrol Challenge Trophy 39
Cecotto, Johnny 93, 97, 99, 102, 133, 135, 142, 150, 155
Celebrity Squares TV programme 181
Cessna aircraft 156
Champion spark plugs 125
Channel Nine TV 200
Channel Ten TV 200, 210, 214
Charles, Prince 117
Charlwood home 82, 118, 121, 149, 156, 178, 195
Chimay 93, 135
Claessens, Henk 64
Clark, Jim 139
Clermont-Ferrand 54, 77
Cobb, Nigel 174-175, 181
Coleman, Andrea (née Williams) 25, 118
Coleman, Barry 150, 152
Cooper, Henry 122, 124
Cooper, John 32, 45
Cooper, Vernon 131
Coulon, Philippe 99, 102
Crawford, Michael 124
Croft 30
Crookes, Eddie 43
Crosby, Graeme 153, 155, 161, 163, 166, 168-169
Croxford, Dave 35, 63
Crystal Palace 17
Cvitanovich, Frank 51
Czech GP 1975 85

DAF Trucks 150, 189-191
Daily Express 117
Daily Mail 71, 117
Daily Mirror 117
Daily Telegraph 212
Darlington Park, Brisbane 204
Dawson, Les 181
Daytona 51, 53, 59, 65, 67, 80, 85, 90, 96, 111, 117, 141
    24-hour race 114
    200-mile race 37, 55, 64
de Vries, Jan 45
Derbi 38, 44-45
    50cc 26
    250cc 45, 48
Desert Island Discs radio programme 109
Dirt-track racing 133
Ditchburn, Barry 60
Dodds, John 49, 55
Donington Park 124, 139, 141, 152, 155, 159, 163, 177-178, 185, 188, 191, 204, 207, 212
Doohan, Mick 196, 200-201

Douglas 18
Driver, Paddy 25
Ducati 48, 130
    50cc engine 19
Dundrod 43
Dunlop tyres 64-65, 141, 161, 166, 200
Durnford, Irene 71
Dutch TT 1971 44; 1974 78; 1976 96; 1982 178

Earls Court motorcycle show 96
East German GP 1971 45
Easter Match Races – see Transatlantic Challenge
Eastlake, Darrell 200
Ecclestone, Bernie 199
Ekerold, Jon 167, 172
Endurance racing 35
Enstrom helicopter 156
Essex, David 130
Estrosi, Christian 93
Excelsior 250 18

Fabergé 'Brut' 89, 109, 122, 124, 181, 199
Farrell, Mike 204
Fastest motorcycle race in history 87, 101-103
Fernandez, Patrick 99
Ferrari, Virginio 99, 134, 139, 141-142
FIM 53, 150, 152
Findlay, Jack 54, 67, 77-78
Finnish GP 111; 1967 35; 1971 44; 1975 85; 1978 135-136; 1979 142; 1980 155; 1981 163
Fletcher, Ken 153, 156, 161, 166, 186, 189
Fogarty, Carl 147, 201
Fogarty, George 147
Fontan, Marc 159, 166, 168
Ford 26
    GT40 114
    rally cars 71
    Thames van 19, 30-31, 37
    V8 203
Forester, Piers 71, 113-114, 117
Formula One cars 124, 127, 201
Formula One class 171
Formula 750 40, 53, 59-60, 63, 67, 85, 90
Francis, Clare 127
French GP 1973 77; 1974 78; 1975 85, 117; 1976 93; 1977 99, 104; 1978 117, 135; 1980 153; 1981 161, 167; 1982 168; 1983 186; 1984 190
Frutschi, Michel 159

Gardner, Wayne 199-200, 204, 207
Gauloises 168
German GP 1974 78-79; 1975 85; 1977 97, 99; 1978 128; 1979 141; 1983 186; 1984 190
Gibson, Grant 23, 25-26
Goodwood 203-204, 207, 213
    Lennox Cup races 204, 207
    Revival 204
Goodyear tyres 90, 133
Gould, Rod 32, 46, 48
Graham, Les 35
Graham, Stuart 28, 35, 37
Grant, Mick 60, 67, 71, 82, 106, 130, 139, 191, 196, 214
Guardian, The 113

Hagon, Will 199-200
Hailwood, Mike 31, 106, 109, 122, 130
Hameenlinna circuit 54
Hardy, Fred 25
Harley-Davidson 133
Harris Performance Products 150, 153, 182, 185, 189-190, 199
Harris, Steve 167-168
Harrison, George 109, 114, 117, 124, 127, 134, 193, 195
Harrison, Olivia 117
Hartog, Wil 11, 102, 134-136, 139, 141-142, 153
Haslam, Ron 139, 147, 190-191
HB team 185-186, 188-189
Hengelo 44
Hennen, Pat 93-94, 96-97, 99, 101, 105, 133-135
Heron Group 89, 134, 147
Heron Suzuki Team 89, 94, 104, 141, 153, 178, 185, 189
Herron, Tom 93, 118, 141, 210
Hesketh F1 team 71; motorcycle 117
Hesketh, Lord 71, 117
Hill, Damon 203
Hill, Graham 139
Hilzinger, Melanie 199
HM Queen Elizabeth II 127
Hockenheim 40, 54, 97, 99, 159, 186
Holt, Dr John 214
Honda 53, 74, 161, 168-169, 184, 188, 190, 196, 199-200
    NR500 168
    V3 168
    V4 181
    750 Four 53

Huewen, Keith 172, 184, 186
Hughes 500E helicopter 196
Hughes of Beaconsfield 191
Hunt, James 71, 87, 94, 114, 117, 124, 190

Igoa, Patrick 171-172
Imatra 102, 139, 147, 149, 152-153, 186
Imola 49, 54, 60, 63, 77-79, 94, 99, 141
    200 race 59
Isle of Man 18, 23, 28, 40, 43, 55, 130, 210
    Manx TT 18-19, 28, 35, 38, 40, 43, 60, 78, 93, 122, 130, 133
    Southern 100 race 28
Italian GP 1974 78; 1975 85; 1978 135; 1980 153, 155; 1983 185-186; 1984 190
Ito, Toshiya 181
Itoh, Mitsuo 65
Itom 50cc 17, 19
ITV 139, 141, 155, 177, 191
Ivy, Bill 23, 31, 35, 63

Jackson, Robert 150, 156, 159, 169, 177-178
Jaguar 25
Jansson, Börje 38, 44
Japanese GP 1967 35
Jarama 43, 45, 153, 159
Jawa V4 31
John Player 94, 168, 177
Johnson, Dick 201
Johnson, Jilly 71
Jones, Brad 203
Just Amazing! TV programme 51, 181, 193

Kammela 111
Kanaya, Hideo 82
Kanemoto, Erv 159, 161
Karlskoga 135, 163
Katayama, Takazumi 168
Kawasaki 35, 53, 59, 82, 108
    500 35
Knight, Maurice 37-38, 53-54, 89, 109, 131, 147, 178
Koike, Hisaeo 156
Kreidler 50cc 40, 45
Kyalami 49

Länsivuori, Teuvo 'Tepi' 82, 85
Lauda, Niki 87
Lawill, Mert 59
Lawson, Eddie 159, 182, 184, 189-190, 199
Le Mans 93, 114, 142, 188
Lichfield, Patrick 113-114, 117
London Evening Standard 96, 209, 212
Long Beach 117, 124

Loudon 79
Lowe, Chris 139
Lucchinelli, Marco 93, 131, 134, 153, 161, 163
Lynch, Kenny 181

Machin, Steve 45
Mackay, Don 32, 37, 43, 46, 53, 82, 89-90, 139, 166
Magee, Kevin 199
Maico 38
Mallory Park 19, 30, 35, 45-46, 49, 60, 139, 156, 158
    Race of the Year 60, 63, 67, 96, 163
Mamola, Randy 8, 142, 153, 155-156, 161, 168, 177, 182, 185-186, 188, 190
Mang, Toni 188
Mann, Dick 48
Manship, Steve 139
March, Lord 204
Marlboro 150, 168
Marshall, Roger 139
Mashe jeans 109
Massot, Joe 181
Matchless 25
    G50 26, 204, 207
Matsui, Tadao 136
Mayfair magazine 117
MBA 125 171
McCoy, Garry 196
McElnea, Rob 181
McLaren 117
McLean, Clive 117
McLean, Roman 117
McLean (later Sheene), Stephanie 12, 71, 96, 106, 109, 117-118, 121, 127, 135, 153, 159, 171, 174, 177-178, 181, 185, 195-196, 199, 210, 212, 215
MCN Superbike championship 53, 55, 60, 67, 71, 80, 90, 96, 105, 108, 133, 139
Melbourne 199
Mercedes-Benz 500SE 111
Michelin 125, 190, 200
Middelburg, Jack 147, 164, 168, 171-172
Mills, Tony 64-65
Miss World contestants 112
Mitsui Machinery Sales Ltd 150, 155-156, 159, 169, 177
Montjuich Park 21, 38, 53
Monza 40, 44, 74, 161, 186
Morbidelli 44
Mortimer, Chas 26, 28, 31-32, 43, 45, 111, 113, 204
Mortimer family 25
Moss, Stirling 59
Motor Circuit Developments (MCD) 139, 155
Motocourse 97, 104, 150, 189
MotoGP 26, 74, 96-97, 133, 141, 150, 168
Motor Cycle News 30, 48, 163, 184, 191, 212, 214

Man of the Year 55, 60, 96, 122, 131
Motor Cycle Weekly 32, 49, 89, 188, 191
Motorevue 212
Mott, Sue 212
Mugello 93, 189-190
Murdoch, Rupert 109
MV Agusta 40, 45-46, 49, 53, 59-60, 63, 67, 73-74, 78-79, 82, 85, 93, 204
MZ 38

Newbold, John 67, 85, 89-90, 94, 210
News of the World 63
Nieto, Angel 8, 38, 43-45, 204
Nixon, Gary 59, 64, 79, 97, 158-159
Nogaro 168
North-West 200 race 26, 89, 141, 210
North, Alan 11
Northern Daily Mail 130
Norton 40, 191
    Commando 53
    Manx 203-204, 207
Nürburgring 43, 78-79, 139, 152-153

O'Herlihy, Gavan 181
Okamoto, Mitsuru 136
Oliver's Mount, Scarborough 60, 130, 156, 163, 189, 191
Olio-Fiat, Nava 141
Opatija 43
O'Rourke, Mike 25
Oulton Park 30, 49, 60, 130, 139
Ovett, Steve 124

Packer, Kerry 200
Parkinson TV programme 106, 109
Parkinson, Michael 106
Parlotti, 44
Parrish, Steve 'Stavros' 11, 96-97, 99, 102, 105, 114, 134, 139, 141, 158, 166-167, 177-178, 181, 190-191, 210, 214-215
Pasolini, Renzo 74
Patterson, Ken 139
Paul Ricard circuit 99, 153, 161, 186, 190
Pellandini, Sergio 188
Percy, Win 191
Phillip Island 8, 207, 214
Phillips, Mick 214
Pietermaritzburg, Roy Hesketh circuit 49
Pietri, Roberto 97, 174
Plomley, Roy 109
Potter, Dave 139
Putney town house 71, 118, 121

Queen Square premises, Holborn 17-19, 23, 25-26, 31, 38, 46, 49, 56, 89, 106, 113-114, 118, 190
Queensland Raceway, Historic National Title races 204

RAC British Saloon Car Championship 191
Rainey, Wayne 128, 200
Ravens, Jan 181
Read, Madeleine 63, 80
Read, Phil 23, 31, 35, 46, 48, 60, 63, 67, 73-74, 78-80, 82, 85, 93-94, 111, 122, 204
Redman, Jim 204
Reggiani, Loris 188
Richardson, Sir Ralph 108-109
Riders for Health MotoGP charity 118, 150
Rijeka 141, 161, 169, 190
Roberts, Kenny 8, 11, 59-60, 67, 94, 96, 103, 105, 128, 133, 135-136, 139, 141-142, 144, 147, 150, 152-153, 155-156, 159, 161, 163-164, 166-169, 171-172, 185, 188-189, 200
Roche, Raymond 184, 190
Rohan, Denys 178, 186
Rolls-Royce 71, 80, 111, 114, 130, 185
Romero, Gene 60
Ronson, Gerald 89, 134
Rosberg, Keke 195
Rossi, Graziano 153
Rossi, Valentino 111, 124, 153, 201
Rougerie, Michel 11, 93-94, 102, 134
Rourke, Bob 97
RPM TV programme 201
Ryuyo test circuit 73, 75, 79

Saarinen, Jarno 46, 48-49, 74
Sachsenring 31
Salzburgring 26, 40, 135
San Carlos 97
San Marino GP 1983 188
Sarron, Christian 159
SBS TV 199
Schwantz, Kevin 128, 181, 200
Seeley frames 46, 53
Seeley Suzuki 750 56
Seeley, Colin 38, 40, 53
Shand, Camilla 117
Sheene Bultaco 21, 25, 30
Sheene team 32
Sheene, Arthur 18
Sheene, Barry
    alternative treatment 209, 212-214
    appearance/image 46, 55, 83, 89, 122, 131, 185, 212, 214-215
    autobiography 26, 28
    belief in God 209
    bike collection 35, 195, 204

business and property interests 106, 108, 113, 149, 193, 195-196
    character and personality 17, 49, 53, 117, 122, 128, 130
    charisma 23, 25, 49, 113, 216
    classic bike racing 204, 207, 210
    courage 32, 51, 63, 80, 117, 175, 177-178, 184, 213, 216
    crashes 26, 38, 49, 51, 55, 60, 63-65, 71, 78-80, 82, 85, 87, 96, 105, 111, 117, 128, 141, 155-156, 158, 163, 169, 171-172, 174-175, 177-178, 185, 189-190, 207
    death 22, 53, 64-65, 204, 207, 215-216
    dislike of Isle of Man TT 18
    education 22, 26
    emigration to Australia 35, 106, 121, 181, 193, 199-200
    fame 40, 49, 51, 53, 77, 85, 87, 111, 117, 124-125, 128, 195, 203
    fans 32, 46, 53, 67, 80, 87, 89, 105, 128, 130-131, 139, 152, 175, 177, 216
    fastest laps 189
    first GP ride 38
    flying 118; helicopters 111, 121, 156, 158-159, 181, 196, 199, 210, 212-213
    Formula One test 124, 127
    girls 22-23, 26, 30, 46, 71, 112, 114
    helmets 30, 32, 35, 48, 53, 73, 89, 135, 147
    illnesses and asthma attacks 19, 22, 25-26, 31, 186; cancer 199, 207, 209-210, 212-214; mystery virus 134-135
    injuries and X-rays 21, 49, 51, 53, 55, 60, 64-65, 67, 71, 78-80, 82, 85, 87, 93, 96, 99, 117, 141, 155-156, 172, 174-175, 177-178, 181, 186, 195, 199
    jet and water-skiing 153, 195
    jobs 26, 30, 108
    languages 22, 152
    lap records 102, 147
    last motorcycle race 191
    magazine columns 49, 96, 130, 163, 184, 188, 191, 214
    marriage 118
    MBE 12, 127
    mechanical understanding 25, 32, 164
    mischief 22-23, 39, 46, 191, 196, 199
    pole positions 85, 93-94, 99, 102, 105, 128
    precociousness 25-26, 30, 40
    prizes 39, 48, 111

racing number '7' 59, 89, 101
racing licence 28, 204
retirement from racing 35, 177, 182, 188-191, 193
riding style 25, 32, 54, 87, 97, 133, 149
saloon/touring car racing 191, 203
smoking 22, 46, 51, 71, 135, 174, 212
sponsorship 32, 89, 96, 108-109, 111, 131, 147, 150, 172, 181, 189
swimming 22
titles 32, 39, 53-55, 73, 109, 133, 139, 207; World Championships 94, 97, 104-106, 117, 121-122, 186, 190
truck racing 191, 203
TV and film career 181, 193, 199-201
wins 30, 40, 45-46, 49, 53-55, 63, 67, 79, 85, 94, 99, 102, 104-105, 134, 142, 155-156, 163, 167, 191, 204, 207, 210, 213; first GP 28, 44, 204; last GP 163-164
Sheene, Frank 17-19, 21-23, 26, 28, 31-32, 37-38, 43, 46, 56, 80, 89-90, 93, 99, 114, 118, 127, 135, 139, 147, 172, 174, 177, 181, 185, 195-196, 214
Sheene, Freddie 8, 15, 193, 196, 214
Sheene, Iris 17-19, 21, 23, 31, 46, 55, 80, 109, 114, 117-118, 127, 177, 185, 195-196
Sheene, Joyce 21
Sheene (later Smart), Margaret 18, 21, 23, 39, 48-49, 78, 195-196, 209-210, 212-213, 215
Sheene, Marjorie 21
Sheene, Sidonie 15, 118, 193, 195-196
Sheene, Stephanie – see McLean

Shell Australia 201
Shellsport 500 series 53, 55, 63, 90, 96, 105, 133, 139
Shepherd, Lesley 63
Silverstone 54-55, 60, 82, 89, 105, 124, 139, 142, 144, 147, 163, 169, 171, 185, 189 'British GP' 1971 46; 1974 79
Simmonds, Dave 35, 37-38
Six Million Dollar Man TV series 177
Smart, Maggie – see Sheene, Margaret
Smart, Paul 12, 18, 38-39, 48-49, 53-54, 59, 63, 74, 77, 97, 109, 117, 133, 158, 204, 212-215
Smart, Scott 12, 153, 210, 215
Snetterton 30, 35, 38, 139 Race of Aces 32, 38, 105
Solitude 26
South African GP 1983 182, 185, 189; 1984 182, 189-190
Spa-Francorchamps 28, 43-44, 46, 85, 87, 94, 102-103, 142, 150, 152
Space Riders film 181, 188
Spain, King of 159
Spanish GP 1970 38; 1971 38, 74; 1978 117; 1979 141; 1980 153; 1983 186; 1984 190
Speedway racing 18, 196, 204
Spencer, Freddie 155, 159, 168-169, 185, 188, 199
Spondon Engineering 171
Sporting Motorcycle Show 48
Sports Writers Association 124 Sportsman of the Year 85, 124
Stedelman, Hans 99
Sugo 156
Sun, The 71
Sunday People 63
SuperBike magazine 131
Superbikes 40
Surtees F1 team 124, 127
Surtees, John 124, 127, 203-204

Suzuki 26, 38, 46, 48, 53, 55, 59-60, 63, 65, 67, 73, 75, 77-79, 82, 85, 89-90, 93-94, 96-97, 102, 108-109, 113, 117-118, 125, 131, 134-136, 139, 147, 149-150, 153, 155, 159, 161, 163, 166, 168, 171, 178, 181-182, 184, 186, 189-190, 193; 196, 200, 210; MotoGP team 196
GS750 89, 96
GT550 55
RG500 53, 75, 79, 85, 89, 131, 141, 159, 178, 190; Mk8 185-186; XR14 77, 204
RGA500 134
T500 Titan 37
TR500 (XR05) 37, 40
XR45 engine 189
125cc 28; RT67 35, 37-38, 40, 195, 204
250cc 43
500cc 45-46, 49, 51, 54, 56, 67, 73-74
750cc 53-54, 80
1000cc 139
Suzuki GB 37, 53, 67, 89 Beddington Lane HQ 131
Suzuki USA 55, 59, 64, 89
Suzuki, Nijmag 141
Swedish GP 1971 44; 1974 60; 1975 85; 1976 94; 1977 105; 1979 142; 1983 188; 1984 190

Taylor, Dave 67
Taylor, Garry 113, 131, 196
Texaco 89, 93-94, 104, 124-125, 147, 150, 199
Thames Television 51, 109
This Is Your Life TV programme 108-109
Thruxton 500-mile race 35
Toracca, Armando 82, 99
Touring Car series 191
Townley, Pammie 71

Toyota Supra 191
Tramps, Jermyn Street 71, 114, 117
Transatlantic Challenge series 59, 79, 94, 96, 103, 105, 130, 133, 139, 155, 167-168
Trials bikes 23, 25, 67
Triumph 40, 48
Tiger Cub 25
Trident 53

Ubbiali, Carlo 204
Ulster GP 38
Uncini, Franco 8, 99, 131, 153, 168-169, 188
Uphill, Malcolm 38, 50
US 750 Superbikes 79

van Dulmen, Boet 159, 164, 168, 188-189
Venezuelan GP 1977 97; 1978 134-135; 1979 141
Vermeulen, Chris 196
Villa 32
Vogue 71

Waibel, Alfred 171
Walmsley, Fred 207
Wells, Jim 189
West German GP 26
White, Rex 37-38, 53-54, 67, 85, 89, 133
Whitsunday Islands 195
Williams, Jack 25
Williams, John 67, 89, 93-94, 210
Williams, Keith 195
Williams, Peter 25, 60, 63
Winter World Cup series 163
Winton 203
Wisbech home and workshop (Ashwood Hall) 55-56, 64, 80, 114, 118, 121
Wogan, Terry 109
Wooldridge, Ian 71
Woodman, Tony 26

Woods, Stan 53-54, 67, 85
World of Sport TV programme races 87, 139, 155-156, 163, 191
World Series 150, 152-153
World Superbike Championship 147, 201
Wright, Merv 64, 89-90, 93-94, 109

Yamaha 31, 35, 38, 46, 48-49, 53, 67, 74, 82, 85, 93, 97, 99, 102, 108, 133-135, 141-142, 147, 149-150, 153, 156, 159, 161, 166, 168-169, 172, 178, 184, 188, 200
LC350 177
OW54 159, 161
OW60 168
TD250 32, 46
TZ500 150, 155; TZ500G 150
TZ750 59, 67, 117, 150, 155-156
V4 168-169, 171, 174, 178
250cc 48-49, 171
350cc 48, 85
351cc 93
354cc 48
Yamsel 38, 40
Yorkshire Television 51
Young, Lewis 28
Yugoslavian GP 1983 186

Zolder 155

125cc championships 31, 45-46, 48; British 32, 37, 39; World 40, 77, 113
250cc championship 31, 46, 48; World 32, 74, 133, 159
350cc World Championship 93
500cc World Championship 35, 53, 55, 60, 77, 85, 104, 159, 190, 196, 199-200
500cc 'World Cup' 177
750cc series 53, 55, 94

BIBLIOGRAPHY

Motocourse 1976 to 2002 (Hazleton Publishing)

The Sheene Machine by Andrew Marriott (Pelham Books, 1979)

Barry Sheene: The Story so Far by Barry Sheene with Ian Beacham (Star Books, 1976)

Barry Sheene: A Will to Win by Michael Scott (W.H. Allen, 1983)

Leader of the Pack by Barry Sheene with Ian Beacham (Queen Anne Press, 1984)

Team Suzuki by Ray Battersby (Osprey)

Barry Sheene 1950-2003: The Biography by Stuart Barker (CollinsWillow, 2003)